To my parents

A Hiker's Guide to
California
Native Places

Interpretive Trails, Reconstructed Villages, Rock-Art Sites and the Indigenous Cultures They Evoke

Nancy Salcedo

WILDERNESS PRESS

BERKELEY

First Edition September 1999

Photos by Nancy Salcedo, except as noted
Maps by Chris Salcedo
Edited by Paul Backhurst
Book and cover design by Larry B. Van Dyke

Library of Congress Card Number 99-41684
ISBN 0-89997-241-1

Manufactured in the United States of America

Published by **Wilderness Press**
             1200 5th Street
             Berkeley, CA 94710
             (800) 443-7227; FAX (510) 558-1696
             mail@wildernesspress.com
             www.wildernesspress.com
Contact us for a free catalog

Cover photos: *(background)* **Petroglyph Sunrise** © 1999 by Daniel J. Cook;
             (inset) **Reconstructed Miwok Village, Indian Grinding Rock
             State Historical Park** © 1999 by Larry Ulrich

Frontispiece: **Vasquez Rocks, home to "people of the south-facing slope"**
             © 1999 Nancy Salcedo

 Printed on recycled paper, 20% post-consumer waste

Library of Congress Cataloging-in-Publication Data

Salcedo, Nancy.
    A hiker's guide to California native places : interpretive trails,
reconstructed villages, rock-art sites and the indigenous cultures
they evoke / Nancy Salcedo. -- 1st ed.
        p.   cm.
    Includes bibliographical references and index.
    ISBN 0-89997-241-1 (alk. paper)
    1. Hiking--California Guidebooks. 2. Natural history--California
Guidebooks. 3. California Guidebooks. I. Title. II. Title:
California native places.
GV199.42.C2S25   1999
917.9404'53--dc21   99-41684
                                                     CIP

Table of Contents

Shoshonean – South Coast & Peninsular Ranges

Chumash – Central Coast, Transverse Ranges, & Channel Islands   73

The Hikes:

Ohlone – Central Coast & Coast Ranges 145

The Hikes:

Guided Walks:

Coast & Bay Miwok – North Coast & Coast Ranges 163

The Hikes:

Pomo, Yuki, & Lake Miwok – North Coast & Coast Ranges   179

Washoe – Tahoe Sierra Nevada   195

Acknowledgments

A special thank you to the tribal members who work with the parks to interpret their cultures for visitors. Their personal contributions provide an invaluable perspective for our modern culture. Thank you to the members of the Hupa Tribe and the Agua Caliente Band, and to the residents of the Tule River Reservation for providing the opportunity to walk their lands with their interpretation. Thank you to the staff of parks and open spaces which interpret Native California places. The work of volunteers, docents, rangers, staff archaeologists, and cultural historians who tirelessly share their wealth of knowledge of the Native California cultures has provided our society with a series of outdoor "museums." I greatly appreciate the efforts of Professor M. Steven Shackley and Stephen W. Silliman from the Phoebe Hearst Museum of Anthropology and the Anthropology Department at the University of California—Berkeley, respectively, who greatly improved the technical accuracy of this book but bear no responsibility for my interpretations. Thank you to Daniel J. Cook for the use of his cover photograph. I am grateful to the staff at Wilderness Press for their expertise, and to Caroline Winnett, for her support and patience in the development of this project.

—Nancy Salcedo
Stinson Beach
August, 1999

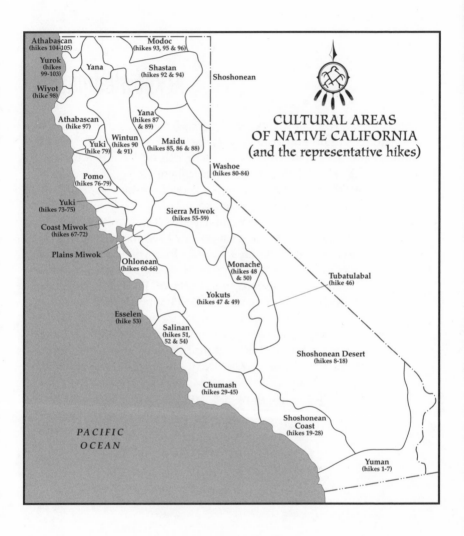

CULTURAL AREAS OF NATIVE CALIFORNIA (and the representative hikes)

Athabascan (hikes 104-105)

Modoc (hikes 93, 95 & 96)

Yurok (hikes 99-103)

Yana

Shastan (hikes 92 & 94)

Shoshonean

Wiyot (hike 98)

Athabascan (hike 97)

Yana (hikes 87 & 89)

Wintun (hikes 90 & 91)

Maidu (hikes 85, 86 & 88)

Yuki (hike 79)

Washoe (hikes 80-84)

Pomo (hikes 76-79)

Yuki (hikes 73-75)

Sierra Miwok (hikes 55-59)

Coast Miwok (hikes 67-72)

Plains Miwok

Ohlonean (hikes 60-66)

Monache (hikes 48 & 50)

Tubatulabal (hike 46)

Yokuts (hikes 47 & 49)

Esselen (hike 53)

Salinan (hikes 51, 52 & 54)

Shoshonean Desert (hikes 8-18)

Chumash (hikes 29-45)

Shoshonean Coast (hikes 19-28)

PACIFIC OCEAN

Yuman (hikes 1-7)

Introduction

The Yurok, in what could be a representative Native Californian response, believed that a trail was a living thing, worthy of great respect. Rest stops were designated at choice places along important routes. The Yurok traveled attentively along the trails, taking care to treat them properly and stopping to enjoy the special resting places. To have done otherwise would have shown disrespect. In leaving a resting place, a traveler would ask the spirits, "May I come this way again?"

This guide focuses on indigenous cultures of California, as they were before the encroachment of the modern world, when the native people lived in their ancestral homelands according to their own traditions. The hikes include interpretive trails, native plant trails, reconstructed villages, mortars, pictographs, petroglyphs, and geographic features that are the subject of Native Californian stories. Despite its wealth of native places, this book does not disclose unprotected or otherwise vulnerable archaeological sites or places considered sacred to Native Americans. In addition to hike descriptions, the chapters provide background on the tribes, their languages, and the regionally adapted cultures. Following this discussion, museums and other places to visit are listed for more information. Not-to-be-missed guided walks are also described. Consider the Yurok attitude toward the trail as you sample these hikes; with the proper respect there is so much that can be learned and shared. As the native cultures of California enter a renaissance, living descendants are relearning native languages, dances, and art forms, and sharing many of them with the rest of us. It is a fascinating time to visit Native California.

Geography

This guide covers many of the ancient cultural sites scattered throughout California that, in my opinion, best reflect the traditional lifeways of the indigenous cultures. Though petroglyphs, hunting grounds, middens, and village sites exist throughout the state, many are now on private property, are lying under reservoirs, or are planted over by fields of crops. Many of our modern cities began as Native California villages, and many of the highways in California originated as ancient trade routes. Yet less-disturbed pockets remain of the Native California cultural landscape. Their prehistoric significance shrouded, the ancient sites may now seem like nothing more than beautiful and tranquil places in the wild that resonate with a significance that the eye alone cannot take in.

Village sites were chosen for access to food and water, and for protection from bad weather and flood waters. Most were concentrated along rivers, creeks, lakes, or the seacoast. There were also seasonal camps near oak groves for acorn gathering and in pine groves during the pine nut harvest. Hunting and gathering grounds, and trading routes lined creeks, ridges, and canyons. Besides areas necessary for material sustenance, petroglyphs mark important sites throughout the state. In some rock-art sites, the rock itself marks the entrance to the spirit world, and is treated with utmost respect (Whitley, 1996). Villagers along the coastline harvested shellfish, leaving behind middens mostly composed of bleached shell fragments. People of inland villages ground acorns harvested from oak groves, and their mortars remain in the bedrock. In the Sierra, middens are recognized by a substantial layer of dark soil— the leavings of charcoal and animal oils from ancient fires. Obsidian flakes can still be seen in the soil of ancient tool-making sites.

Archaeology

From the contents of middens—the village refuse heaps—archaeologists determine the material culture of a village and begin to reconstruct prehistoric society. In a campsite, the midden is a thin layer, but in a village site it may be 12 inches thick or more. The thicker the midden, the more intensive was the use of the site (whether that means a longer period of habitation or simply more people). Middens in Chumash territory and in many other areas of California have been found to be 40 feet deep. Shell fragments, grinding tools, and bone remnants convey information about food sources. The existence of materials not endemic to the area where they were found tells us about trade routes. For example, routes between coastal villages, villages in the Central Valley, and villages east of the Sierra have been identified, based upon shell-fragment finds from the Pacific Coast in Great Basin village sites, and from Sierra obsidian finds in Central Valley and coastal sites.

From the presence of trace elements in rock implements, archaeologists have been able to identify the source of rocks used in early tools. For some, their origin was a great distance from where the tools were found, illuminating not only trade routes but also the distribution of prehistoric technology.

It is easy to see the importance of letting archaeologists, rather than hikers, unearth artifacts. Archaeological investigation has been likened to a jigsaw puzzle in that the position of an object in relation to another is as important as what the object is. Never disturb an item you suspect may be an artifact. Instead, note the location and inform park staff, or the nearest natural-history museum or historical society. The Federal Antiquities Act of 1906 makes it illegal to "appropriate, excavate, injure or destroy any prehistoric ruin or object of antiquity" on Federal lands. Park regulations further protect archaeological resources with severe criminal and civil penalties. Hikers in Point Reyes National Seashore were recently prosecuted for moving some bones in order to show them to park staff. Most parks do not give information about vulnerable prehistoric cultural sites in an effort to protect them from degradation. State and local regulations protect archaeological sites on other lands. Check with the administrative agency listed for a particular hike for more information.

Anthropology and Ethnography

To help make sense of information gathered about Native California, anthropologists have developed cultural- and language-area classifications, as well as a chronological system. Native California is divided into six geographically distinct culture areas: Southern, Central, Colorado River, Great Basin, Northwestern, and Northeastern. Each area contained several distinct tribes sharing similar cultural attributes. Ethnographers have also divided California cultures into the Yuman, Uto-Aztecan, Penutian, Hokan, Yukian, Athabascan, and Algonkin language groups.

In classifying California into language groups by region, anthropologists have learned a bit about chronology and development of these prehistoric cultures. Some anthropologists believe that the Early Horizon people were Hokan speakers who, in some areas, were displaced by Penutians around 1000 BC. The chronological system includes the Paleo-Indian Period (such as the San Dieguito people, around 7000 BC), followed by the Milling Stone Horizon (such as the La Jolla and Oak Grove peoples, around 5000 BC), and the Late Prehistoric Period (such as the Yumans, around 1000 BC). Milling Stone Horizon village sites contain the earliest mortars and metates throughout the state. This culture apparently increased the distribution of plant material in the diet.

The Acorn Maidens

The acorn was the staple throughout much of California, obtained through trade in those few spots where it was not plentiful. Prolific oak groves meant a wealthy society. Extended families participated in the gathering of at the ancestral groves for the acorn harvest. Young children as well as men shook the acorn-laden branches and others would gather the nuts that fell to the ground. Grinding holes, where the nuts were milled, were the scene of village conversations. Many calendars and feasts of ancient California revolved around the acorn harvest. The myth of the Acorn Maidens shows its importance.

Many years ago, the Acorn Maidens lived upon a cloud. They went about their days weaving baskets until one day, the wind pushed a hole in the cloud and the Maidens could see, for the first time, the earth below. The people they saw were thin, and always busy looking for food. The Maidens felt sorry for these California Indians, because they had to work so hard to find food. The Maidens chose to stop their basket weaving and travel to earth to become acorns to feed the people. As the first Maiden finished her ample and well-woven basket, she placed it upon her head and went to earth as the acorn of the valley oak, which is a plump one with a large cap. When the next sister finished her basket, she became the acorn of the coast live oak, which is a thinner acorn with a smaller cap. The third sister, seeing her other two sisters already as acorns on earth, rushed to finish her basket so she could join them. Due to her rush, her basket was messy. She became the acorn of the tanbark oak, which has a bristly cap. To make up for her basket, Tanbark Acorn became the best-tasting one for acorn soup. Every year the sisters grow plump on the branches of the oak trees in preparation for the fall harvest. When they fall to the ground you can examine their woven caps.

Acorns were ground into flour in stone mortars. The flour was then leached in a creek in a basket for several days to remove the tannic acid. The flour could then be placed in a basket with heated rocks to make acorn soup. Today, acorns are ground in a blender, the flour is placed in a cloth bag in the sink, and water run through it overnight. Acorn soup may still be made from the flour, or an acorn bread resembling a tortilla may be made of acorn flour, water, and salt. The acorn was once considered for modern agriculture as it requires no preparation of the soil and no irrigation, and is rich in nutrients. The acorn and the grinding rock are the most conspicuous symbols of Native California cultures.

How To Use This Guide

The state is divided into chapters each focusing on the cultural group of a region. The hikes in each chapter are preceded by background information under these headings: "Landscape and People," and "Natural Resources and Material Culture." Museums and visitor centers are also listed. The hikes are chosen for their interpretive facilities, beauty of the natural landscape, and archaeological or mythological significance of the site visited. They range in length from less that 1 mile to over 15 miles. All mileages given in the headers are round-trip. Where it exists, wheelchair accessibility is noted. Most hikes are ideal for families and group field trips. The hikes are arranged in order from south to north in the state.

Accompanying the descriptions of many of the hikes are graphic icons used to show you, at a glance, some of the features you will find. Below is a list of the icons, and what they represent:

 Ethnobotanical Exhibits, Gardens, and Native American Plant Use Trails

 Grinding Rocks

 Rock-Art Sites

 Reconstructed or Re-created Villages

 Places Informed by a Native Story or Myth

 Archaeological Sites

 Trade Routes and Prehistoric Trails

 Trails and Exhibits on Tribal Lands

Keep in Mind

Many of the trails do not allow bikes or dogs due to the vulnerable nature of the sites. Follow trail etiquette and hiking safety practices. Bring water, snacks, and appropriate clothing. Note the hours of operation posted at park entrances. Keep children close to you on the trails. Many parks charge a day-use fee, and some national forests require a parking pass. Phone numbers are listed for each hike in case you have specific questions.

About Maps and Directions

The book has a map of the region of each chapter. These maps show trailheads, the roads leading to them, geographic features, and points of interest. Trailheads are cross-referenced by hike number on the maps, and are labeled either by hike name (with the arrowhead icon) or park name (with the evergreen icon). Though most of the trails described are well marked, it may be useful to carry a map showing trail-side amenities. Several of the trails in the book are interpretive hikes for which brochures are available. For the most complete information, request a park map from the administrative agency. On the following pages are 105 hikes in Native California, each with highlights listed in the Cultural Feature Listing (see Appendix 1). You can choose the ones that spark your interest.

Hiking in the backcountry entails unavoidable risk that every hiker assumes and must be aware of and respect. The fact that a trail is described in this book is not a representation that it will be safe for you. Trails vary greatly in difficulty and in the degree of conditioning and agility one needs to enjoy them safely. On some hikes routes may have changed or conditions may have deteriorated since the descriptions were written. Also trail conditions can change even from day to day, owing to weather and other factors. A trail that is safe on a dry day or for a highly conditioned, agile, properly equipped hiker may be completely unsafe for someone else or unsafe under adverse weather conditions.

You can minimize your risks on the trail by being knowledgeable, prepared and alert. There is not space in this book for a general treatise on safety in the mountains, but there are a number of good books and public courses on the subject and you should take advantage of them to increase your knowledge. Just as important, you should always be aware of your own limitations and of conditions existing when and where you are hiking. If conditions are dangerous, or if you're not prepared to deal with them safely, choose a different hike! It's better to have wasted a drive than to be the subject of a mountain rescue.

These warnings are not intended to scare you off the trails. Millions of people have safe and enjoyable hikes every year. However, one element of the beauty, freedom and excitement of the wilderness is the presence of risks that do not confront us at home. When you hike you assume those risks. They can be met safely, but only if you exercise your own independent judgement and common sense.

The author and the publisher of this book disclaim any liability or loss resulting from the use of this book.

Map Legend

Ocean	*PACIFIC OCEAN*	Large City	**SAN FRANCISCO**
		Medium City	● Vallejo
		Small City	● Tomales
Lakes & Islands	*Clear Lake* Angel Island		
		Highway	—
Rivers & Creeks	*Russian River*	Secondary Roads	—
		Tertiary Roads	—
Large Geographic Features	C o a s t R a n g e	Dirt Roads	- - - - -
Small Geographic Features	Point Arena	Highway Shields:	
		Interstate	⬭80
		US Highway	⬭50
Mountains	Mount Lassan	California State Highway	⬭89
		Other State Highway	⬭37
		County Road	▭17
Parks	MENDOCINO NATIONAL FOREST		
C h u m a s h W i l d e r n e s s	MACKERRICHER STATE PARK	International Boundary	M E X I C O
		State Boundary	N E V A D A

Trailheads:

Trailhead	▲ *Pictograph Trail* (hike 4)	Point of Interest	■ *Big Flat*
Trailhead, when labelled as park name	▲ MACKERRICHER STATE PARK (hike 79)		

Compass Rose, Scale, & Title

0   5   10 miles

MIWOK TERRITORY

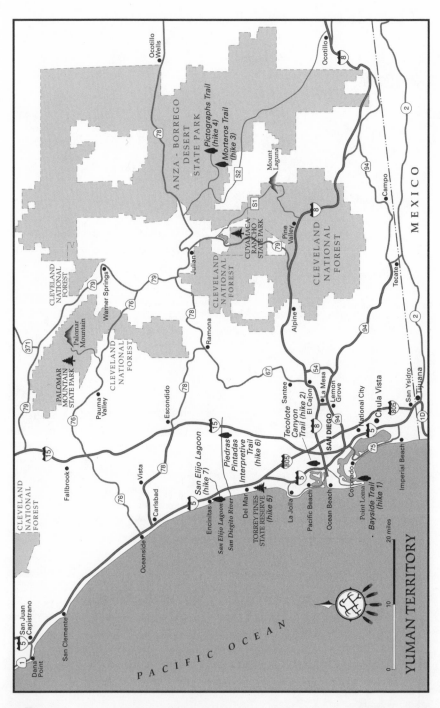

Yuman
Southern Coast, Peninsular Ranges, & Colorado Desert

Landscape and People

San Diego and Imperial counties were inhabited during the Late Prehistoric by the Yuman people. The landscape ranges from coastal lagoons through the Cuyamaca Mountains and river valleys to the Colorado and Mojave deserts. One Yuman tribe is the Kumeyaay, known as Ipai north of the San Diego River and Tipai south of the river. During the mission period the Kumeyaay also became known as the Diegueño people. In the Mojave Desert near the banks of the Colorado River other Yuman tribes were the Yuma, the Mojave, the Halchidhoma, and the Kamia. The Halchidhoma were displaced by the Chemehuevi people in the 1800s. The Yuman language is part of the Hokan family, together with Chumash, Pomo, Salinan, Shastan, and Yana. The prehistoric Yuman population is thought to have reached 9,000.

Much of the recent development in San Diego County has triggered mandated archaeological investigation. Developments around Lomas Santa Fe, Del Dios, Del Mar, and the Fairbanks Ranch have led archaeologists to conduct surveys that have yielded significant findings. The San Diego River estuary was home to two distinct cultures that came before the Yuman (Late Prehistoric Period): the San Dieguito (Paleo-Indian Period) and the La Jollan (Milling Stone Horizon).

Because of the extensive findings within the San Dieguito River Valley, archaeologists refer to this culture as the San Dieguito people. The San Dieguito are most widely accepted as the earliest people. Carbon-dated remains suggest that the San Dieguito people lived in the region between 8,500 and 4,000 years ago. Compared to La Jolla middens, theirs contain less shellfish remnants, and substantially greater signs of game hunting and vegetation harvesting. Cobble choppers (large tools flaked from stones quarried in the alluvium of the San Dieguito River Valley) provide archaeologists with a distinguishing artifact of the San Dieguito culture.

About 4,000 years ago, the San Dieguito culture gave way to a new culture which lasted approximately 3,000 years. The people of this next cultural generation are called the La Jolla people, as several large camps were found in the La Jolla area. Their territory ranged from southern Orange County to Central Baja. Middens reveal that the favored foods were scallops, abalone, shark, barracuda, and bonito. The earliest mortars and metates in the region were found among the remnants of La Jolla villages. Eight La Jollan sites have been documented at locations including La Jolla, the north bank of the San Diego River, the south side of Mission Bay, the shore side of San Diego Bay, and the bay side of Point Loma. The people migrated up San Diego's rivers, camping in hundreds of small sites to hunt game and gather plants.

About 1,000 years ago, the La Jolla people were displaced by Yuman people, who migrated here from the desert. The Yuman people flourished in large, permanent settlements throughout coastal San Diego County and south to Ensenada, Mexico. A large Ipai village of 170 people once stood near what is now the Del Mar racetrack. There was another large settlement known as Pauma in Pauma Valley on the lower flanks of Mount Palomar. (Oral histories have been recorded here by ethnographers from the University of California.) Yuman middens have yielded pottery, arrow points, metates, manos, beads, shell pendants, soapstone pendants, cobble choppers, and flake scrapers. Archaeologists have also attributed gravel pictographs, trail shrines, and polychrome pictographs to the Yuman culture.

The Kumeyaay moved into the Cuyamaca Mountains from the desert around AD 1500, as climatic changes dried Lake Cahuilla, an episodically filling lake in what is now Imperial Valley. The Kumeyaay name for the Cuyamacas is *Ah-ha-Kwe-ah-mac*, or "place beyond the rain." An ancient trade route between the coast and the desert follows Green Valley through the Cuyamaca Mountains. As trading partners with the people of the coast, the Kumeyaay bartered acorns and agave in exchange for salt, dried seafood, greens, and abalone shells. With the desert people, the Kumeyaay traded acorns and granite mortars in exchange for river fish and vegetable crops. The Kamia of the Imperial Valley traded watermelon to the Kumeyaay for acorns.

Natural Resources and Material Culture

Traditional Kumeyaay plant foods include acorns, grass seeds, roasted bladderpods, sage, jojoba, curly dock, pickleweed, coast saltbush, and coastal sagebrush seeds. The stems of curly dock were boiled and eaten much like rhubarb. Leaves of sea blite and sea lettuce were boiled and eaten as greens. Sea rocket and lady fingers were eaten raw. Fruits and berries of prickly pear cactus, toyon, and lemonade berry were eaten both raw and cooked, or crushed for drinks. The Kumeyaay gathered clams, mussels, and surf fish. Animal foods included deer, elk, antelope, and rabbit.

A black dye made from sea blite and an orange dye made from salt-marsh dodder were used for baskets. Saltmarsh dodder was also used as a scouring pad, and to cure the bite of the black widow. White sage was used as a shampoo, hair straightener, and deodorant. In their paddle-and-anvil pot construction, the Kumeyaay added juice of beavertail cactus to clay as a binder. Houses were seasonal structures, made of rounded willow frames covered with brush or bark in the desert, or tule and rush near the coast.

Influenced by Southwestern culture, the Yuman people in the desert practiced agriculture. As the only early farmers in California, about one-half of the desert Yuman tribes' plant diet was obtained through cultivation. Settlements were chosen for proximity to bottom-land plots where crops could be planted in floodplain silts after the spring floods. Crops consisted of several varieties of maize, beans, gourds, and pumpkins. The Kamia, for example, lived almost entirely on cultivated maize, beans, pumpkins, gourds, watermelons, and cowpeas. If crops failed, mesquite beans were collected and river fish were caught in weirs.

Pottery appears for the first time in California in middens of the Yumans. It was produced only in the southern part of this region, by Kumeyaay, Yuma, Mojave, Cocopa, and Kamia. The Kumeyaay and the Kamia are known for their high-quality pottery. Some of the vessels recovered from archaeological sites are decorated with red or, occasionally, black lines. Clay pigments were also used in face and body painting.

The desert region holds a specific form of rock art known as "intaglios," which are huge motifs of animal and human-like figures, concentric circles, and rattlesnakes, scraped into the desert varnish. Some are 250 feet across, and some have been dated at over 3,000 years old. Several intaglios remain along the shore of the Colorado River between *Avikwal*, the spirit house at the southern end of the river now known as Pilot Knob, and *Avikwa'ame* (Spirit Mountain), where the world was mythically created. The Blythe Intaglios, which date back 1,100 years, were created by the Yuman people, while others nearby were created by the Mojave and the Quechan people.

Museums and Interpretive Sites

The **Colorado River Reservation Museum** in Parker, Arizona, provides exhibits on local cultures and the Blythe Intaglios. The museum is open daily from 8 A.M. until noon, and from 1 P.M. until 5 P.M., (520) 669-9211.

The **Blythe Intaglios** include three human figures, a mountain lion, a concentric circle, and a spiral. On BLM land, the Blythe Intaglios are fenced for their protection, and can be visited by the public. They are located between Highway 95 and the Colorado River 13.5 miles north of Blythe.

The **Museum of Man** in San Diego's Balboa Park lets you experience the world of Native Americans and early man, and features the best collection of Kumeyaay baskets in the country, (619) 239-2001.

Also in San Diego, near Mission Bay, the **Tecolote Canyon Nature Center's** natural history display includes a native plant garden with a reconstructed Kumeyaay dwelling (see hike 2), (619) 581-9952.

The **Torrey Pines Visitor Center** has a native plant garden complete with Kumeyaay plant names and uses (see hike 5), (619) 755-2063.

The museum at **Cuyamaca Rancho State Park Headquarters** interprets the Kumeyaay of the Cuyamacas, (760) 765-0755.

The **Kwaaymii Trail** passes through a native plant garden in the Laguna Mountains of Cleveland National Forest, (619) 445-6235. Labeled plants include deer grass used in basket-making, wild lilac fashioned into throwing sticks for hunting, manzanita used as a long-burning firewood, and cactus which was squeezed into clay as a binder in pot manufacturing. The trail leads through a grove of pinyon pine and islay (holly-leaved cherry), to mortars and metates used by the Kumeyaay for grinding the fruits, seeds, and nuts of their harvest.

hike 1

Bayside Trail

Roundtrip Distance	1.5 miles
Location	Coastal Kumeyaay territory
Administration	Cabrillo National Monument (619) 557-5450
Map	Point Loma Ecological Preserve

The remains of a village of the La Jollan people lie, underwater just offshore, beneath the bluffs along the bayside of the Point Loma Ecological Preserve. Thought by archaeologists to have originated at least 4,000 years ago, this La Jollan site flourished at a time when sea level was considerably lower than it is today. The rising sea level flooded all but the later (and higher) settlements of these people, such as those found at La Jolla and Topanga. Later, the Kumeyaay lived here, traveling the open ocean to fish in reed canoes, traversing the headlands to hunt deer, antelope, and rabbit, and gathering plant materials. The preserve features the vegetation of the Kumeyaay, with coastal sage scrub mantling the bluffs.

Trailhead

Exit I-5 at Rosecrans St. (Hwy. 209) in San Diego. Head southwest on Hwy. 209 to Canon St. Turn right and go to Catalina Blvd. Go left and continue to the entrance station (fee required) and the road's end in the parking area for Cabrillo National Monument.

On The Trail

The 1.5-mile Bayside Trail features signs interpreting the human history as well as the natural history of the coastal sage scrub community on Point Loma. The signed BAYSIDE TRAIL begins as a paved walkway at the east side of the lighthouse. Follow the Bayside Trail south, traversing through the black and white sage, bladderpod, encelia, and California sagebrush that cover the headland. In 0.25 mile the Bayside Trail follows a gravel pathway to the left (east), descending toward the bay along the north side of a canyon, to where the interpretive signs begin. The first panels explain the Kumeyaay use of plants found in the coastal sage scrub community. Continue down the trail to where it levels off at the blufftop. Rather than cultivated specimens, the headland presents a full palette of this pure, wild, and complete plant community. Follow the blufftop north, meandering in and out of small canyons, and passing interpretive signs on flora and fauna, and a drinking fountain. In 0.75 mile, the last sign marks the trail's end. Return by the same route.

Offshore Point Loman archaeological site of the La Jollan culture

hike 2 Tecolote Canyon Trail

Roundtrip Distance	2 miles
Location	Coastal Kumeyaay territory
Administration	Tecolote Canyon Natural Park (619) 581-9952
Map	Tecolote Canyon Natural Park

Tecolote means "owl" in the Spanish language. Tecolote Canyon Natural Park demonstrates the Kumeyaay use of native plants. The canyon once supported Kumeyaay villages, its native plants utilized for food and shelter. Middens remain in the lower canyon. The Kumeyaay collected and scattered grass seed for propagation, redirected the waters of Tecolote Creek for irrigation, and burned non-productive vegetation. The plants growing here now help demonstrate the ancient ways of the Kumeyaay. Live oaks and pinyon pines provided the acorn and pinyon nut staple for *shawii*, or "mush." Berries of lemonade berry and toyon were boiled to make a drink. Black sage produced seed for a flour. Wild gourd furnished a cleansing lather. The branches and leaves of the arroyo willow were coiled to make baskets that repel pests in storage. Because of the insect-repellent nature of the willow leaf, the baskets could safely be used to store acorns and pine nuts.

To ward off development interests in the 1960s, Kumeyaay descendants joined the residents of the canyon to form a citizen-advisory committee to purchase the canyon for a park. Kumeyaay elders on the committee developed and now implement a master plan for the park. For the park's dedication ceremony, Kumeyaay tribal members from San Diego and northern Baja came to applaud the preservation of such ancient places, and the commemoration of traditional ways.

Trailhead

Take I-5 to the Tecolote exit east of Mission Bay in San Diego. Go east on Tecolote Rd. to the Tecolote Nature Center at 5180 Tecolote Rd. Tecolote Canyon Natural Park is open from dawn to dusk daily.

Tecolote Canyon Trail explores Kumeyaay plant-use

On The Trail

The Tecolote Canyon Trail takes in this lovingly preserved piece of Kumeyaay ethnobotany. Walking east from the parking area you pass through a gate and can wander the fenced native garden on the right side of the trail. The garden features labeled native plants, and a reconstructed Kumeyaay house. From the native garden, go right and follow the trail east, up the canyon floor along the south side of Tecolote Creek. The trail follows the canyon bottom for 1 mile before winding north toward the Tecolote Canyon Golf Course. The trail continues along the canyon with the golf course on the left, and on the right the coastal sage scrub community, much as it was when Kumeyaay traveled along the creek to the mesas. When you are ready, retrace your steps to the parking lot.

hike 3   Morteros Trail

Roundtrip Distance	0.4 mile
Location	High desert of seasonal Kumeyaay territory
Administration	Anza-Borrego Desert State Park (760) 767-5311
Map	Anza-Borrego Desert State Park

Anza-Borrego Desert State Park has recently hosted the excavation of several archaeological sites of early man. The people who lived in the region 10,000 years ago knew a greener Anza-Borrego Desert with wooded hills and lush valleys. The early people hunted now-extinct camels and mammoths. Later, the desert lands were divided between the Cahuilla in the north around present-day Borrego Valley, and the Kumeyaay in the south near Blair Valley. An ancient Native American trail between the Laguna Mountains and the desert passes through Blair Valley.

The Morteros Trail visits an ancient Kumeyaay village site. The Kumeyaay band in Blair Valley used this winter village, while traveling to gather seasonal foods. The site can be identified by grinding holes left in boulders where mesquite pods, pine nuts, and chia seeds were ground into flour.

Trailhead

Exit Hwy. 78 at Rd. S2 in Anza-Borrego Desert State Park (fee required) 12 miles east of Julian. Follow Rd. S2 about 6 miles southeast to Little Blair Valley Rd. Turn left and go about 3.8 miles to the parking area signed MORTEROS VILLAGE. (This site can be visited in conjunction with the Pictographs Trail—hike 4.)

On The Trail

Cooler than the lower desert, Blair Valley has a pinyon and juniper woodland above sandy washes and rocky outcrops. The trail climbs 0.2 mile from the trailhead to a village site which dates back at least 800 years. Bedrock mortars (morteros), and cupules (stones with smaller depressions that were used in rituals) lie along the trail behind a large boulder. Nearby, black-lined pictographs were painted during a boy's initiation ceremony. After exploring the grounds, retrace your steps to the parking area.

After dark, the village might have seemed belittled by the intensity of the stars in the desert night sky. Perhaps because of the optimal viewing conditions here, stars—each considered a spirit—figured often in Southern California rituals and songs. In Kumeyaay culture, too, the Pleiades were once girls, pursued here by Coyote, the nearby bright red star that we call Aldebaran. The Milky Way is regarded by many California cultures as a path of dead spirits. To the southern cultures, the Milky Way is *Wanawut*, who personifies the sacred chord of life, and is often associated with *towish*, "the spirit of the dead." Wanawut is sometimes depicted as a stick figure in pictographs from boys' initiation ceremonies.

A reconstructed Kumeyaay dwelling

hike 4

Pictographs Trail

Roundtrip Distance	2 miles
Location	High desert of seasonal Kumeyaay territory
Administration	Anza-Borrego Desert State Park (760) 767-5311
Map	Anza-Borrego Desert State Park

The Kumeyaay left pictographs in Blair Valley thought to be the culmination of a girl's initiation ceremony. The ceremony signified a girl's eligibility for marriage, and required that each participant get a spirit helper from the supernatural world. The Blair Valley pictographs' location marks the finish line of a footrace girls ran after having ingested native tobacco to produce an altered consciousness. The painting of the pictographs was the final requirement in the ceremony, where the girls, under the watchful eye of a shaman, recorded their visions of acquired spirit helpers. The rattlesnake, depicted with zigzag lines and diamond chains, was considered the most appropriate spirit helper for a girl. Red, associated with the west and the setting sun, was considered the female color, and is found in many such ceremonial painting sites.

Trailhead

Exit Hwy. 78 at Rd. S2 in Anza-Borrego Desert State Park (fee required) near Julian. Follow Rd. S2 southeast about 8 miles to Blair Valley Camp Rd. Turn left and go about 5.3 miles to the Pictographs parking area. (This site can be visited in conjunction with the Morteros Trail—hike 3.)

On The Trail

The Pictographs Trail brings you to a boulder painted in red zigzag and diamond-chain designs of the rattlesnake associated with the Kumeyaay girl's ceremony. From the parking area, walk east following granite boulders along the trail through a dry wash. Climbing a ridge through intermittent pinyon and juniper, the trail ascends east over a small saddle before passing into Smugglers Canyon. At 0.8 mile, look for the pictographs on a large and conspicuous boulder on your right, along the south side of the canyon, slightly shrouded by an overhang. If you want to keep hiking, the trail continues on into the narrows of the canyon before coming to a 200-foot dry waterfall. Eventually, retrace your steps to the parking lot.

hike 5   Guy Flemming Loop Trail

Roundtrip Distance	0.65 mile
Location	Coastal Kumeyaay territory
Administration	Torrey Pines State Reserve (619) 755-2063
Map	Torrey Pines State Reserve

The village of Ystaguay once flourished on a knoll above Los Penasquitos Lagoon, near the entrance to Torrey Pines State Reserve. The Kumeyaay people who lived here gathered pine nuts and other materials from the reserve's 330 species of plants, which they found in coastal sage scrub, upland chaparral, and salt marsh plant communities. A native plant garden in the courtyard of the reserve's visitor center features labeled specimens with their ancient uses. In addition to listing the botanical name, these labels have the Kumeyaay name. You will see that *aakul* is "yucca," which was used for its roasted seed flour, *hamuchi* is "chamise," used as firewood and in arrowshafts, *'ehwiiw* is the "Torrey pine," used in baskets, and *ehpaachewuu* is "coast prickly pear," which was sliced and cooked. Acorns, pine nuts, and seeds of chia and black sage were ground into flour for pinole. A midden below the visitor center's bluff establishes that shellfish were collected from the lagoon. Fishing was done from the shore and from tule canoes. Florence Shipek's *Autobiography of Delfina Cuero*, which is available in the bookstore here, preserves the recollections of a Kumeyaay descendant who lived at Torrey Pines.

Trailhead

Exit I-5 at Carmel Valley Rd. in Del Mar. Go 1.5 miles west to oceanfront Torrey Pines Rd. Turn left and go 1.7 miles south to the Torrey Pines State Reserve entrance (fee required) on the right, across from Los Penasquitos Lagoon. From the entrance station, drive 0.2 mile up to the Guy Flemming parking area on the right. The visitor center is 0.25 mile farther at the road's end.

On The Trail

The Guy Flemming Loop Trail meanders through the reserve's North Grove, providing plant-identification opportunities and a view of the Kumeyaay village site by Los Penasquitos Lagoon. From the parking area, the loop trail heads west toward the bluff, along the upper slopes of a canyon that animals use as a transportation corridor. The trail soon winds north to pass along the blufftop overlooking the ocean, where Kumeyaay boats once patrolled offshore waters. Soon, the trail turns northeast and passes beneath the cover of pines, where pine nuts and basketry materials were gathered. The North Grove overlooks Los Penasquitos Lagoon and the ancient site of Ystaguay, which was situated on a knoll above the lagoon shore, just southeast of the reserve's entrance kiosk. The trail soon rejoins the loop, and returns to the parking lot.

The North Grove Trail takes in the Kumeyaay coast

hike 6   Piedras Pintadas Interpretive Trail

Roundtrip Distance	3.8 miles
Location	San Dieguito River Valley of Kumeyaay territory
Administration	San Dieguito River Park (619) 235-5445
Map	San Dieguito River Park

One of the earliest known archaeological sites in San Diego County is the Harris Site, located along the western reaches of the San Dieguito River Valley. Artifacts found at varying depths within the Harris Site reveal what evolutionary changes occurred in village material culture over a period of 8,000 to 11,000 years. Included here are early stone hunting artifacts of the San Dieguito people, whose subsistence focused on the hunting of large game. The upper levels of the site hold more recent artifacts attributed to the La Jolla people of the Early Milling Stone Horizon, who relied more upon the gathering of plant materials and shellfish than hunting. Later, the San Dieguito River marked the northern boundary of Kumeyaay territory. Fifteen hundred years ago, the Kumeyaay village Shnyau-Pichkara thrived in the area surrounding the Piedras Pintadas Trail. The trail's name, which in Spanish means "painted rocks," refers to a regional style of rock art known as Rancho Bernardo Style that incorporates maze-like designs. Though not accessible at this site, the rock art is described in an interpretive panel at the beginning of the trail.

Trailhead

Exit I-15 at West Bernardo Dr./Pomerado Rd. in Rancho Bernardo. Go 0.5 mile north on West Bernardo Dr. to the Bernardo Bay Natural Area parking lot (no fee) of the San Dieguito River Park on the left (west) side the road.

On The Trail

The Piedras Pintadas Interpretive Trail follows the winding San Dieguito River past interpretive panels on Kumeyaay pottery, basketry, plants, tools, and rock art. From the southwest corner of the parking area, the trail heads southwest through coastal sage scrub. Passing interpretive panels on Kumeyaay technology, you walk down a hill and across a drainage to a trail fork near an exposed pipe. Take the left fork and continue southwest around a knoll to a second trail fork. Turn right and pass through the riparian corridor along Green Valley Creek, lined by willows, mulefat, and other plants (interpreted by panels on Kumeyaay ethnobotany), to a bridge in 0.5 mile. From the bridge, follow the trail to the right, passing through a marshy area to the south shore of Lake Hodges. An oak tree at 0.8 mile reminds walkers that before the Lake Hodges dam was built, there were many oak trees in this area, which provided the Kumeyaay with acorns and hot-burning firewood ideal for firing pottery. The trail climbs via switchbacks to a waterfall view at 1 mile, then descends into a wetland. At 1.5 miles you cross a stream to a trail fork which marks the beginning of the 0.8-mile loop trail. Bear right, passing interpretive panels on Kumeyaay ethnobotany, and then climb to a ridgetop overlooking the mountains to the east. Continue the length of the ridge until the trail descends to the valley floor. An interpretive sign underneath an ancient oak describes the role of acorns and nearby grinding rocks. Continue south, past subsequent Kumeyaay interpretive panels to the end of the loop trail at 2.3 miles. Retrace your steps to the parking lot.

hike 7   San Elijo Lagoon

Roundtrip Distance	2.5 miles
Location	Coastal La Jollan cultural site
Administration	San Elijo Lagoon Conservancy (760) 436-3944
Map	San Elijo Lagoon Ecological Reserve

Within the San Elijo Lagoon Ecological Reserve, archaeologists from the San Diego Museum of Man have uncovered 10 ancient sites, five of which they attribute to the La Jollan culture. In prehistoric times, the lagoon was a salt marsh flushed with the fresh water of Escondido Creek. The lagoon sustains large populations of migratory shorebirds and waterfowl, 20 species of fish, and 300 species of plants. Shellfish, seaweed, bulrush, arrowweed, and rye grass were gathered from the wetlands and coastal waters. Over time, the lagoon waters cut bluffs in the cobble-dotted sandstone, exposing rounded cobbles prized by the La Jolla people for use in the manufacture of stone tools. (On Manchester Avenue at the northwest corner of the lagoon is a nature center and a self-guiding nature trail.)

Trailhead

Exit I-5 at Lomas Santa Fe Dr. in Solana Beach, and go east to North Rios Ave. Turn left and go 0.8 mile north to the road's end at the trailhead (no fee).

On The Trail

The hiking trail takes in an interpretive exhibit along the lagoon shore, an important site to the La Jollan culture. From the end of North Rios Ave., follow the gated fire road north, down toward the lagoon. Where the fire road cuts into the sandstone bluff above the lagoon, it reveals the cobbles prized in the manufacture of stone tools. Enjoy ocean views extending to the horizon as you descend the bluff. In the Kumeyaay creation myth, all beings are born of the Sun Mother and the Sky Father, where they meet at the western horizon, beyond the sea. Near the water, the Hiking and Equestrian Trail extends both east and west along the lagoon's south shore. The western route ends in 0.4 mile, near the railroad bed. Instead, go east, where interpretive signs explain the plant and animal life in the marshes and surrounding coastal sage scrub. Continue 1.25 miles to the spur trail leading into Holmwood Canyon Narrows, where eroded sandstone cliffs create a surreal canyonland. Retrace your steps to the parking lot.

San Elijo Lagoon from the bluff

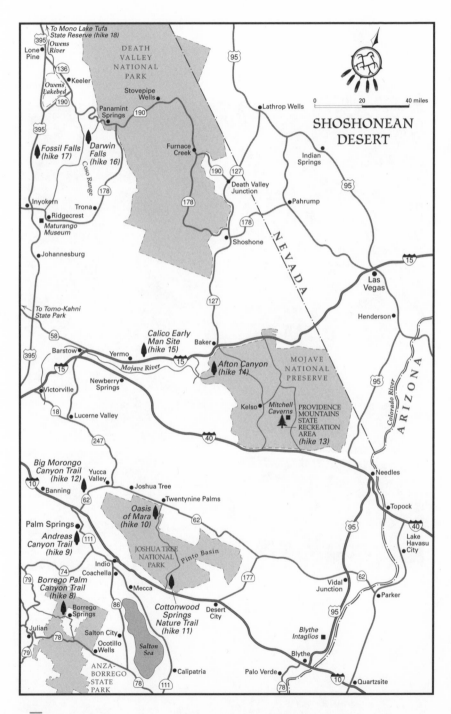

To Mono Lake Tufa
State Reserve (hike 18)
Owens
River
Lone
Pine
395
136
Keeler
Owens
Lakebed
190

DEATH
VALLEY
NATIONAL
PARK

Stovepipe
Wells
Panamint
Springs
190

95

Lathrop Wells

SHOSHONEAN
DESERT

0   20   40 miles

395

Fossil Falls
(hike 17)
Darwin
Falls
(hike 16)

Coso Range

Furnace
Creek

190   127

Death Valley
Junction

Indian
Springs

95

178

178

Inyokern
Trona
Ridgecrest
Maturango
Museum

178

Shoshone

Pahrump

Johannesburg

NEVADA

15

Las
Vegas

Henderson

To Tomo-Kahni
State Park

58

395

Barstow   Yermo

Mojave River

15

127

Calico Early
Man Site
(hike 15)   Baker

Afton Canyon
(hike 14)

MOJAVE
NATIONAL
PRESERVE

95

Victorville

Newberry
Springs

18   Lucerne Valley

Kelso

Mitchell
Caverns

PROVIDENCE
MOUNTAINS
STATE
RECREATION
AREA
(hike 13)

ARIZONA

Colorado River

247

40

Big Morongo
Canyon Trail
(hike 12)   Yucca
Valley

10   Banning

62

Joshua Tree

Twentynine Palms

Needles

Topock

Palm Springs

Andreas
Canyon Trail
(hike 9)

111

Oasis
of Mara
(hike 10)

62

95

62

40

Lake
Havasu
City

74

Borrego Palm
Canyon Trail
(hike 8)

79

Indio
Coachella

Mecca

86

JOSHUA TREE
NATIONAL
PARK   Pinto Basin

177

Cottonwood
Springs
Nature Trail
(hike 11)   Desert
City

Vidal
Junction

95

Parker

Julian   Borrego
Springs

78

Salton City

79   Ocotillo
Wells

Salton
Sea

ANZA-
BORREGO
STATE
PARK   78   111

Calipatria

Blythe
Intaglios

Palo Verde

Blythe

10   Quartzsite

Shoshonean
Mojave & Colorado Deserts

Landscape and People

In the desert, Shoshonean territory stretches from northern San Diego and Imperial counties in the south, through San Bernardino and Riverside counties, and north to Inyo County. The southern landscape is that of the arid Mojave and Colorado deserts, with villages centered around oases. The northern landscape is typified by basin and range country, with smaller population groups living along rivers.

The Shoshone migrated to California from the Great Basin, ultimately occupying a third of the state. Once in California, the Shoshonean people spread throughout the southern desert to the sea, becoming separate tribes. The desert Shoshone spoke languages in the Numic subgroup of the Uto-Aztecan language family, while Shoshone living along the coast spoke languages of the Lakic subgroup. The Shoshone of the Kern River drainage spoke in the languages of the Tubatulabalic subgroup. Uto-Aztecan speakers share a common ancestry with the Hopi and the Aztec peoples.

Shoshonean tribes include Northern Paiute (also known as Paviotso), Panamint Shoshone (a.k.a. Koso), Chemehuevi (a.k.a. Southern Paiute), Kawaiisu (a.k.a. Tehachapi), Monache (a.k.a. Western Mono), Kitanemuk (a.k.a. Tejon), Alliklik (a.k.a. Tativum), Mohineyarn (a.k.a. Vanyume), Serrano, and Cahuilla. The prehistoric desert Shoshone population is estimated to have reached 8,500 people. These people occupied the largest yet most sparsely populated territory in the state, with low population density correlating with limited food and water resources. Tribal boundaries were not firm and settlements were seasonal, so the people could gather pinyon nuts or mesquite pods where and when they were plentiful.

In the south, the desert climate was cooler and its vegetation more lush in prehistory than it is today. Over time, movements along the earthquake faults have changed groundwater tables and redirected rivers and underground flows to ancient lakes and oases. In places, the only signs of prehistoric lushness are the salt beds of ancient lakes now blistering in the sun. Despite the summer's heat, oases of the Colorado Desert remain cool with a moist, tropical atmosphere reminiscent of the ancient landscape.

To the north, huge lakes dating from the Pleistocene once filled lake basins as far as Death and Panamint valleys. Diversions of natural water courses toward modern settlements also changed the landscape. The Owens River diversion left riverbeds dry in the volcanic landscape of the western Mojave Desert. Despite desertification, many native peoples retain their ancestral homelands: the Agua Caliente Band of Cahuilla in Palm Springs, whose stewardship of the oases in the Indian Canyons is ancient; and the Panamint Shoshone in Death Valley. These peoples continue one of North America's oldest residencies.

Archaeological evidence has been found in desert caves and rock shelters, and along the shores of ancient rivers and lakes. In the southeastern corner of Joshua Tree National Park lies the Pinto Basin, which 10,000 years ago supported an ancient culture. A wide river promoting lush vegetation once flowed through Pinto Basin. Fossil remains of many now-extinct animals such as ground sloths, hyena-like dogs, and extinct species of horses and camels have been uncovered by the bank of the former riverbed. Similar remains from the time of the Pinto people have been unearthed along the Owens River and in Death Valley.

In the Providence Mountains State Recreation Area are the Mitchell Caverns. They are not far from Foshay Pass, where the ancient Mojave Trail crosses the Providence Mountains. Smoke-blackened cave walls, hidden caches of food and tools, and spirit offerings indicate that Chemehuevi Indians used them for perhaps 500 years on a seasonal basis, while hunting for game and harvesting pinyon pine nuts in this area. The caves were excavated by the Los Angeles County Museum of Natural History in 1934. Many of the items recorded were textiles, such as seed beaters, a winnowing tray, basketry fragments, sandals, and cordage. The Mojave Trail is an ancient route leading from Colorado River Mojave villages through the desert, passing springs and caves en route to the coast. Cajon Pass was another major trade route between the desert and the sea.

Natural Resources and Material Culture

Practical foods and material culture of this region were limited by the carrying capacity of a nomadic society. Regional plant foods from the juniper/pinyon woodland include mesquite, pine nuts, and seeds and flowers of the joshua tree, prickly pear, and saguaro cactus. The Cahuilla divided the year into seasons pertaining to the growth of their staple mesquite, with seasons named "blossoming of trees" and "time of ripening seed pods." The Cahuilla supplemented their staple with the agricultural production of crops. The Chemehuevi also practiced agriculture, while the Owens Valley Paiute cultivated seed crops. Meats consisted mainly of small mammals and bighorn sheep, which were attracted by hunters banging on a rock to imitate the sound of two rams fighting with their horns. Lizards and insects were valuable sources of protein. The Owens Valley Paiute collected the larvae of the pandora moth, and the grasshopper. Rock-salt deposits were found in the Owens Valley.

Rectangular houses were built over 3-foot pits with wooden posts and arrowweed thatching, and then covered with earth. Perhaps the region is best known for its petroglyphs, which include animal and human figures as well as geometric patterns. The Cahuilla, being both desert and inland-coastal dwellers, produced both the pictographs typical of the coastal people and the petroglyphs typical of the desert people. The Cahuilla are also known for their high-quality pottery vessels produced in grays, reds, and browns, with red lines. Panamint Shoshonean baskets are known for quality and intricate designs.

Museums and Interpretive Sites

Cahuilla Ethnobotanical Loop at The Living Desert Reserve in Palm Desert offers an ideal, wheelchair-accessible introduction to the lifestyle of the desert Cahuilla. There are botanical gardens representing 10 desert ecosystems. The Cahuilla Loop includes labeled (also for sight-impaired) plants used by the Cahuilla, bedrock mortars, day jars (a.k.a. ollas), bark strippers, arrowheads, and a reconstructed *kish* (Cahuilla house). The Living Desert is open daily, (760) 346-5694.

Agua Caliente Cultural Museum in Palm Springs contains photographs displaying Cahuilla life, and Cahuilla artifacts (see hike 9). There is also a botanical garden of plants used by the Cahuilla, and a reconstructed kish, (760) 323-0151.

Oasis of Mara Visitor Center at Joshua Tree National Park is on Utah Trail, just off Highway 62 east of Twentynine Palms. Exhibits illustrate the natural and human history of the desert, from simple artifacts of the Pinto people to more recent, intricate artifacts of the Serrano and

Chemehuevi peoples (see hike 10). The visitor center is open daily, (760) 367-7751.

The **Mousley Museum of Natural History** in Yucaipa features exhibits on the cultures of the Serrano, Cahuilla, Luiseño, and Mojave, along with some others in the state and the US, (909) 790-3163.

Morongo Reservation/Malki Museum is owned and administered by the Cahuilla. The museum features baskets, pottery, ceremonial costumes, and a gift shop with Native arts and books. The museum is located on the Morongo Reservation in Banning (see hike 12). The museum is open Wed–Sun from 10 A.M. to 4 P.M., (909) 849-7289. The Malki Museum Fiesta and Powwow is held annually in May.

The **Maturango Museum** in Ridgecrest features exhibits on the Shoshonean and Yokuts cultures, and offers guided tours of Little Petroglyph Canyon. Since that is one of the greatest rock-art sites in the world, book your trip months in advance. The museum is open daily, (760) 375-6900.

The **Antelope Valley State Indian Museum** about 15 miles east of Lancaster in Antelope Valley features exhibits on the culture of the Shoshonean people, (805) 946-3055.

The **Furnace Creek Visitor Center** in Death Valley features baskets, arrowheads, a small diorama, and a petroglyph exhibit, as well as exhibits on geologic formations, flora, and fauna. The visitor center is open daily, (760) 780-2331.

The **Paiute/Shoshone Indian Cultural Center** has cultural displays and reproductions of local petroglyphs. Indian owned and operated, the museum is located in Bishop on the Bishop Indian Reservation, (760) 873-4478.

The **Mono Basin National Forest Scenic Area Visitor Center** in Lee Vining features a reconstructed Mono summer house, basketry, and other artifacts. It documents the brine larvae harvest in the shallows of Mono Lake. *Of Fire and Ice* is a 20-minute film narrated by a Mono Shoshone woman living in Lee Vining, illustrating many aspects of Shoshonean life from a first-hand source. The visitor center is closed Tuesdays and Wednesdays, (760) 647-3044.

hike 8   Borrego Palm Canyon Trail

Roundtrip Distance	3 miles
Location	Desert oasis in Cahuilla territory
Administration	Anza-Borrego Desert State Park (760) 767-5311
Map	Anza-Borrego Desert State Park

The northern portion of Anza-Borrego Desert State Park in the Borrego Valley was inhabited by the Cahuilla. Seemingly a land of boulders, sand, sun, and wind, this part of the desert is blessed with the surprising comfort of California fan palm oases, which range from Baja to Death Valley. The Cahuilla enjoyed the pleasant climate of the palm oases throughout their territory. Within Anza-Borrego State Park, there are 25 native palm oases. Within the oases, park archaeologists have recorded pottery shards and bedrock mortars used in grinding nuts and seeds. The Cahuilla harvested the palm fruit for food. They used the fronds to build shelters, and to make sandals and baskets.

In lower Palm Canyon, metates (shallow mortars used to grind seed) remain in boulders. To craft a metate hot coals were used to crack the rock's surface. The coals were then worked into the fissure, which was worn deeper with use. Upstream, a midden remains near a growth of honey mesquite, which was a staple of the Cahuilla people. The seed pods were ground and formed into cakes. Nearby, petroglyphs remain both in the canyon and at Borrego Palm Campground.

Trailhead

Exit Highway 78 at Rd. S3 (Yaqui Pass Rd.) 19 miles east of Julian. Turn left and follow Rd. S3 12 miles to Rd. S22 (Palm Canyon Dr.) in Borrego Springs. Turn left on Palm Canyon Dr. and go 1 mile to a junction. Turn right just before the visitor center and go 1 mile to the Borrego Palm Canyon Campground. The trailhead is at the west end of the parking area (fee required).

On The Trail

The Borrego Palm Canyon Trail is a self-guiding nature trail that leads past morteros and metates, past labeled plants used by the Cahuilla for food, and through an ancient Cahuilla campsite. The trail then leads to a side canyon featuring an oasis around Palm Canyon Creek, with over 800 native California fan palms. The Borrego Palm Canyon trailhead is well marked at the northwest end of the parking area, near the refreshment cart. The boulder-lined trail leads up along an alluvial fan, climbing gently northwest. En route, interpretive panels describe flora, fauna, and cultural history. At 1 mile, the interpretive panels end with a sign describing the native palms, and the palm oasis comes into view. The oasis is at 1.5 miles. Depending on the season, it can be 20 degrees cooler within the oasis. Explore Palm Canyon Creek from within the tropics of its fan palms before retracing your steps to the parking area.

Morteros in Borrego Palm Canyon

hike 9

Andreas Canyon Trail

Roundtrip Distance	0.5 mile
Location	Desert oasis in Cahuilla territory
Administration	Agua Caliente band of Cahuilla (760) 325-1053
Map	Indian Canyons

Located on the lands of the Agua Caliente band of Cahuilla, as is much of the land within the Palm Springs area, Indian Canyons convey a fabulous sense of Native California. Centuries ago, each of the Indian Canyons held a substantial Cahuilla village beside its cool stream shaded by the oasis. The Cahuilla summered in the canyons, and moved to the mineral springs on the desert floor (now the Palm Springs spa) in the winter. Standing over the canyons is Tahquitz Peak, which rises immediately from the floor of the Coachella Valley. The mountain is sacred to the Cahuilla people as a creator of storms. The historical significance of the Indian Canyons is marked by their listing on the National Register of Historic Places. The canyons encompass the first (Palm Canyon), second (Andreas Canyon), and fourth (Murray Canyon) largest palm oases in the world. More than 150 species of plants thrive throughout the oases, many of which provided material used by the Cahuilla for food, medicine, and basket making. Bedrock mortars remain along the creeks. Melons, beans, squash, and corn were grown with water from irrigation ditches and reservoirs to supplement the Cahuilla diet.

The Cahuilla rock art in this area includes both pictographs and petroglyphs. Nearby, a rock shelter that contains pictographs utilizing both red and black pigments is thought to have been made by shamans within the past several hundred years. Figures include concentric whirlwind circles thought to symbolize a shaman's ability to fly, and a diamond chain, thought to represent the potent rattlesnake spirit-helper. Cupules (cup-shaped depressions) were perhaps carved by sick people visiting the sites to make offerings and pray for recovery.

Trailhead

Take the Hwy. 111 exit from I-10 in Palm Springs. Follow Palm Canyon Dr. through the town of Palm Springs. (The Agua Caliente Cultural Museum is on Palm Canyon Dr. at Ramon Rd.) Continue as Palm Canyon Dr. veers to the southwest and becomes South Palm Canyon Dr. Continue to the toll gate (fee required). Several hundred yards past the entrance, take the paved one-lane road to the right (southwest) 0.75 mile to the Andreas Canyon trailhead. The Indian Canyons are open daily.

Along the Andreas Canyon Trail

On The Trail

The Andreas Canyon Trail takes you through an oasis with a village site, rock art, and grinding rocks. An interpretive sign at the trailhead gives cultural information about these ancient tribal lands. From the trailhead, the route winds upstream to the west under the palms on the north bank of Andreas Creek. Fan palm fruit was harvested, and if not immediately eaten raw, sundried for storage. When needed, it was reconstituted in water, and ground in bedrock mortars along the creek. A palm fruit tea was made from the soaking water. There is a cumulative 200-foot elevation gain over several rocky scrambles both in and out of the palm shade before the trail reaches the creek crossing at a fence in 0.25 mile. Rest in the grove of sycamore, willow, and fan palm before crossing the creek and exploring the south stream bank on your return to the parking area.

hike 10   Oasis of Mara Nature Trail

Roundtrip Distance	0.5 mile
Location	A desert oasis in Chemehuevi territory
Administration	Joshua Tree National Park (760) 367-7511
Map	Joshua Tree National Park

Ten thousand years ago, a wide river flowed through the Pinto Basin. Archaeologists describe Pinto people living among lush vegetation. As the climate warmed, the river flow diminished, villages were moved to the springs and oases, and people began to practice agriculture. When the Serrano people lived at the Oasis of Mara, there was still enough water to sustain the main village of the region, and enough to divert irrigation water to grow corn, beans, squash, and melon. Houses were built from palm trunks fashioned into poles and beams, covered with palm-frond thatch. The Serrano people were followed by the Chemehuevi people, who made similar use of the oasis.

Trailhead

Exit Hwy. 62 just east of Twentynine Palms on Park Blvd. The Twentynine Palms Visitor Center is one block south on the right (fee required).

On The Trail

The Oasis Nature Trail visits the site of the village that thrived at the Oasis of Mara for thousands of years. The Chemehuevi called this oasis "place of little springs and much grass." The paved, wheelchair-accessible nature trail leads northwest from the Twentynine Palms Visitor Center and ultimately encircles the oasis. Head down the path toward the oasis. The trail is lined with signs interpreting the oasis and its vegetation. Keep in mind that the area looked quite different in ancient times. The water table was higher and the area was much greener. At one time there were 29 California fan palms at the oasis, hence the name of the visitor center and the nearby town.

There are three defining criteria of an oasis, and long ago all three were present here. But, since the time of the earliest people, the Pinto fault has been diverting the underground flow of water from the oasis. Now all that remains is the "ecotone " (the transitional zone, where oasis meets desert). The oasis "proper" (where water is near but below the surface), and the natural "hydric zone" (standing water) are not present. Since the flow stopped in 1942, the National Park Service now pumps water to keep the oasis alive, but the plants and animals depending upon standing water are gone.

The trail leaves the small, artificial hydric zone and encircles remaining vegetation and ethnobotanical specimens. The labeled mesquite beans and palm fruit along the trail once sustained the village. Arrowweed stems were cut and peeled, then worked back and forth between the grooves of a heated stone arrow straightener to make arrowshafts. The Chemehuevi practiced periodic burning to eradicate shrubs and promote the growth of deep-rooted edible plants and grasses with edible seeds. The Chemehuevi believed the dead palm fronds could harbor evil spirits, and burned them to remove that possibility. The burns also improved the palm fruit yield. At the trail's end, retrace your steps to the visitor center and parking lot.

hike 11   Cottonwood Springs Nature Trail

Roundtrip Distance	1.2 miles
Location	A desert camp of the Cahuilla
Administration	Joshua Tree National Park (760) 367-7511
Map	Joshua Tree National Park

S everal cultures inhabited Joshua Tree National Park, beginning with the Pinto people, who were followed by the contemporaneous Serrano, Chemehuevi, and Cahuilla peoples. In the southeastern corner of the monument lies the Pinto Basin, which 10,000 years ago supported the culture known to anthropologists as the Pinto people. A wide river once flowed through the Pinto Basin, with lush vegetation and many now-extinct animals such as ground sloths and camels. With the warming climate, the Pinto River dried up, and the people moved alongside springs and oases to gather plant materials and practice agriculture. The interpretive signs along the trail describe the foods gathered here by the Cahuilla.

Cahuilla grinding hole near Cottonwood Springs Oasis

Trailhead

Exit I-10 on Cottonwood Spring Rd. 25 miles east of Indio. Follow Cottonwood Spring Rd. 8 miles north to the Cottonwood Springs Visitor Center and the entrance to Joshua Tree National Park (fee required). Turn right and head 1 mile west to the campground on the left. The trailhead is near Site 13.

On The Trail

The Cottonwood Springs Nature Trail details ethnobotany of the Cahuilla en route to Cottonwood Springs. From the trailhead at the end of the campground, follow the path down through a sandy wash past paloverde trees—which accounted for up to three-quarters of the Cahuilla diet—ironwood, ocotillo, and cholla cactus. In 0.5 mile, pass through the Cottonwood Springs parking area to the continuation of the trail on its southwest side. A short but steep descent leads to the heart of the oasis. Continue several hundred yards farther southwest along the Lost Palms Oasis Trail. At 0.6 mile, bountiful wildflowers bloom in the spring around an interpretive sign describing the Cahuilla's "supermarket" of foods. Their mortar holes are in a boulder nearby. Retrace your steps to the trailhead.

hike 12   Big Morongo Canyon Trail

Roundtrip Distance	1 mile (with 12-mile option)
Location	A desert oasis in Serrano territory
Administration	Big Morongo Canyon Reserve (760) 363-7190
Map	Big Morongo Canyon Reserve

Ancient cultures have used Big Morongo Canyon as a stopping place in seasonal journeys between the high and low desert for thousands of years. Located between the Mojave and Colorado deserts, the canyon provided an easy passage, with ideal camping both in nearby caves and at the oasis at the canyon mouth. Five archaeological sites have been identified within the canyon, where fire rings, pottery shards, manos, metates,

Big Morongo Canyon is an ancient route

and mortar holes have been recorded. The Morongo, the last people to live here, are a band of the Serrano Tribe, which now has a reservation near Banning. The canyon holds a year-round creek and several springs, which are now famous among watchers of birds and bighorn sheep. Vermilion flycatchers frequent this lush, riparian habitat. The oasis, one of the ten largest natural desert oases in California, has the greatest variety of flora and fauna and the largest cottonwood/willow stands.

Trailhead

Exit I-10 at Hwy. 62 in Palm Springs. Go 9.5 miles north on Hwy. 62 to East Dr. Turn right and go several hundred yards to the Big Morongo Canyon Reserve parking lot (no fee) at 11055 East Dr. The main trailhead has a natural history display with trail information.

On The Trail

The Canyon Trail revisits the ancient route through Big Morongo Canyon. Beginning from the covered interpretive kiosk at the southwest end of the parking area, the trail passes through a meadow lined with sycamore trees and skirts park buildings to the Mesquite Trail at 0.2 mile. Follow the Mesquite Trail down a sunny, south-facing slope to the boardwalk at 0.35 mile, and follow the boardwalk through the marsh. Continue down stairs, over bridges, and through a thicket to the intersection of the Yucca Ridge and Canyon trails at 0.5 mile. Turn right (south) on the Canyon Trail and go to the oasis at the boardwalk's end in the canyon mouth. (From here, the Canyon Trail extends 5.5 miles to Indian Avenue for an optional 12-mile round-trip). Continue south, going as far as you wish down canyon before returning as you came.

hike 13   Mary Beal Nature Study Trail

Roundtrip Distance	0.5 mile
Location	A Chemehuevi camp in Mojave National Preserve
Administration	Providence Mountains State Recreation Area (760) 389-2303
Map	Mary Beal Nature Study Trail brochure

Providence Mountains State Recreation Area gives you a panoramic perspective of Mojave National Preserve's stark dry desert from a lofty 4,200-foot eleva- tion. Table Mountain, a 1,900-foot mesa visible 15 miles to the northeast, was a landmark used by the Chemehuevi when traveling the Mojave Trail. Tecopa, El Pakiva, and Medicine caves, now collectively known as Mitchell Caverns, sheltered Chemehuevi travelers for over 500 years. The caves' fire-blackened walls and hid- den food-and-tool caches give you the timeless feeling that a trading party is yet to return. The Chemehuevi used Mojave sage in the food caches to repel rodents with its strong aroma.

Trailhead

Exit I-40 at Essex Rd. 99 miles east of Barstow. Follow Essex Rd. to its end 16 miles northeast at Providence Mountains State Recreation Area Headquarters and Visitor Center (fee required).

On The Trail

The Mary Beal Nature Study Trail features the plant materials used by the Chemehuevi. The trail begins just north of the picnic tables by the visitor center. Letters along the trail refer to plants described in the brochure (available at the visitor center). Labeled plant specimens along the trail include creosote bush—a tea made from its leaves cured as many ailments as we cure with antibiotics—and both squawberry and banana yucca, which were used in basketry. Barrel cactus buds, flowers, and fruits were harvested, then either boiled and eaten immediately, or dried for later use. The trail features a wood rat's nest—similar to those found in nearby caves—containing Chemehuevi artifacts such as food and pottery shards. Radiocarbon-dating of wood rat nests indicates some date back hundreds of years, housing countless generations of rats, which habitually raided Chemehuevi food caches, returning to their nests with what are now ancient artifacts.

The trail descends slightly, then veers left (west) to traverse the plant community along the lower slope of several 7,000-foot peaks. Then, the trail climbs 400 feet in 0.25 mile to benches near the highest point of the hike (beside a sage specimen). From there, the trail offers incredible views of the mountains. Pinyon pine can be seen on the steep slopes. The large nuts were a staple of the Chemehuevi. While descending 400 feet to the trail's end, you traverse the exposed lower flank of Fountain Peak. The trail then climbs south just before the picnic area. Guided tours of Tecopa and El Pakiva caverns are available daily.

hike 14   Afton Canyon (Mojave Trail)

Roundtrip Distance	4 miles
Location	A Mojave Desert trade route
Administration	BLM, California Desert Information Center in Barstow (760) 255-8760
Map	USGS 7.5-minute series: Dunn and Cave Mountain quadrangle

Containing one of the few year-round water holes in the Mojave Desert, Afton Canyon lies along an important trade route between the former Shoshonean villages along the coast and those along the Colorado River. The trade route came to be known as the Mojave Trail. Archaeologists have unearthed stone tools and pottery estimated to be at least 8,000 years old in the area. Afton Canyon was carved by water draining from ancient Lake Manix. Other than the Mojave Trail, maintained as an ungraded four-wheel-drive road, there are no official hiking trails. The Mojave River still trickles along the canyon floor here, while elsewhere it flows underground to the Mojave sink near Soda Lake.

Trailhead

Exit I-15 at the AFTON CANYON CAMPGROUND exit 33 miles east of Barstow. Turn right and head south along the graded dirt road for 4.4 miles to the campground (shaded picnic tables, chemical toilets, and fire pits). The trailhead is at the entrance to the campground (no fee) before the railroad bed.

On The Trail

The hike in Afton Canyon along a section of this former Mojave Desert trade route includes caves used as early campsites. From the parking area, follow the road bed (actually a section of the Mojave Trail) to the right, heading east toward Afton Canyon. Within 0.25 mile, pass a right turn to a pond flooding a small portion of the Mojave Trail. (This is a great wildlife-viewing area when off-road vehicles are not fording the shallow water.) A levee extends ahead for a short way before crumbling to the river wash. Climb down toward the river. Several trails crisscross the wash heading toward the canyon narrows. To avoid off-road vehicles, stay on the footpaths through the wash. The canyon walls tower over you as you hike north toward Cave Mountain at 2 miles. Caves there sheltered early travelers along this trade route. From here, the Mojave Trail continues through Afton Canyon to the Colorado River, with many accessible side canyons open for exploration. When you're ready, retrace your steps to the parking lot.

hike 15   Calico Early Man Archaeological Site

Roundtrip Distance	0.3 mile
Location	A desert site of early man
Administration	BLM, Barstow Resource Area (760) 261-3591
Map	Calico Early Man Archaeological Site

Convinced that stones found at the Calico Early Man Archaeological Site were human-altered, Dr. Louis Leakey obtained funding from the National Geographic Society to excavate three master pits. Stone tools had been found during a commercial excavation adjacent to the site that exhibited ancient use-wear patterns. At the time the Calico stones were altered, which is dated at 200,000 years ago, Pleistocene Lake Manix filled the basin here. Pinyon pine, live oak, and juniper grew in the valley. Sloths, saber-toothed cats, and mammals roamed the area. Providing some of the earliest evidence of human occupation in North America, the stone tools were fashioned by nomadic hunters who stopped here for silica rocks. The hand-held tools were used in digging, skinning hides, and working wood. They included scrapers, choppers, perforators, and sawing tools, and were made of chert, jasper, chalcedony, and siliceous limestone. Though a semicircle of cobbles was excavated at Master Pit II, and excavation is still in progress in Master Pit III, there have been no fire rings or other remains suggesting life here. While Dr. Leakey's "favorite tool" at the visitor center presents evidence of human, rather than chance, alteration, a recent consensus in the scientific community holds that Calico is not a valid site due to extraneous materials having eroded into earlier deposits here.

Trailhead

Exit I-15 at Minneola Rd., 15 miles east of Barstow. Follow Minneola Rd., a graded dirt road, 2.5 miles north to the site (no fee). Guided tours lead into the main pits. A visitor center houses displays of artifacts and a technical library. The site is administered by the BLM, Barstow Resource Area.

On The Trail

Listed on the National Register of Historic Places, the Self-Guiding Trail tours Dr. Leakey's three master excavation pits on the slope above the former shoreline of Pleistocene Lake Manix. From the parking area the trail leads north up-canyon, skirting the commercial pit before swinging west, toward Master Pit I. From here, the trail continues to a viewpoint over the valley before climbing again along a ridge. The highest point of the site lets you examine a T-shaped trench and Master Pit II. From here, the trail descends past Master Pit III and the stockpile of round cobbles before returning to the parking lot.

hike 16 Darwin Falls

Roundtrip Distance	1.5 miles
Location	A desert spring in Shoshonean territory
Administration	Death Valley National Park (760) 780-2331
Map	Death Valley National Park

Remains of early campsites, rock shelters, and rock art are scattered throughout Death Valley. All sites have been restored to the descendants of the Panamint Shoshone Tribe. The Timbisha Shoshone still live at Furnace Creek.

In the heat of summer, Shoshonean villages were moved to the cooler heights. Oases and natural springs were choice camps. Darwin Falls is 3,100 feet above the valley floor. From here, the people could gather roots, berries, and pinyon nuts. With obsidian tools and pottery utensils, they could catch fish and hunt game. Mesquite pods and sand grass seeds were gathered and either eaten raw or ground into flour and stored.

Death Valley was once filled by Pleistocene Lake Manly, with villages around the shore and in the canyons

Trailhead

Exit I-395 at Hwy. 190. Head east for 48 miles to the intersection of Darwin Canyon Rd., 1 mile west of Panamint Springs. Following the sign to Darwin Falls, turn right, and head 2.5 miles south on the dirt road. Bear right at the fork and continue 0.3 mile to the Darwin Falls parking area (fee required). The visitor center at Furnace Creek interprets the site.

On The Trail

The Darwin Falls trip takes you along a lush canyon that once hosted seasonal Shoshone camps at an important water source. The Shoshone have lived in Death Valley for the last 10,000 years. Before the Shoshone, Lake Manly filled much of what is now Death Valley. The Pinto people had lived at the springs and along the shore of the huge Pleistocene lake. The hike follows a sandy wash 0.25 mile up-canyon, to where several lesser trails cross spring-fed Darwin Creek. As the canyon narrows at 0.5 mile, the vegetation becomes more lush with ferns and cattails, then cottonwoods and willows. At 0.75 mile, an intricate pattern of falling streams fill a pool surrounded by tules and cattails. Water means life in this canyon, and as in prehistoric times, people, birds, and animals are drawn here. Retrace your steps to the parking lot.

hike 17

Fossil Falls

Roundtrip Distance	0.5 mile
Location	A river camp in Owens Valley Paiute territory
Administration	BLM, Ridgecrest Resource Area, (760) 384-5400
Map	USGS 7.5-minute series: Pearsonville quadrangle

The Fossil Falls area was covered in molten lava 20,000 years ago, then sculpted by the Owens River. It has had a long history of human habitation dating back to 4000 BC. While the Pinto people lived around Fossil Falls and Little Lake, the Owens River flowed through Indian Wells Valley eroding the lava. The resulting canyons provided shelter for the early cultures. The Pinto people were succeeded by the Paiute beginning 1,000 years ago. From the Pinto people, archaeologists have found petroglyphs, grinding rocks, obsidian flakes, and rock rings that once held Paiute brush-and-tule shelters. Although the water is gone now, you can feel how smooth it made the otherwise rough lava around the falls. Obsidian quarried in the Coso Range to the east was used in tool manufacturing; remaining obsidian flakes dot the edge of the gorge.

Trailhead

Exit Hwy. 395 at Cinder Cone Rd. 20 miles north of Inyokern. Following the signs to Fossil Falls, turn east and continue 0.6 mile to a fork in the road. Bear right (south) and continue another 0.6 mile to the trailhead parking area.

On The Trail

The Fossil Falls Trail features the prehistory of the ancient Owens River bed. Marked by orange blazes painted on the rock, the trail begins next to the picnic table at the east side of the parking area. It meanders south over uneven lava toward the former path of the Owens River at 0.25 mile. The trail then follows the riverbed several hundred yards south to the first dry falls, then continues another several hundred yards to the second. While it ends here, you can continue along the riverbed to flat, sandy areas downstream. Explore the ancient landscape, using caution near cliff-like edges as the gorge is steep. Retrace your steps to the parking lot.

hike 18   Mono Lake Self-Guiding Trail

Roundtrip Distance	1 mile
Location	A summer harvest site in Shoshonean territory
Administration	Mono Lake Tufa State Reserve (760) 647-6331
Map	Mono Lake Tufa State Reserve

Though many tufas at Mono Lake Tufa State Reserve are 13,000 years old, they were underwater when the Paiute lived in summer houses near the lakeshore. It was not until recent water diversions that the lake level was lowered to reveal them. At 700,000 years old, Mono Lake is the oldest remaining lake in California. The tufas along the shoreline host enormous populations of brine flies, whose pupas wash up along the shore in late summer. The pupas were collected in baskets by the local Kuzedika Paiute for food, and for trade with neighboring peoples. At harvest, a pupa was rolled between the hands to separate the protective shell from the protein-rich body the size of a grain of rice. The resulting *kootsabe* could be stored for several months. In fact, the Yokuts name for brine fly is *mono*, which survives today as both the lake's name and a reference to this protein-rich food.

Trailhead

Exit Hwy. 395 at Hwy. 120, 5.5 miles south of Lee Vining. Go 5 miles east on 120 to the signed Mono Lake Tufa State Reserve. Follow the dirt road north to the parking area on the left (no fee). The site is interpreted by the Mono Basin National Forest Scenic Area Visitor Center in Lee Vining, (760) 647-3044.

On The Trail

Besides a close view of Mono Lake and its tufa spires, the loop along the South Tufa Trail takes in the traditional harvest of the Kuzedika Paiute. From the parking area, the trail meanders through previous lakeshores to the current shore. From the shoreline, go east among the tufa castles, watching for the brine fly pupa. Paoha and Negit islands are visible in the middle of the lake. The brine flies attract more than 80 species of migratory birds that nest on the islands. The migratory waterfowl also provided an important food source for the native people, who would travel by boat to the islands to collect eggs from nesting birds. Follow the loop east, then south as it circles back to the parking lot.

 # Guided Walks

Extensive petroglyphs in the Coso Range were created by the Paiute and Kawaiisu cultures. People traveled from as far away as Wyoming and Utah to visit these sites. Shamans traveled great distances to reach the Coso Range because it was the best place to gain power for influencing the growing season. In pristine condition, the petroglyphs in Little Petroglyph Canyon—with panels extending along both sides of a wash—are very impressive. The oldest panel dates back 19,000 years, while the most recent dates to the early 1900s. Guided walks are available in **Little Petroglyph Canyon** on spring and fall weekends through the Maturango Museum in Ridgecrest. All-day tours (fee required) are booked months in advance through 100 E. Las Flores Ave, Ridgecrest, CA 93555, (760) 375-6900.

At **Mitchell Caverns Natural Preserve**, smoke-blackened walls, hidden food-and-tool caches, and offerings to the cave spirits indicate that Chemehuevi Indians used the caves for perhaps 500 years on a seasonal basis, while hunting for game and harvesting pinyon pine nuts in this area. The caves were excavated by the Los Angeles County Museum of Natural History in 1934. Many textile items were recorded such as seed beaters, a winnowing tray, basketry fragments, sandals, and cordage. Guided walks are available through the Providence Mountains State Recreation Area Visitor Center on a daily basis, (760) 389-2303.

Tomo-Kahni State Park features a guided walk to a Kawaiisu village site near Tehachapi. The site includes pictographs that feature bears. A grizzly is said to live within a crack in the cave. It will emerge to frighten away visitors who approach without respect. A guided walk (1.5-mile hike with 800-foot elevation gain) is offered through the Lancaster Office of the California State Parks at (805) 942-0662.

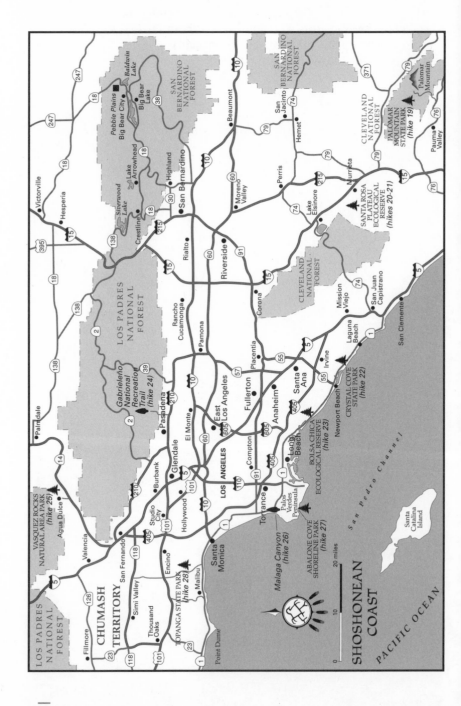

Shoshonean
South Coast & Peninsular Ranges

Landscape and People

The area of Los Angeles and Orange counties and the northern section of San Diego County were inhabited by the Shoshone people. The landscape is coastal-range mountains and valleys, and Pacific shore. Shoshonean people belong to the Uto-Aztecan language family, which is the largest in California. The family is divided by linguists into the Lakic (mainly people living near the coast), Numic (people living in the desert), and Tubatulabalic (people living near the Sierra) subgroups. The Shoshone first began their extensive migrations to Southern California from the Great Basin in approximately 500 BC.

Many southern coastal groups of Shoshone were renamed by the Spanish according to the names of their nearby missions. Along the coast of Los Angeles and Orange counties and on Catalina and San Clemente islands the Gabrieleño culture had three distinct languages. The Juaneño and Luiseño lived to the south of the Gabrieleño, along the coast. The Mountain Cahuilla lived in the mountains from Riverside to the Coachella Valley. The Nicoleño lived on San Nicholas Island. To the north, in the San Fernando Valley, lived the Fernandeño. In the southeastern section of the Transverse Ranges lived the Serrano. The Shoshonean population in the south coastal region is thought to have reached 11,000 in prehistoric times.

The largest of the Gabrieleño villages was Yanga, located near what is now Olvera Street in downtown Los Angeles. Near the Los Angeles River, the site was once shaded by a canopy of alder, cottonwood, sycamore, and ash, beside tule-bordered wetland. Yanga was home to more than 200 Gabrieleños. A large sycamore tree functioned as the council tree, in whose shade chiefs from neighboring villages would gather to discuss the issues of their day. The tree is no longer alive, but is believed to have been located along what is now a center median on Highway 101. The city's mayor is considering a request to plant a new sycamore in its spot to commemorate the millennium. At the foot of coastal bluffs between Abalone and Malaga coves are asphaltum seeps used by the Gabrieleños to seal boats and baskets.

Numerous Gabrieleño and Juaneño archaeological sites and shell middens remain along the Los Angeles County coast. Mineral hot springs in Orange and northern San Diego counties also have satellite archaeological sites. Dried fish, shells, and otter skins were the main barter of coastal people with inland villages. The coastal villages would receive acorns and tobacco in trade from Yanga or Sibango, which later became the San Gabriel mission site. Places of special interest include the Malaga Canyon archaeological site, where archaeologists have dug down through four distinct cultural layers of habitation, revealing at the bottom evidence of a civilization from the late Pleistocene. The steatite quarries on Catalina Island were known throughout the region. Neighboring people would travel to the island to trade for the heat-resistant, easy-to-carve stone used in the manufacture of cooking pots, pipes, and charmstones.

Natural Resources and Material Culture

Coastal Southern California plant foods featured the produce of the coastal sage scrub community. Yucca was the staple of many uses. The Gabrieleño people ground the seeds into flour; they ate the flowers boiled and the fruits raw. Another important food source, holly-leaved cherry was used as an ingredient in pinole. A tea was made from flowers of California buckwheat and chia, and sugarbush berries. Seafood consisted mainly of clams and abalone, whose discarded shells were left in great quantities in middens along the coastline. The people of the coastal villages obtained meat from sea otters, dolphins, sea lions, and beached whales. Also found within the coastal Shoshonean middens are the remains of sea gulls, brown pelicans, deer, antelope, badgers, rabbits, and squirrels. Coastal houses, known as *wickiups*, were willow-framed domes with thatch of tule or grass.

Money was manufactured from clamshell beads strung in 2 ½-foot-long *ponkos*, four of which were worth one Spanish real. Arrow points were made from local chert, volcanics, and imported obsidian, as were symmetrical, ceremonial knives. Fishhooks were carved from abalone shells. Coastal Shoshone fashioned treasure boxes from abalone shells sealed together with asphaltum. Small chipped, wheel-shaped stones have been found in the coastal region, but archaeologists have not determined their use. The Cogged Stone Site atop a bluff overlooking Upper Bolsa Bay has yielded 400 such stones dating back to 2500 BC. Throughout the western hemisphere, cogstones have been found only in central Chile and southern California.

Perhaps the best-known story of coastal Shoshonean culture is the "Island of the Blue Dolphin." It is a true story about a Nicoleño girl who jumped ship as her people were being forcibly relocated from their village on San Nicholas Island. She swam back to the island, and was found 18 years later in 1853, living alone in a home on the headland. She was wearing a cormorant feather skirt that is now on display in Rome. Faintly visible from the Palos Verdes Peninsula on a very clear day, San Nicholas Island contains ancient petroglyphs of killer whales, dolphins, and sharks. Abalone shell fishhooks lie in middens along the shore. Today, San Nicholas Island is managed by the Navy, and is strictly off-limits to the public.

The Gabrieleño were highly acclaimed for their craftsmanship. Boats were finely constructed of driftwood logs split into planks and bent into shape, fastened with fiber rope, and then sealed with asphaltum. Diaries of the early European travelers through the region record the beauty of Gabrieleño women, with flowers in long hair falling over their shoulders. Yucca fiber hairbrushes and yucca bulb shampoo cared for the hair, while red ochre provided a sunscreen and make-up. Jewelry made from steatite, whalebone, or shell was worn by men and women. Yucca and milkweed were finely woven into a linen-like cloth and used in basketry.

Museums and Interpretive Sites

Southwest Museum in Pasadena features dioramas and exhibits on all California cultures and basketry, (310) 221-2163.

Los Angeles County Museum of Natural History features exhibits of all California cultures, and displays the work of well-known Native American artists, (310) 744-3411). Traditional dance performances and festivals are held under their auspices.

Lake Perris State Recreation Area. *Ya' Heki'*, which means "Home of the Wind," Regional Indian Museum southeast of Riverside contains information on the Luiseño, Juaneño, Cahuilla, and other desert tribes, (909) 940-5603, 5608.

Point Vicente Interpretive Center exhibits pottery shards, arrowheads, and other artifacts found in the Palos Verdes Peninsula area, (310) 377-4444. Interpretive displays fan out from a model of the peninsula, labeled with the former Gabrieleño villages.

hike 19

Doane Valley Nature Trail

Roundtrip Distance	1 mile
Location	A Luiseño seasonal camp in the coastal mountains
Administration	Palomar Mountain State Park (760) 765-0755
Map	Palomar Mountain State Park, Doane Valley Nature Trail brochure

P alomar Mountain State Park contained three seasonal villages plus ten temporary camps and gathering stations along the sheltered route up Pauma Creek into Doane Valley. This route was traveled by the Luiseño people in summer and fall to gather pine nuts, acorns, elderberries, and seeds. In the upper valley at 4,600 feet is the Doane Valley Natural Reserve, which has bedrock mortars and metates, and the plants sought by the Luiseño. Wavainai, the Luiseño name for the mountain, was divided among the separate territories of several groups of Luiseño. The main Luiseño village of Pauma was lower, at the foot of the mountain, by the creek bearing the name.

Trailhead

Exit I-15 at Hwy. 76, 15 miles north of Escondido. Head east for 21 miles to County Rd. S6. Turn left, heading north for 6.5 miles to County Rd. S7. Turn left and continue for 3 miles to the Palomar Mountain State Park entrance kiosk (fee required). Pass the park headquarters, bearing right on the signed road to the Doane Valley Pond parking area.

On The Trail

The Doane Valley Nature Trail interprets the ethnobotany of the Luiseño, with labeled plants explaining their significance to the early culture here. The trail is posted with numbered signs corresponding to the brochure available at the trailhead. The signed nature trail begins at the southwest corner of the parking area and heads west, down a wooded path that crosses the park road within several hundred feet. The trail then traverses a hillside just above Doane Creek, passing specimens of stinging nettle, whose fibers were used for thread and whose young leaves were eaten as greens. Wild rose found here was used for both medicinal and religious purposes. The nature trail bears right at the Weir Trail junction and circles northeast, passing western raspberry, mountain currant, and wild strawberry, which were harvested in summer by the Luiseño. Cross Rattlesnake Creek within 0.5 mile. Forest opens out to meadow as the Doane Valley Nature Trail bears right again at the French Valley Trail junction. Meandering past oak, bracken fern (whose tender shoots were prized by the Luiseño for their walnut-like taste), and deer grass (used in basketry), the trail ends at the Doane Valley campground in 0.75 mile. Follow the road through the campground to the right, back to the parking lot.

hike 20   Oak Tree Trail

Roundtrip Distance	2.4 miles
Location	Coastal mesa hunting grounds in Luiseño territory
Administration	Santa Rosa Plateau Ecological Reserve (909) 677-6951
Map	Santa Rosa Plateau Ecological Reserve

For more than 2,000 years, the Luiseño used the Santa Rosa Plateau for hunting, and for gathering acorns in the fall. The plateau marks the southern extent of the Santa Ana Mountains, which parallel the coast 20 miles inland. Though the creeks dry in summer months, deep springs in the basalt creekbeds hold water year around, attracting deer and other wildlife that were hunted by the Luiseño. Remnants of a Luiseño camp still exist beside the creek along the Oak Tree Trail. Mortar holes and metates—shallow depressions in rock for grinding smaller seeds—are found in the granite outcrops.

Trailhead

Exit I-15 at Clinton Keith Rd. 16 miles north of Murrieta. Head west for 7.8 miles, for now bypassing the visitor center (open on weekends) to the Hidden Valley trailhead and parking area on the left.

Crossing the Santa Rosa Plateau

On The Trail

The Oak Tree Trail passes near a seasonal Luiseño campsite along a perennial creek with deep *tenajas* (holes worn in the creekbed that hold water year around). The trail passes through stands of Engelmann and coast live oaks, and rolling grassland brimming with wildflowers whose edible seeds the Luiseño gathered. The trailhead is marked by an interpretive sign. Pass through the gated entry and bear left along the Coyote Trail, walking southeast for 0.6 mile to the junction with the Trans Preserve Trail at Cole Creek. Head left along the Trans Preserve Trail for 0.3 mile, following Cole Creek through rolling grassland toward the junction with the Oak Tree Loop Trail. Turn left. Along this trail, you can recognize Engelmann oak by its short, rounded acorns, gray-colored leaves, gnarled branches, and fissured bark. Coast live oak acorns are long and slim, and its leaves are a deeper green. The trail soon doubles back to return along Cole Creek. Explore the creekside before retracing your steps to the parking lot.

hike 21   Vernal Pools Trail

Roundtrip Distance	2 miles
Location	Coastal mesa hunting grounds in Luiseño territory
Administration	Santa Rosa Plateau Ecological Reserve (909) 677-6951
Map	Santa Rosa Plateau Ecological Reserve

The Luiseño used the Mesa de Colorado (a.k.a. Santa Rosa Plateau) for hunting deer, rabbits, and waterfowl. It holds one of the largest vernal pools in the state. There is water here, and usually migrating waterfowl, from December through May. As the pool evaporates, plants bloom in rings along the shore. The plateau is topped with oak woodland, bunchgrass prairie, and coastal sage scrub.

Trailhead

Exit I-15 at Clinton Keith Rd. 16 miles north of Murrieta. Head 10.2 miles west, for now passing the visitor center (open on weekends) to the Vernal Pool trailhead and parking area next to the road.

On The Trail

The Vernal Pools Trail crosses Mesa de Colorado to two pools. Vernal pools provide seasonal wetlands for migrating waterfowl. Of the 14 remaining vernal pools in southern California, this ecological reserve

Nearing a vernal pool

protects 13. From the east side of the road, the Vernal Pools Trail heads east through rolling grassland. Backed on one side by an oak woodland, the trail continually offers excellent views of the surrounding vernal pools and the mesa to the southeast. Past the Trans Preserve Trail intersection, you ascend a small rise near an oak-lined ridge; then, descend to an interpretive sign explaining the life within the vernal pools. Ahead is the largest vernal pool. Note the piles of rock near the water. Though their origin is unknown, it is speculated they were used by the Luiseño as duck blinds. A boardwalk loops along the shore giving you a closer look. Retrace your steps to the trailhead.

hike 22   Crystal Cove Beach Walk

Roundtrip Distance	6.4 miles
Location	Coastal canyons in Gabrieleño territory
Administration	Crystal Cove State Park (949) 494-3539
Map	Crystal Cove State Park

The Gabrieleño people lived near the mouth of El Moro Canyon for over 4,000 years, hunting deer and rabbit and harvesting acorns, black sage, lemonade

Lush vegetation along the coast at Crystal Cove

berry, and sugarbush in the drainage of seasonal El Moro Creek. From the shore at Crystal Cove State Park, exposed 50-foot bluffs reveal layered remnants from California prehistory. Archaeologists have identified the remains of several Gabrieleño village sites, shell mounds, and artifacts within the park. Running through Crystal Cove are 3.5 miles of undisturbed sandy beach, reef, and tide pools backed by marine terrace and the San Joaquin Hills. From the blufftop, a healthy, coastal sage scrub community extends to the sandstone caves in the canyons. Fish, shellfish, and seaweed were collected along the beach, which is lined with tidepools of the Irvine Coast Marine Life Refuge. The tidepools are brimming with eel grass, sea cucumbers, and sea urchins, whose eggs were harvested by the Gabrieleño. They also collected mussels, clams, and limpets, and fished for shark, mackerel, and surfperch.

Trailhead

Exit Hwy. 1 at the Pelican Point entrance to Crystal Cove State Park, 1.3 miles south of Corona del Mar. There is a visitor center next to the El Moro Canyon parking area (fee required).

On The Trail

The trails along the beach and the bluff explore early Gabrieleño hunting and gathering grounds. From the parking area, both the beach route and the paved, wheelchair-accessible blufftop Walk and Bike Trail extend the length of the park, covering 3.2 miles to the mouth of El Moro Canyon. To start, follow the Walk and Bike Trail 0.3 mile south to the first of several, concrete beach-access trails. Follow the shoreline southeast. In 2.2 miles, the bluffs are broken by a string of cottages lining Los Trancos Creek. Continue south, rounding Reef Point, to where the park jurisdiction ends at the mouth of El Moro Canyon. (From here other trails explore the inland areas of the park.) Double back to Reef Point and climb the beach-access trail to return via the blufftop. The Walk and Bike Trail winds 3 miles northwest along the bluffs to Pelican Point. You could chose to ramble awhile along this route through the coyote brush, watching for meadowlarks. (Optionally, you could return along the beach to the parking lot. The northernmost beach-to-bluff access trail is well marked.)

hike 23   Cogged Stone Site

Roundtrip Distance	1.6 miles
Location	Coastal wetland in Gabrieleño territory
Administration	Bolsa Chica Ecological Reserve (714) 846-1114
Map	Bolsa Chica Ecological Reserve

More the 8,000 years ago, an ancient culture lived along the bluffs here at Upper Bolsa Bay. For a time—about 4,500 years ago—these people milled cogstones: 1-inch-thick stone disks from 3 to 5 inches in diameter with notched edges and holes bored through the centers. Having found no signs of wear on the disks, archaeologists assume their purpose was ceremonial. Throughout the western hemisphere, cogstones have been found only in central Chile and southern California. The Cogged Stone Site at Bolsa Chica has yielded 400 such stones dating back to 2500 BC. The cogstone milling site was located on a bluff overlooking Upper Bolsa Bay.

More recently, the Gabrieleño harvested spiny rush and bulrush from the bay for use in basket weaving. The bay estuary once provided a prolific food supply of spawning fish, crabs, shellfish, ducks, and plants for the people who lived here. The surf zone provided grunion and pismo clams. The site is interpreted by the Bolsa Chica Conservancy Interpretive Center.

Trailhead

Exit Hwy. 1 in Huntington Beach across from Bolsa Chica State Beach (a couple hundred yards south of Warner Avenue). Park in the lot on the bay side of Hwy. 1.

On The Trail

The trailhead is marked by an interpretive sign on the reserve history. The Reserve Trail heads northeast along the boardwalk over water before heading northwest, between the water and the bluffs. Walk among pickleweed and cordgrass, past a salt marsh interpretive display. The trail

The Cogged Stone Site across Upper Bolsa Bay

continues northwest, crossing several levees. There is good bird-watching along the route, which makes up for the bustle from the Pacific Coast Highway and the Signal Oil Company. Migrating waterfowl and shorebirds congregate here, once contributing to the bountiful harvest of both Gabrieleño and earlier cultures. At the trail's northernmost point near 0.8 mile, a spur trail ascends a bluff where several signs interpret the cogstone milling site. From this vantage, the entire marsh and coastline are visible. After crossing a tide gate in the bay, the loop trail returning to the parking area closely parallels the highway. For a more peaceful walk, retrace your steps via the Reserve Trail.

hike 24   Gabrieleño National Recreation Trail

Roundtrip Distance	5.2 miles
Location	Mountain canyon in Gabrieleño territory
Administration	Oak Grove Ranger Station, Angeles National Forest (818) 790-1151
Map	Big Santa Anita Canyon, Angeles National Forest

The Gabrieleño National Recreation Trail is named for the early Native people who traveled these canyons in the Front Range fishing, hunting, and gathering plants.

The Gabrieleño came here seasonally because the deep canyons sheltered important seed-bearing plants and wild game. The creeks provided fish and year-round water. The chaparral included oaks with bounties of acorns, and chamise for firewood. As a result of the National Scenic Trails Act in 1970, the Forest Service mapped a 29.5-mile network of pathways through the San Gabriel Front Range, meandering along the banks of tributaries of the San Gabriel River. In its entirety, the Gabrieleño National Recreation Trail first climbs from its origin near the Oak Grove Ranger Station in Altadena, along the Arroyo Seco to over 4,600 feet at Red Box. From there it descends the canyons of the West Fork of the San Gabriel River, then passes down through Santa Anita Canyon to Chantry Flat. This area was the mountain homeland of the Gabrieleño.

Along the Gabrieleño National Trail in Big Santa Anita Canyon

Trailhead

Exit I-210 at Santa Anita Ave. in Arcadia. Drive 6 miles north into the San Gabriel Mountains, to the Chantry Flat parking area. A National Forest Recreation Pass is required, and can be purchased at the Oak Grove Ranger Station (open weekdays).

On The Trail

Big Santa Anita Canyon offers a glimpse of the Gabrieleño mountain world. From the Chantry Flat parking area, the marked Gabrieleño National Recreation Trail descends into the canyon for 0.6 mile along the paved fire road. On the canyon floor, the trail is shaded by oaks and alders as it winds among the chaparral of the San Gabriel Mountains. At 0.7 mile, the trail crosses the Winter Creek bridge to a trail junction. The Gabrieleño Trail bears right, following the creek 1 mile upstream to the Sturtevant Falls Trail fork. Here, the Gabrieleño Trail heads left, and you continue 1 mile more uphill to the Cascade Picnic Area above the falls. Retrace your steps to the parking lot.

hike 25   Vasquez Rocks History Trail

Roundtrip Distance	2 miles
Location	Mountain canyon in Alliklik territory
Administration	County of Los Angeles Department of Parks and Recreation (805) 268-0840
Map	Vasquez Rocks Natural Area Park

Pictographs, middens, ovens, stone tools, and burial grounds throughout Vasquez Rocks Natural Area Park indicate that the Alliklik (a.k.a. *Tataviam*, "people of the south-facing slope,") inhabited the area for 4,300 years. The rocks provided shelter from the elements at Agua Dulce Spring. The Vasquez Rocks area is situated along a trade route between the people of the coast and the people of inland valleys and deserts. Acorns, yucca, yerba santa, chia, and islay (holly-leaved cherry) were plentiful food staples, and chamise was readily available for firewood. Deer, rabbit, and birds were hunted with an *atlatl*, a spear or dart thrower that preceded the bow and arrow. Homes were constructed of bent cottonwood and juniper branches, and thatched with bunches of grass sewn together with yucca twine. Grinding stones were used to crush acorns, juniper berries, and seeds.

Trailhead

Exit I-5 at Hwy. 14 in Santa Clarita and go 15 miles north to the VASQUEZ ROCKS/ESCONDIDO canyon exit. Go 2.2 miles north to the park entrance (no fee), and continue past the ranger's house to the camping area. The signed trailhead is near the beginning of the camping area. The park is administered by Los Angeles County Parks and Recreation. The park ranger's office is open weekdays, but beware of the dog.

On The Trail

Ethnobotany of the Alliklik near ancient dwelling sites is the History Trail's draw. The trail leads through a juniper woodland plant community, passing labeled specimens whose ancient uses are described in the trail brochure (available at the park ranger's office). The trail climbs gently southeast, ascending a dry wash. It meanders past rock formations and ends at the south side of the Famous Rocks. Explore the rocks at your own pace, and then retrace your steps to the parking area.

Plants featured along the way include yucca, islay, ceanothus, juniper, California sagebrush, and California buckwheat. Yucca was one

Shelter, water, and food attracted the Alliklik to Vasquez Rocks

of the most useful plants to the Alliklik people. Seeds, flowers, and fruits were eaten. Leaves were also soaked and peeled, then rolled into a strong fiber cord. Leaves were also soaked and worked into a lather for shampoo. Holly-leaved cherry flesh was made into a beverage, and its kernel was leached and ground into a meal. Ceanothus blossoms were used in a soap, while the roots were crushed to make a red dye. Juniper berries were either dried and ground into meal, or they were brewed to make a liquid that killed fungus on contact. The bark of the juniper was shredded to make a dye, and used as insulation in dwellings.

hike 26   Malaga Canyon

Roundtrip Distance	2.5 miles
Location	Coastal canyon with archaeological sites
Administration	Torrance County Beach (310) 372-2166
Map	None needed

Malaga Canyon was excavated by archaeologists from the Southwest Museum in 1936, and again in 1961. It is regarded as one of the few important archaeological sites in California containing evidence within its layers

of prehistoric human evolution. Under a 1955-period condominium complex on the bluff north of the canyon is an archaeological site that is four complexes (stratified levels of human habitation) deep, dating back as far as 500 BC.

The artifacts at the deepest level included shells, whose contents do not appear to have been cooked, and microliths of chert used for drilling and cutting. Second-level artifacts included metates and manos, revealing a diet largely dependent on acorns, seeds, and roots. There were still no hunting tools, and few shells and mammal bones. The third level, however, contained carved abalone fishhooks, bone harpoon barbs, and the skeletal remains of sea lion, sea otter, porpoise, fish, coyote, deer, and rabbit. The top layer included carefully fashioned chert and chalcedony arrow points, steatite arrow-shaft straighteners, and a basket-hopper mortar (a bottomless basket made to top the stone mortar).

Archaeologists learned enough to realize there was much more valuable information to be excavated at this site. But before they could complete their investigation, a condominium was built on the bluff. In 1961 the owner of the adjoining property found several artifacts while excavating for a tennis court. The site became known as Malaga Cove II, and a three-month study by the Southwest Museum followed. Excavation at Malaga Cove II revealed 500 artifacts.

Trailhead

Exit Hwy. 1 at Palos Verdes Blvd. in Torrance. Go 2 miles south to Paseo de la Playa. Turn right and head 1 block west to the blufftop parking area at Torrance County Beach (fee required seasonally).

On The Trail

This walk takes you along the beach and up through Malaga Canyon near the archaeological sites. From the parking lot, a steep ramp leads down to Torrance Beach. Follow the sandy beach left (south), passing under bluffs which get higher as you approach the rocky Palos Verdes Peninsula headland. Continue 0.75 mile south until the peninsula juts sharply west, and the sand gives way to rocks. This marks the start of the most prolific tidepools in the area, which were harvested for thousands of years by the villagers living atop the bluff. Near where the rocks begin, a path climbs among them to traverse the base of the coastal bluff. By 1 mile, the trail turns east to ascend Malaga Canyon. A paved 0.25-mile road leads up along the south side of the canyon to the bluff overlooking Malaga Cove Sites I and II. Behind a blufftop meadow, Malaga Cove I is located near the a large, white multilevel condominium visible through the trees to the north. Retrace your steps to the parking lot.

hike 27   Abalone Cove Beach Walk

Roundtrip Distance	2 miles
Location	Coastal village in Gabrieleño territory
Administration	Abalone Cove Shoreline Park (310) 545-4502
Map	None needed

Once brimming with red, green, and black abalone, Abalone Cove was valued by the Gabrieleño for centuries for its abundant shellfish. Besides being an important food source, the shells were fashioned into valuable beads. In prehistoric times, people as far away as the Grand Canyon sought abalone shells in trade. The Gabrieleño believed a person wearing this iridescent shell was protected from rattlesnake venom. During construction of a parking lot near Portuguese Point, a large kitchen midden was discovered and inventoried by archaeologists. They unearthed shell beads, broken mortars, and a pipe. Another midden was uncovered in the cove that revealed broken shell bits. The ocean-facing bluffs are the more recent in a series of 13 exposed marine terraces on the Palos Verdes Peninsula riddled with coves and caves. The terraces denote former sea levels. Before the Ice Age, the peninsula had been an island; it was later connected to the mainland by silt and sediment from the surrounding mountains.

Trailhead

Follow I-110 south to its southern end in San Pedro, where Gaffey St. begins. Continue 2 miles south on Gaffey St. to 25th St. Turn right (west) and drive until it becomes Palos Verdes Dr. S. in 2.5 miles. Follow Palos Verdes Dr. S. as it circles west on the peninsula for 3 miles to the Abalone Cove Shoreline Park entrance (fee required).

On The Trail

This beach walk visits the abalone harvest site of the Gabrieleño. From the east side of the parking area, the trail heads 0.25 mile down to the beach. There are no formal trails along the beach, only the sandy and rocky shoreline with tidepools, and occasional unsigned trails up the bluffs. Following bluffs, you can go 0.5 mile northeast up a small canyon to the top of Portuguese Point, where a gated road circles the edge of the 170-foot cliffs for a view of the peninsula coastline. As many as 10 Gabrieleño villages once graced this coastline. Alternatively, follow the sandy shoreline 0.25 mile east toward the Portuguese Point headland. Continue east where the route becomes cobbles and round the point to a watercourse. There is a sea cave here passable only when the tide is low. The reef-rock shoreline extends around Portuguese Point into Smuggler's Cove. Because of restocking efforts aimed at restoring abalone to their former abundance, you may be able to see them there. Then retrace your steps to the parking area.

Abalone Cove was valued for its abundant shellfish

hike 28   Santa Ynez Canyon Trail

Roundtrip Distance   6 miles
Location   Coastal mountains in Gabrieleño territory
Administration   Topanga State Park (424) 455-2465
Map   Topanga State Park

Topanga Canyon once delimited the territories of the Chumash to the north and the Gabrieleño to the south. Yet the site of Topanga State Park was a home to the Gabrieleño people, and "Topanga" is a Gabrieleño place name. At the mouth of Topanga Canyon archaeologists have uncovered remnants of a major settlement that had been a center of the Milling Stone Horizon culture. Within its lowest layers, the Topanga Site also contains evidence of the earlier San Dieguito culture: large stone tools such as chipped crescents and domed scrapers along with stone implements of their seed-gathering culture.

Trailhead

Exit Hwy. 1 at Topanga Canyon Blvd. and head 4.8 miles to Entrada Rd. Turn right and go 1 mile to the Topanga State Park entrance (fee required), and Trippet Ranch parking area, near the visitor center.

On The Trail

Rock shelters and bedrock mortars remain along the Santa Ynez Canyon Trail. From the Trippet Ranch parking area, continue up the road several hundred yards east toward the barn/visitor center. Just before the barn, follow the fire road to the right, switchbacking one hundred yards up (south) to a T-junction. Go left, heading southeast under an oak canopy up to the intersection with the Santa Ynez Fire Road. Go left for 0.25 mile to the Santa Ynez Canyon Trail, hiking along a grassy ridge. Follow the Santa Ynez Canyon Trail to the right (south) down to the canyon floor. Tiger lilies seasonally line Santa Ynez Creek as it winds through oak, willow, and sycamore. Watch for rock shelters and other traces of the past among the sandstone cliffs. Wander along the bottom of the canyon for up to 3 miles, until the path ends at Palisades Drive trailhead. Retrace your steps to the parking area.

 # Guided Walks

To the Serrano people, **Pebble Plains** is the birthplace of all wildflowers. When the Serrano Creator was cremated here, his ashes drifted throughout the valley, each one becoming a blossom. Then wildflowers appeared on earth for the first time. From Big Bear Valley, they spread all over the world. Today, over 300 species of wildflowers bloom in the valley, the largest display of rare flowering plants in the continental United States. Big Bear checkerbloom, eyestrain monkeyflower, California dandelion, Bear Valley sandwort, Munz's hedgehog cactus, and slender-petaled mustard thrive in this vernal meadow's clay soil. Bald eagles winter here. The north shore of Baldwin Lake in the San Bernardino Mountains was the homeland of the Serrano people, who hunted ducks and grizzly bears and gathered pinyon pine nuts here in summer and fall. Information on guided walks through the Big Bear Valley Ecological Preserve in wildflower season is available at Big Bear Ranger Station and Discovery Center, (909) 866-3437.

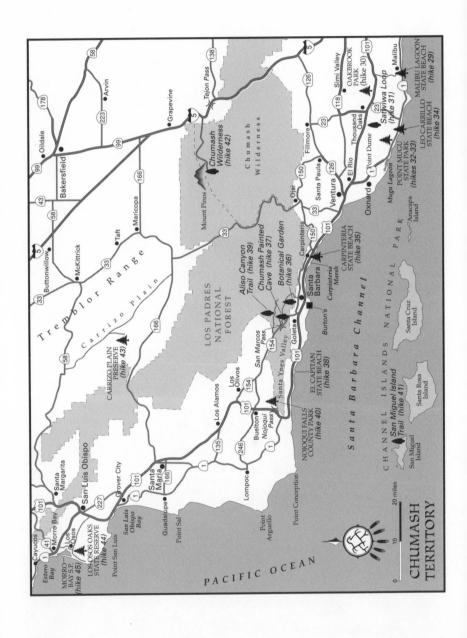

CHUMASH TERRITORY

Chumash
Central Coast, Transverse Range, & Channel Islands

Landscape and People

The ancestral homeland of the Chumash includes what are now San Luis Obispo, Santa Barbara, and Ventura counties. The Coast Range and Transverse Range mountains adjoining the coast, as well as the northernmost of the offshore Channel Islands, are principal features of this landscape. The word "Chumash" is perhaps derived from *Michumash*, a Chumash name for the people of Santa Cruz Island. *Michumash* literally means "makers of shell-bead money." Chumash residency in this area dates back perhaps 6,000 years.

The Chumash language belongs to the Hokan group. Hokan speakers occupy widely dispersed regions of California, each with its own linguistic variation. They range from the Diegueño in San Diego to the Karok of the Klamath River region. Among the Chumash, there are eight distinct languages. The scientific consensus is that when the Hokan speakers first arrived in California, they shared a single culture. Over time they adapted to the varying circumstances of their adopted lands. The wide variance among Hokan speakers could only have developed over many thousands of years, proving this language group's antiquity in California and throughout the Southwest.

Within Chumash territory, major settlements once lined the coast and the offshore islands of the Santa Barbara Channel, usually near marshes or river mouths. The Arroyo Burro and Mono Alamar trails were trade routes through the foothills linking coastal villages with those in the Central Valley. Chumash villages on the northern Channel

Islands of Santa Barbara, Santa Cruz, Santa Rosa, and San Miguel traded with the mainland villages. While many Chumash artifacts found on the islands date back about 1,000 years, certain older artifacts found there carbon-date back 8,000 years. More than 170 largely undisturbed archaeological sites have been mapped on Santa Rosa Island alone. The Chumash population is estimated to have reached 13,650 in prehistoric times. Many people of Chumash descent still live in the region, and are actively relearning and passing on the ancient ways.

The Chumash were the most ocean-oriented of the Native Californians. They traveled great nautical distances in plank canoes (*tomols*), fished the channel with bone hooks, hunted marine and land mammals, and exchanged the ocean's bounty for what they lacked within their region. The Channel Island Chumash would trade shell beads and knife points on the mainland for deerskins and antlers, chia, wild cherry, acorns, and pine nuts. The Chumash traveled to *Hitya* (Soapstone), the Chumash name for Santa Catalina Island, for the valuable and easily carved steatite quarried there. Chumash living in the Santa Ynez Valley traveled over what is now Refugio Pass Road to Quasil (now Refugio Beach) to trade for shell beads, tar, fish, and shellfish. They traveled interior trade routes through Sycamore Canyon and Santa Barbara Canyon (the Mono Alamar Trail) to trade with the Yokuts of the Central Valley and the Tehachapis for obsidian, honeydew sugar cakes, and tobacco. They traded with the Mojave for pottery, woven blankets, and hematite—the red pigment of their cave paintings.

Chumash territory is more fragmented north of Point Conception. Unprotected rocky coves and bluffs with pocket sandy beaches line the coast to Point Sal. From here, a coastal plain of sandy beaches full of pismo clams and backed by dunes stretches north to Point San Luis. Along the coast of present-day San Luis Obispo Bay, Chumash villages of *Nipolnit* (Village) and *Pisinit* (Tar) flourished. The nearby Nipomo Dunes contain archaeological sites 9,000 years old. At the northern limit of this satellite Chumash settlement, Cave Landing, a rock face protruding 150 feet into the surf was utilized by the Chumash as a fishing platform.

One of the most important archaeological digs providing information about early Chumash culture was that of the village of Syuxtun, on what was later known as Burton's Mound. Burton's Mound was one of two hillocks once 30 feet above the Santa Barbara waterfront, at Chapala Street. Occupying one of the mounds, Syuxtun had been home to 600 people. The mounds were excavated in 1923 by linguist and ethnographer John P. Harrington in conjunction with the Smithsonian and the Museum of the American Indian in New York. Twenty-five hundred artifacts were uncovered and sent to the Museum of the American Indian. Before the dig could be completed, however, the 30-acre property was subdivided into residential lots. A bond measure to secure it as a beach-front park failed. Instead, Burton's Mound—the village site of Syuxtun—was graded almost flat. Today, a plaque in Ambassador Park along the Santa Barbara waterfront marks the spot. The recovered artifacts remain in New York, while Harrington's field notes are in the Smithsonian's National Anthropological Archives in Washington, DC.

Natural Resources and Material Culture

Traditional Chumash plant foods included acorns, pine nuts, walnuts, cattail pollen, chia, sage, manzanita, miners lettuce, wild rose hips, holly-leaved cherry (islay), and yucca. Important seafoods included seaweed, abalone, clams, and fish. Seals, sea lions, dolphins, and stranded whales were also eaten. Animal foods included ducks, geese, quail, rabbit, deer, and bear.

Families lived in circular, willow-framed, tule-thatched homes with central fire pits. In large villages houses were built in rows with connecting passageways. Each village had a *temescal,* a Nahuatl word the Spanish applied to the sweathouse, and a common area, which included a playground and a ceremonial dance area. Communal space was allocated for making stone tools, canoes, and shell beads. Each town along the coast had several plank canoes.

Bead money was fashioned from olivella shells. Projectile points were made from chert. Mortars were hollowed out of sandstone or whale vertebrae. Whale vertebrae were used also as stools. Easy-to-carve steatite was used to make bowls and charmstones. Digging tools were given heft by the application of serpentine weights around their handles. The Chumash ate and drank from wooden bowls and plates, and from baskets sealed with asphaltum.

The *tomol,* the Chumash word for "pine," is one of the masterpieces of Native California. A tomol was a canoe made from driftwood or pine which had been shaped with tools of antler, bone, and shell, tied together with rope made from the milkweed plant, painted red with a mixture of pine pitch, red ochre, and asphaltum, and brilliantly decorated with abalone shell. Canoes were made only by members of the Brotherhood of the Canoe, some of the most highly accomplished and respected members of a community. Society members could paddle farther and faster into the channel, catch the biggest fish, and bring back the heaviest loads from the Channel Islands. A one-way trip to San Miguel Island being over 45 miles away, this was an impressive feat.

The Chumash are also known for brilliant cave paintings in the interior of their region. Chumash rock art is epitomized by the Chumash Painted Cave State Historic Park and the Painted Rocks at Carrizo Plain Preserve. Some of the most brilliant pictographs of Native California contained Chumash rock-art colors derived from minerals. Purple, red, and orange were obtained from iron oxide. Diatomaceous earth found near Lompoc provided a white pigment. Yellow came from limonite. Both blue and green were derived from serpentine. Black could be obtained from either manganese, charcoal, or burnt graphite. Pigment cakes were diluted with water, milkweed juice, animal oil, or bird eggwhites to add permanence. Figures were either painted on cave walls with brushes made of soaproot or yucca, or drawn with the pigment cakes themselves. Symbols overlap and cover each other. Beautiful sunlike circles, and curious, curved lines split at both ends adorn the cave walls. Their meaning is linked to universal symbols for fertility, water, and rain. Clearly, the Chumash produced one of the most advanced material cultures in Native California.

Museums and Interpretive Sites

Chumash Interpretive Center at Oakbrook Park is open from 10 A.M. until 5 P.M. (closed Mondays) and features artifacts and interpretive displays on Chumash culture, 3290 Lang Ranch Parkway, Thousand Oaks (see hike 30). Guided walks are available weekends, (805) 492-8076.

Satwiwa Native American Indian Culture Center at Rancho Sierra Vista in the Santa Monica Mountains National Recreation Area, open weekends, features exhibits on Chumash daily life. Artifacts include abalone shell fishhooks, soapstone fish fetishes, deer bone tools, a harpoon, rope made of yucca, a tomol sealed with asphaltum, and a piece of sharkskin (to demonstrate its use as sandpaper). The Satwiwa Sunday Guest Host Program brings native descendants to the site who share traditional knowledge with visitors, (805) 375-1930. (See also hike 31.)

Santa Barbara Museum of Natural History, open Mondays through Saturdays, features dioramas of southern Chumash village life. Exhibits include steatite pots, mortars and pestles, a copy of Painted Rock at the Carrizo Plain Preserve, and a replica of John Harrington's plank canoe. The early 1900s anthropologist first recorded the ethnography told to him by Kitsepawit. Though he was a mission-born Chumash, Kitsepawit had visited his elders to relearn the traditions of his people. Much of the information we rely upon today about the Chumash originated from this work. The museum also sponsors field trips to the Chumash Painted Cave State Historic Park, (805) 682-4711.

Morro Bay State Park Museum of Natural History in Morro Bay features a diorama of Chumash life, steatite pots, and whale charmstones. Charmstones were believed to attract whales, causing them to be stranded on the beach. Then they could be killed and eaten, (805) 772-7434.

Channel Islands National Park's mainland visitor center at Ventura harbor features Chumash artifacts, (805) 658-5730. Island Packers, next door, has charter boat trips to the islands. Call (805) 642-1393 for reservations (see hike 41).

The **Goodwin Educational Center** at Painted Rocks in Carrizo Plain Preserve interprets the geology and flora and fauna here, with a brief description of the Chumash rock art. The museum is open 9 A.M. to 5 P.M. Thursday through Sunday, from December through May. Other than March 1 through July 15, when they are closed to protect nesting falcons, the Painted Rocks are accessible all year, (805) 475-2131. (See also hike 43.)

hike 29   Malibu Lagoon

Roundtrip Distance	0.5 mile
Location	Coastal wetland in Chumash territory
Administration	Malibu Lagoon State Beach (818) 880-0350
Map	Malibu Lagoon State Beach

A large Chumash village once flourished along the shore of the lagoon at the mouth of Malibu Creek. Malibu was the territorial transition between the Gabrieleño and Chumash peoples. Human habitation of the area dates back 7,000 years. "Malibu" is derived from *Maliwu*, the name of the Chumash village here. The Chumash word *Maliwu* means "sound of crashing waters." The village sat atop Vaquero Hill, a small bluff overlooking Malibu Lagoon. The site is now occupied by the Adamson House, whose garage houses the Malibu Lagoon Museum with its Chumash exhibits. The Chumash people fished in the lagoon and collected shellfish nearby.

Trailhead

Exit Hwy. 1 at Cross Creek Rd. in Malibu. Go south to the road's end at the Malibu Lagoon Public Access parking area. (The Malibu Lagoon Museum and the Adamson House are at 23200 Pacific Coast Hwy. The museum is open from Wednesday through Sunday.)

On The Trail

At the parking area, an interpretive kiosk depicting the lagoon's natural history marks the beach trail. A maze of footpaths weave around the shore. Head west through tule, bulrush, and pickleweed, over a system of boardwalks and bridges. Malibu Lagoon provides habitat for abundant waterfowl and shorebirds. Continue to the sandy beach within 0.25 mile. Surfrider Beach and the Malibu Pier are classics of the Southern California shore, which features a mild climate and calm seas. Wander the shoreline another 0.25 mile to the left (south), and wade across the outlet of Malibu Creek, which is shallow or dry in summer but may divide Surfrider Beach in the wet season. Just beyond the outlet is a pathway leading up the bluff to the Adamson House and Malibu Lagoon Museum on Vaquero Hill. Signs throughout the house grounds and in the museum interpret the Chumash village site. Retrace your steps to the parking lot.

hike 30 Oakbrook Canyon Trail

Roundtrip Distance	1 mile
Location	Inland canyon in Chumash territory
Administration	Oakbrook Regional Park (805) 492-8076
Map	Oakbrook Regional Park

In this inland canyon in eastern Chumash territory, a single, 12-inch-long upright swordfish drawn in hematite on the wall of a rock shelter suggests that some of the people living here belonged to a special swordfish society (Whitley, 1996). Adorned in elaborate swordfish headdresses, the group performed the swordfish dance at their tribe's annual gathering. One such headdress was

Grinding rocks in Oakbrook Canyon

found to date back 2,000 years. Sacred, primordial swordfish were said to live in a rock house in the waters off Point Mugu. Gathering shellfish along the coast, Chumash women would throw a native tobacco and lime mixture in the water as an offering. The swordfish pictograph may be visited along a guided walk arranged through the Chumash Interpretive Center (see "Museums and Interpretive Sites" above).

Trailhead

Exit Hwy. 101 at Westlake Blvd. in Thousand Oaks. Take Westlake Blvd. 4 miles north to Lang Ranch Pkwy . Turn right and go 0.25 mile to Oakbrook Park. Guided walks are available through the interpretive center on weekends.

On The Trail

There is a reconstructed Chumash village and interpretive center staffed by tribal members near the trailhead. From the interpretive center, follow the Canyon Trail east along a dirt road beside the creek up-canyon. The trail leads you through an ancient oak woodland along the base of the canyon. At 0.75 mile there is a farm that nurtures native animals for future reintroduction. After 1 mile, the trail reaches a clearing with grinding holes in boulders. Within several hundred yards, the trail becomes an almost impassable footpath. Retrace your steps to the parking area.

hike 31   Satwiwa Loop

Roundtrip Distance	1.5 miles
Location	Coastal canyons of Chumash territory
Administration	Santa Monica Mountains National Recreation Area (805) 375-1930
Map	Rancho Sierra Vista/Satwiwa Site

Satwiwa was a major Chumash village in Big Sycamore Canyon along an early trade route through the Santa Monica Mountains. Gabrieleño, Chumash, and people from the inland mountains, valleys, and deserts often passed through Big Sycamore Canyon, trading and feasting with the people of Satwiwa. *Satwiwa* is the Chumash word for bluffs, like those seen on Boney Mountain. The prominent cliffs of Boney Mountain were sacred to the ancient people who came here.

Satwiwa is still a cherished natural place in the Santa Monica Mountains used by Gabrieleño and Chumash peoples for weekly, Sunday storytelling and historical presentations; these are open to the public at the Native American culture center here (see "Museums and Interpretive Sites" above). The National Park Service staff named the reconstructed Chumash village after the original Satwiwa.

Trailhead

Exit Hwy. 101 at the WENDY AVENUE exit in Newberry Park. Go 2.5 miles south to Potrero Rd. Turn right and go 1.8 miles west to the park entrance across from Pinehill Rd.

Satwiwa is named for the cliffs of Boney Mountain

On The Trail

For the Satwiwa Loop Trail, walk through the gate at the south end of the parking area of the Rancho Sierra Vista/Satwiwa site. Continue south along a paved fire road, past two park residences. The trail enters the chaparral of the upper reaches of Big Sycamore Canyon in 0.25 mile. Several hundred feet farther south, cross the footbridge on the left over a creek. Signs here at the Satwiwa site interpret traditional Chumash ways. Near the creek, shaded by venerable oaks is a reconstructed *ap* (domed house). To the left is the Culture Center, and straight ahead is the self-guiding Satwiwa Loop Trail. Head east from the Culture Center, bearing right and crossing the creek to pass through a field to a windmill at 0.5 mile. The loop trail now turns south, first descending into, then emerging from, a ravine with periodic views of Boney Mountain's bluffs. A stone-tool manufacturing site once existed below the bluffs, but has since been covered by the debris of the park's ranching days. In 0.75 mile, the trail turns right at a fork to head west over a rise overlooking Big Sycamore Canyon. Continue back toward the now-visible village site. When you've explored the Culture Center and reconstructed village, retrace your steps to the parking area.

hike 32   Chumash Trail

Roundtrip Distance	3 miles
Location	Coastal Chumash territory
Administration	Point Mugu State Park (818) 880-0350
Map	Point Mugu State Park

M uwu was the largest of the Chumash villages along the shores of Mugu Lagoon. The lagoon was home to the Chumash for 7,000 years. One of the archaeological sites along the lagoon's shoreline is listed on the National Register of Historic Places because it has provided California's best and most complete sample of Chumash artifacts. *Muwu* is the Chumash word for "beach." Located where Calleguas Creek enters Mugu Lagoon, Muwu was the lagoon's namesake. As there is no public access to the lagoon, its environs are best seen from the Chumash Trail to Mugu Peak. The Chumash Trail follows the early route connecting the lagoon and the La Jolla Valley.

The archaeological site at Mugu Lagoon has yielded Chumash artifacts

Trailhead

To reach the trailhead, 37 miles west of Santa Monica, exit Hwy. 1 at the large turnout across from the Navy Rifle Range bordering Mugu Lagoon (no fee). You can get a map at the Sycamore Canyon entrance to Point Mugu State Park (see hike 33 trailhead directions).

On The Trail

Beginning near the northern boundary of Point Mugu State Park, the Chumash Trail ascends the flank of Mugu Peak for a view of the Channel Islands, Mugu Lagoon, and La Jolla Valley, all of which had Chumash villages for centuries. As was the Chumash way, the trail ascends straight up the mountain, making no use of switchbacks. From the trailhead, you climb through a ravine to a series of chaparral-clad terraces beginning at 0.5 mile. Shell fragments seen beside the trail are actually part of a Chumash midden of discarded shellfish remains. The route continues up the exposed grade among prickly pear cactus and coastal sage scrub to the Mugu Peak Trail junction. Go straight, continuing northeast over a saddle and into the bunch grass prairie of La Jolla Valley. At 1.5 miles, turn right at the intersection with the La Jolla Loop Trail and follow it to an oak-lined creek. Archaeological evidence reveals that there were large, permanent settlements here in the La Jolla Valley. The loop trail connects with a trail to Mugu Peak and others around the valley for extended hikes. Explore the La Jolla Valley before retracing your steps to the parking area.

hike 33   La Jolla Canyon Trail

Roundtrip Distance	7 miles
Location	Coastal Chumash territory
Administration	Point Mugu State Park (818) 880-0350
Map	Point Mugu State Park

La Jolla Canyon has wind-carved sandstone caves that appear among cliffs interspersed with chaparral. Some 7,000 years ago—before the Chumash—the area supported the Oak Grove people of the Milling Stone

Horizon. This culture inhabited the coast from here northwest to Santa Barbara. The Little Sycamore Shell Mound documented this culture within its layers. (The Oak Grove culture coincided with that of the La Jolla in San Diego.) The La Jolla Valley with its native bunch-grass prairie was dotted later with Chumash villages. The Chumash traveled La Jolla Canyon between inland camps and the coast. The caves are thought to have been used in Chumash religious ceremonies.

Trailhead

Drive 32 miles west of Santa Monica on Hwy. 1 to the Sycamore Canyon entrance to Point Mugu State Park. Follow the park entrance road to the lot (fee required) near the Ray Miller trailhead.

On The Trail

The trailhead is marked by an interpretive kiosk at the north end of the parking area. Pass through a gate and follow the fire road north into a canyon covered by chaparral. Climb 0.75 mile up the canyon's east side, past old mining equipment, until the canyon narrows. Cross the creek

Sandstone caves of La Jolla Canyon

and wander between sandstone cliffs and caves, among coreopsis, yucca, and prickly pear cactus, to switchbacks ascending a ridge. From this vantage point, survey the mountain views and the coastline visible below. Shortly after the trail levels off, it intersects the La Jolla Valley Loop Trail at mile 1.25. Turn right on the loop trail to explore the prairie of La Jolla Valley before retracing your steps to the parking area.

hike 34   Arroyo Sequit

Roundtrip Distance	2 miles
Location	Coastal Chumash territory
Administration	Leo Carillo State Beach (818) 880-0350
Map	Leo Carillo State Beach

Evidence obtained from the Chumash archaeological site near the mouth of Arroyo Sequit Creek at Leo Carillo State Beach suggests that the Chumash people lived here as early as 6,000 ago. Indeed, several important Chumash archaeological sites have been documented nearby along the coast, including the nationally known Little Sycamore Shell Mound near Solromar. The people of the village at Arroyo Sequit collected shellfish in the tidepool near the point, hunted game, and gathered plant material from the surrounding coastal sage scrub and riparian woodland. In the fall, the Chumash traveled to the foothills up-river to harvest acorns and black walnuts, and hunt game. Salmon once spawned in Arroyo Sequit, and in winter the Chumash followed the run upstream to fish. From the beach at Arroyo Sequit, they traveled in tomols to the offshore Channel Islands to collect lobster, mussel, and abalone. Fishhooks were made of abalone shell.

Trailhead

Exit Hwy. 1 at the Leo Carillo State Beach entrance, 13 miles west of Malibu. Pass under the highway and park near the visitor center in the NORTH BEACH parking area.

Sea caves at Sequit Point

On The Trail

The walk begins at the visitor center by the parking area and descends the bluff to the sandy beach. From the beach, follow the shoreline 0.5 mile southeast. A low tide will let you explore sea caves and tidepools at Sequit Point. Continue around the point to the mouth of Arroyo Sequit, where a Chumash village once stood. Beyond the creek mouth, the rocky shoreline extends 0.5 mile to the south boundary of the park. Sea lions and shorebirds make use of offshore rocks. Enjoy the beach before retracing your steps to the visitor center and the parking lot.

hike 35

Asphaltum Seep

Roundtrip Distance	1 mile
Location	Coastal Chumash territory
Administration	Carpinteria State Beach (805) 684-2811
Map	Carpinteria State Beach

A n archaeological investigation in 1929 at Carpinteria Marsh uncovered remnants of the Oak Grove culture, which predated the Chumash. The Chumash succeeded the Oak Grove people here about 6,000 years ago. The San Miguel Campground at Carpinteria State Beach is situated almost directly above Mishopshnow, once a Chumash village of 300 people and a center for tomol building. Intricate woodwork produced here so impressed the Spanish that they referred to Mishopshnow as "La Carpinteria." Mishopshnow was located here because of tar seeps in the nearby cliffs, where asphaltum could be obtained for use in water-proofing the tomols. Tar still seeps from the cliff face.

Site of Chumash tomol-building village of Mishopshnow

Trailhead

Exit Hwy. 1 at Palm Ave. in Carpinteria. Go 1 mile south to the Carpinteria State Beach entrance. Leave your vehicle in the day-use parking area (fee required).

On The Trail

A walk along Carpinteria State Beach takes in the site of Mishopshnow and the tar seeps used by the Chumash in waterproofing tomols, cooking vessels, and baskets. The walk begins at the day-use parking area of Carpinteria State Beach. The Channel Islands, once a destination for tomol voyages, are visible offshore. Follow the shoreline 0.5 mile east, past the lifeguard towers and across the mouth of Carpinteria Creek. Here the beach narrows to wet sand backed by low sandstone cliffs. Continue several hundred yards east to the low, dark bluffs in front of San Miguel Campground. Tar seeps from the cliff face here. The bluffs extend to a tiny cove, where they ooze with more active seeps. Large deposits of asphaltum lie beneath the sand. Exposed tar pits on the beach were found to contain Pleistocene fossils. When you are ready, retrace your steps to the parking area.

hike 36   Plant Fiber Ethnobotanical Exhibit

Roundtrip Distance	0.5 mile
Location	Outdoor exhibit in Chumash territory
Administration	Santa Barbara Botanic Garden (805) 682-4726
Map	Santa Barbara Botanic Garden

The plant-fiber ethnobotanical exhibit at the Santa Barbara Botanic Garden features displays on how Native Californians used plants to create nets, baskets, clothing, and houses. Throughout the exhibit there are labeled plants such as Indian rush, deer grass, and wild grapes, which were coiled and twined into baskets by the Chumash. There are samples of basket-making techniques and clothing styles of Native Californians. Though the riparian canyon site remains in a natural state, the botanic garden hosts native plants from all over California. Streamside vegetation here includes plants used by the Chumash for food and medicine, such as maidenhair fern, milk maid, island alum-root, wild cucumber, currant, black sage, California bay, wood mint, wild ginger, gooseberry, and bladderpod. Mission Creek runs along the bottom of the canyon, while white alder and sycamore shade the canyon floor.

Trailhead

Exit Hwy. 101 at State St. in Santa Barbara. Head 0.5 mile northwest to Los Olivos Rd. Turn right and go 0.5 mile, past the mission to Foothill Rd. (Hwy. 192). Turn right and drive 0.2 mile to Mission Canyon Road. Turn left and head 0.5 mile north to the Santa Barbara Botanic Garden entrance on the left.

On The Trail

The exhibit route is lined with labeled California native plants. Take the trail through the signed MEADOW SECTION, passing UNDER THE OAKS, to the INDIAN TRAIL. (The INDIAN STEPS is a shortcut here.) Pass through the RED-WOODS SECTION to Mission Dam in 0.25 mile. The ethnobotanical exhibit is across the bridge, and just downstream from the dam. The exhibit displays can be seen along a short spur trail that follows the bank of Mission Creek. From the exhibit, return as you came, or continue following the creek along the Canyon Trail for 0.4 mile to Campbell Bridge. Cross the bridge and follow the Campbell Trail back through the DESERT SECTION to the information kiosk, and back through the MEADOW SECTION to the parking area.

hike 37

Chumash Painted Cave

Roundtrip Distance	0.1 mile
Location	Coastal hills in Chumash territory
Administration	Chumash Painted Cave State Historic Park
	(805) 968-3294
Map	Not necessary

Brightly painted pictographs line the walls and ceiling of sandstone caves in the hills behind Santa Barbara. An ancient ceremonial site, the Chumash Painted Cave, has some of the most highly regarded rock art of its kind in the western United States. Because such caves opened pathways to the Chumash spirit world, people unprepared to take those journeys did not visit rock-art sites. Though located near a village site, this cave was carefully avoided by all but the shaman.

The opening of the Chumash Painted Cave

Brilliantly painted in pigments of red, black, and white, the rock art is thought to be no more than 1,000 years old. The red pigment, *'ilil*, is an iron oxide mixture mined both from a deposit east of Santa Ynez and from sites on Santa Rosa and Santa Cruz islands. Different hues represent intentional variation achieved by obtaining hematite cakes from different sources. The black pigment, *wak'shik 'alchoshoy*, is charcoal of oak or ash. The white pigment, *'itshtaqaq*, was ground from diatomaceous earth. Figures include rattlesnakes, guardians of the spirit world, represented here as red zigzags sandwiched between red and white lines. A red centipede, a symbol of death in Chumash mythology, represents the danger of the spirit world.

Circles and sun-like figures are thought to represent celestial events, a black disk signifying a total solar eclipse. There was a total eclipse visible at the cave calculated to have occurred on November 24, 1677, when the sun was closely aligned with Mars and Antares. The triangle formed by a black disk near two red circles with internal crosshatching is thought to record this event. A brochure interpreting the Chumash Painted Cave is available at the Santa Barbara Museum of Natural History (see "Museums and Interpretive Sites" above).

Trailhead

Exit Hwy. 101 in Santa Barbara at Hwy. 154 (San Marcos Pass Road). Go 5 miles northeast to Painted Cave Rd. Turn right and head 2.5 miles east to the CALIFORNIA STATE PARK sign on the left. Park alongside the road. (The Santa Barbara Museum of Natural History offers guided interpretive tours, (805) 682-4711.)

On The Trail

From the roadside, a state park sign marks the steep, rocky trail that ascends the hill a short switchback to the cave opening. Bring a flashlight to illuminate the cave walls from the gate at the cave opening. Back down the hill and across the road, there is another footpath that passes a bedrock mortar along Maria Ignacio Creek.

At the heart of Chumash territory near San Marcos Pass, the terrain is riparian woodland with frequent sandstone outcrops. The Chumash migrated into the canyon in summer and fall to gather acorns and seeds. Hwy. 154 follows an early trade route over San Marcos Pass. The route was used for travel between Syuxtun, the village commemorated in Santa Barbara's Ambassador Park, and the villages of the Santa Ynez Valley.

hike 38   El Capitan Nature Trail

Roundtrip Distance   O.3 mile

Location   Coastal Chumash territory

Administration   El Capitan State Beach (805) 968-3294

Map   Not necessary

A juahuilashmu, the Chumash village site here at the mouth of Cañada del Capitan, was excavated in 1957, but the entire visible coastline from Santa Barbara to Point Conception is riddled with Chumash midden excavations. Well-preserved remnants of shellfish, bones, tools, hammerstones, and projectile points were uncovered at a village site just east of Arroyo Burro Beach County Park. Artifacts between 3,000 and 6,000 years old have been excavated at More Mesa north of Santa Barbara. Remnants of both Chumash and Oak Grove cultures have been found at Goleta Slough. Quasil was the name of the Chumash village to the west at Refugio State Beach. Refugio Pass Road originated as a Chumash trade route between the coast and the Santa Ynez Valley. Located at the ocean end of this trade route, Quasil was an important meeting place for island, coast, and valley Chumash. A Chumash village has been excavated at Gaviota State Park. Farther west, 'Upup, the Chumash word for "shelter," was the name of the village at Point Conception. The sheer, 160-foot bluffs of Point Conception are known to the Chumash as the "Western Gate." All land visible from this point is sacred in Chumash tradition.

Trailhead

To reach the trailhead, 10.5 miles west of Goleta, exit Hwy. 1 at the El Capitan State Beach entrance on the ocean side of the highway. Pass the entrance kiosk and visitor center (with limited information on the Chumash people) and park in the day-use lot (fee required).

On The Trail

The El Capitan Nature Trail passes near the Ajuahuilashmu village site, then connects with the 2-mile blufftop trail west along an early route linking it with the neighboring village of Quasil. From the parking area, follow the park road back toward the entrance to the signed NATURE TRAIL. Head east into the wooded canopy along the riverbed. At the river mouth, the trail ends at the junction of a 2-mile trail joining El Capitan and Refugio State beaches. Walk right (west) along the blufftop, passing an asphaltum seep. The route offers constant views of the coastline and the Santa Barbara Channel so rich in Chumash history. Along the way are several stairways leading to the beach. When you are ready, retrace your steps to the parking area.

hike 39   Aliso Canyon Trail

Roundtrip Distance	2 miles
Location	Inland Chumash territory
Administration	Los Prietos Ranger Station, Los Padres National Forest (805) 967-3481
Map	Santa Ynez Recreation Area of Los Padres National Forest, Aliso Canyon Interpretive Trail brochure

Chumash villages once dotted the shores of the Santa Ynez River. Harvested plants of the hillside chaparral and oak woodland, along with those of the creekside riparian community, sustained their people for thousands of years. Chert, steatite, and hematite outcrops provided material for tools and for use in trade. A strong cord of the milkweed plant fashioned in the Santa Ynez

Valley was sought by tomol makers along the coast. In conjunction with the California Indian Manpower Consortium, the US Forest Service has constructed a trail in Aliso Canyon that interprets the rich Chumash history here. Signposts along the route tell a story of two Chumash children and the things they find in Aliso Canyon.

Trailhead

Exit Hwy. 101 at Hwy. 154 in Santa Barbara. Go 11 miles north, up and over San Marcos Pass and down into the Santa Ynez Valley, to Paradise Dr. Turn right and go 4 miles to the Los Prietos Ranger Station. Turn left and go 1 mile, across the Santa Ynez River, to the trailhead at Sage Hill Campground parking area's northwest corner.

On The Trail

The Aliso Canyon Interpretive Trail explains the Chumash use of many of the natural materials found in the canyon. The last sign displays the trade route over mountains to Refugio Beach, where Chumash of the Santa Ynez Valley would bring deer hides and antlers, acorns, chia seeds, pine nuts, and milkweed-fiber rope for barter. The trail follows Aliso Creek into the canyon, passing numbered signs for islay, elderberry, cattail, willow, poison oak, sycamore, purple and chia sage, basket sumac, toyon, yucca, and yerba santa. A brochure available at the trailhead interprets their use. At the trail's end, retrace your steps to the parking area. (Or follow the Aliso Loop Trail across grassy meadows up to the ridge overlooking Aliso and Oso canyons—adding another 2.5 miles to the walk—before returning to the parking area.)

hike 40

Nojoqui Creek Trail

Roundtrip Distance	1 mile
Location	Inland village in Chumash Territory
Administration	Nojoqui Falls County Park (805) 688-4217
Map	Not necessary

Nojoqui is the Chumash word for "meadow." This is the name of the Chumash village once located in the meadow, near the park's playing fields. In the canyon, Nojoqui Falls tumbles over an 80-foot travertine cliff that is still growing outward as water-borne minerals are deposited by the creek. This is one of the few places in Santa Barbara County where Venus maidenhair ferns grow from a rock face. Chumash still come to the falls to obtain the materials found here.

Trailhead

Exit Hwy. 101 about 4 miles south of Buellton at Alisal Rd. Head east and go 1 mile to the park entrance on the right. Follow the park road past the playing fields to the trailhead and parking area.

On The Trail

Nojoqui Creek Trail follows the creek 0.5 mile up-canyon between its sandstone walls in the shade of oak, bay, and large-leaf maple trees. The trail crosses a bridge over the creek and climbs through the fractured shale of the Jalama Formation, which is found from the upper reaches of the canyon to

Nojoqui Falls

an amphitheater just below the falls. At the falls, stairs descend to a pool. An interpretive sign explains the geology. Retrace your steps to the parking area.

hike 41   San Miguel Island Trail

Roundtrip Distance	15 miles
Location	Channel Islands in Chumash territory
Administration	Channel Islands National Park (805) 644-8262
Map	Channel Islands National Park

Because the last people who settled the Channel Islands in any numbers were the Chumash, the islands remain undeveloped. Undisturbed island caves and well-preserved archaeological sites are laboratories for archaeologists. Important discoveries relating to Chumash and earlier cultures are still being made at Daisy Cave on Santa Cruz Island. Significant archaeological sites on neighboring Santa Rosa Island include human remains dating back 10,000 years. Estimated to be at least 12,000 years old were the charred bones of dwarf mammoths found in ancient fire pits that may date back 37,000 years.

One way to contemplate Chumash life on the Channel Islands is to view them from the mainland heights across the channel. A better way is to travel with Island Packers to one of the islands and take a hike. Though most of Santa Cruz Island is privately held by the Nature Conservancy and not open to the public, Scorpion Valley is National Park land, and Scorpion Ranch's roads are open to visiting hikers. Santa Barbara Island offers the Canyon View Self-Guiding Nature Trail. There is also a self-guiding nature trail on East Anacapa Island. Though there are no trails on Santa Rosa Island, 12 village sites there indicate that the island had thriving settlements from the 1500s through the 1800s. Perhaps the best hiking trail on the islands is the Point Bennett

Trail on San Miguel Island. Once you arrange for access through the National Park Service, you can hike across the island.

Trailhead

Unless you have your own boat, all Channel Island trails begin at Island Packers ((805) 642-1393), 1867 Spinnaker Drive, next door to the Channel Island Visitor Center at 1901 Spinnaker Drive, in Ventura. If you want to hike to Point Bennett, you will need a landing permit and a reserved campsite on the island. There is a two-night minimum. Obtain a landing permit and camp reservations at the visitor center in advance, (805) 644-8262. The trip to San Miguel passes Santa Cruz and Santa Rosa islands along the way, doubling as a tour of the Island Chumash homelands.

On The Trail

San Miguel Island contains over 500 undisturbed archaeological sites. Shell middens here date back thousands of years. The only trail on San Miguel Island leads from Cuyler Harbor along an old Chumash route up-canyon to the plateau, then follows the island crest from east to west, and ultimately reaches the sea lion rookery at Point Bennett. The offshore slope here provides an ideal environment for giant keyhole limpets, whose shells the Chumash strung for trade. Off-trail hiking is dangerous, as the island was used as a bomb-testing range and many remnants are live.

hike 42   Chumash Wilderness

Roundtrip Distance	1.5 miles (with a 4-mile option)
Location	Inland Chumash territory
Administration.	Mount Pinos Ranger Station, Los Padres National Forest (805) 245-3731
Map	Chumash Wilderness, Los Padres National Forest

M ount Pinos in the Chumash Wilderness is perhaps as close as you can get to the world of the Chumash prior to Spanish colonization. Set aside by Congress, the wilderness commemorates the native people that lived here for so many hundreds of years. From Mount Pinos, most of Chumash territory is visible from the inland valleys to the Channel Islands. Chumash living nearby are relearning and reliving traditional lifeways. A traditional solstice celebration takes place on Mount Pinos each June. A remote and roadless area, the Chumash Wilderness is in many places as unspoiled as it was in earlier times. Hopefully, it is pristine enough for condors, who cannot survive near urban sprawl, but seem to be able to live here. The vulnerability of the condor to human lifeways is reflected in Chumash legend. All condors were white until Hutash sent a lightning bolt to give the Chumash fire. Condor, trusting and curious, swooped down for a look (Ah—too close!) and scorched his feathers black. Since then, all condors are black with just a little white left under the wings, where Condor's feathers weren't burned.

Trailhead

Exit I-5 at the FRAZIER PARK exit and go 3 miles west to Frazier Park. Bear right along Frazier Mountain Rd. and continue 2 miles west to Cuddy Valley Rd. at Lake of the Woods. Turn right and go 5 miles to Mount Pinos Hwy. Follow Mount Pinos Hwy. for 9 miles to a dirt road signed CONDOR OBSERVATION POINT. Turn left and continue 2 miles to the Chula Vista trailhead parking area and the Condor Observation Point on Mount Pinos. The Mount Pinos Ranger Station is located in Lockwood Valley.

On The Trail

The trail provides access to the summit of Mount Pinos, and constant views of Chumash territory. At almost 9,000 feet, Mount Pinos is under a blanket of (skiable) snow in winter and spring. In every season, the pinyon and Jeffrey pine forest creates a fragrant and scenic ambiance. From the parking area, head west along the signed, gated fire road. Enjoy the views as you pass beside wind-sculpted trees for 0.75 mile to the summit of Mount Pinos. (From the summit, the Vincent Tumamait Trail (named after a revered Chumash storyteller) continues an optional 2 miles west through rolling pine forest to Sawmill Mountain.) When you are ready, retrace your steps to the parking area.

hike 43 Carrizo Plain Painted Rocks

Roundtrip Distance	0.5 mile
Location	Inland Chumash territory
Administration	The Nature Conservancy (805) 475-2131, 546-8378
Map	Carrizo Plain Preserve Painted Rocks

Inland from San Luis Obispo, near the homeland boundary the Chumash share with the Yokuts, lies the Carrizo Plain. Many occupation sites have been documented here, including one containing over 50 bedrock mortars. The rock art, which is thought to be at most 2,000-3,000 years old, was painted by many different people, suggesting wide-ranging recognition of the power in this site. A unique feature on the otherwise flat grassland, the painted rocks mark an opening to the spirit world. The Spanish named the Temblor Range—to the east—after a Chumash belief that the valley floor would tremble if someone who angered the spirits came here. At the base of the Temblor Range, cutting a swath under the Carrizo Plain, is the San Andreas Rift Zone.

Trailhead

To reach the trailhead, 8 miles north of **San Luis Obispo**, exit Hwy. 101 at Hwy. 58, and head 52 miles east to Soda Lake Rd. Turn right and go 13.5 miles to the Painted Rocks turnoff on the right. Take this dirt road 0.5 mile to Goodwin Educational Center and go another 2.7 miles to your trailhead. (No fee or permit is required.) From **Los Angeles**, take I-5 116 miles north to the Hwy. 58 exit. Go 35 miles west to Soda Lake Rd. Turn left and proceed as above.

On The Trail

Many of the most impressive Chumash rock-art sites are inland. Among these, the Carrizo Plain Preserve Painted Rocks include the most extensive pictographs. From the parking area, walk 0.25 mile down a wide and flat trail. The rocks, resembling a large amphitheater in their arrangement, hold 45 distinct paintings. Figures include humans in ceremonial dance position with elbows bent and palms raised, and four people in a tomol. Animals depicted include rattlesnakes, turtles, and bears, as well as the mythical Coyote and Lizard. Perhaps the most striking of the pictographs is a red snake extending the length of one panel. The snake appears to slip in and out of cracks in the rock face. When you're ready, retrace your steps to the parking area.

hike 44   Chumash Loop

Roundtrip Distance	1 mile
Location	Inland Chumash campsite
Administration	Los Osos Oaks State Reserve (805) 528-0513
Map	Los Osos Oaks State Reserve

The Chumash traveled seasonally inland, stopping at what is now Los Osos to hunt and gather acorns. *Oso* is Spanish for bear. In prehistoric times, California grizzly bears roamed among the oaks shading the valley. The Los Osos Oaks State Reserve features gnarled, 800-year-old coast live oaks thriving along Los Osos Creek. Atop exposed knolls, sheering winds and salty fog have dwarfed the oaks. Covering higher, wind-swept slopes is chaparral, from which the Chumash gathered black sage, holly-leaved cherry, and California sagebrush. Found within the sandy soils are traces of charcoal and shell from Chumash campfires.

Trailhead

Exit Hwy. 101 at the LOS OSOS exit in San Luis Obispo and follow Los Osos Valley Rd. 8.5 miles west to the Los Osos Oaks State Reserve turnout and parking area on the left.

On The Trail

The Chumash Loop starts at the west side of the parking area. Follow the sign marked RESERVE TRAILS over the bridge to the intersection of the Chumash Trail, which leads to the right. Under an oak canopy, the trail climbs slightly, rounding a knoll. From the clearing at its top, you get

360-degree views of this venerable, moss-covered oak forest. As you descend, reentering the canopy, you pass through a Chumash midden. Keep left at the **T**-junction, and follow the loop back to the bridge. Retrace your steps to the parking area.

hike 45   Morro Dunes Beach Walk

Roundtrip Distance	6 miles
Location	Coastal Chumash territory
Administration	Morro Bay State Park (805) 772-2560
Maps	Morro Dunes Natural Reserve

The midden of a seasonal clam-gathering village can still be seen along the sandspit at Morro Dunes Natural Reserve. This extensive midden, excavated by archaeologists at the Morro Bay State Park Museum of Natural History, is 40 feet deep, indicating a long period of seasonal habitation. Found among the layers of shell bits were spreaders covered with asphaltum, charm-stones of sandstone, granite, schist, and steatite, and projectile points of chert. Besides gathering clams, the Chumash must have come to the sandspit to seal their tule balsa canoes with asphaltum, and hunt sea mammals. They carried charmstones to bring good luck in the hunt.

Morro Bay marked the northern boundary of Chumash territory, and the culture of the people here differed from that of the people in the Santa Barbara Channel region. Unlike the tomols of the southern people, the local Chumash made balsa-style canoes from tule stalks sealed with asphaltum. For the people of these northern villages, the pismo clam was a staple, and an important reason for traveling to the Morro Dunes. From here, they traveled inland, responding to seasonal harvest patterns. Bedrock mortars at White Point (near the museum) and on Turtle Hill (east of the Morro Bay estuary) attest to this migration.

Trailhead

Exit Hwy. 101 at the LOS OSOS exit in San Luis Obispo and follow Los Osos Valley Rd. 15 miles west until it becomes Pecho Valley Rd. Continue southwest on Pecho Valley Rd. to Sandspit Dr. Turn right on Sandspit Dr. and continue several hundred yards to the parking area at the road's end.

On The Trail

Stretching north for 3 miles, the sandspit gives you a feeling of the reserve's prehistory. An interpretive sign marking the trailhead includes a drawing of what the seasonal Chumash village here might have looked like 4,000 years ago. Follow the boardwalk west, through the dunes to the sandy beach, and then walk north (right) following the shoreline. Sheltered areas within the dunes must have made ideal campsites for Chumash collecting the pismo clam. Wander as much of the sandspit as you like before retracing your steps to the parking area.

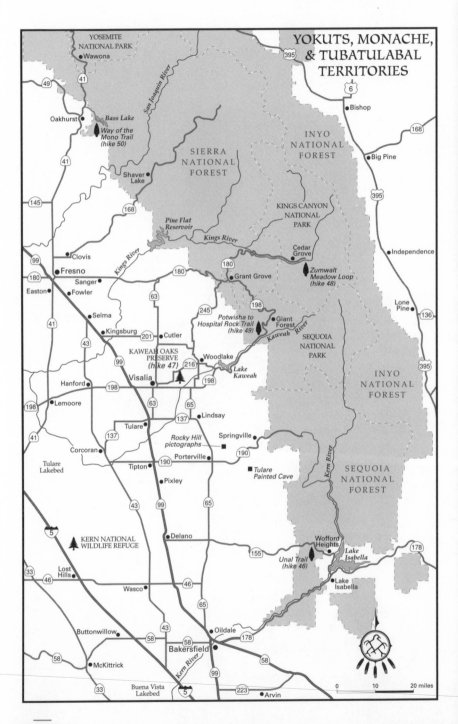

YOKUTS, MONACHE, & TUBATULABAL TERRITORIES

YOSEMITE NATIONAL PARK
• Wawona

49
41

Oakhurst • | • Bass Lake
🔺 Way of the Mono Trail (hike 50)

41

Shaver Lake •

145
168

Pine Flat Reservoir

Kings River

99
Clovis •
180
Fresno
Sanger •
Easton • • Fowler
63
41
• Selma
43
• Kingsburg
201 • Cutler

KAWEAH OAKS PRESERVE *(hike 47)*
99
Hanford • 198
Visalia
198
Lemoore •
41
63
Tulare •
137
137
Corcoran •
Tipton •
190
• Pixley

Tulare Lakebed

43
99

KERN NATIONAL WILDLIFE REFUGE 🔺

33
46
Lost Hills •
Wasco •
46
65

Buttonwillow •
58
33
58
McKittrick •
Bakersfield
58
58
Buena Vista Lakebed
33
5
223
• Arvin

SIERRA NATIONAL FOREST

San Joaquin River

INYO NATIONAL FOREST

395
6
• Bishop
168
• Big Pine
395

KINGS CANYON NATIONAL PARK

Kings River

Cedar Grove
🔺 Zumwalt Meadow Loop (hike 48)

• Independence

180
Grant Grove •
198
Giant Forest •
245
🔺 Potwisha to Hospital Rock Trail (hike 49)

Lone Pine •
136

SEQUOIA NATIONAL PARK

Kaweah River

Woodlake •
216
Lake Kaweah
198

INYO NATIONAL FOREST
395

65
137 • Lindsay
Springville •
■ Rocky Hill pictographs
190
Porterville •
190
■ Tulare Painted Cave

65

Kern River

SEQUOIA NATIONAL FOREST

Delano •
155
Wofford Heights •
Lake Isabella
178
🔺 Unal Trail (hike 46)
• Lake Isabella

Oildale •
178
Kern River

0   10   20 miles

Yokuts, Monache, & Tubatulabal

San Joaquin Valley & Sierra Nevada

Landscape and People

Yokuts, Monache, and Tubatulabal homelands cover most of the San Joaquin Valley and the southern Sierra foothills. The Monache and Tubatulabal people migrated from the Owens Valley over the Sierra Nevada to the Kern Plateau about 600 years ago. Until then, the Sierra posed a barrier to trade and migration between Great Basin and Central California cultures that was rarely bridged. West of the barrier, the Central Valley was the heartland of prehistoric California. Before the advent of modern agriculture, the abundant natural resources here sustained one of the densest human populations in the state.

Yokuts

The Yokuts are Penutian speakers. Their homeland is the eastern floor of the Central Valley, from the San Joaquin River south to Tehachapi Pass. Yokuts villages dotted the banks of the Kaweah, Kings, Tule, and Kern rivers from the valley floor to the foothills. Over 40 distinct tribes developed out of the Yokuts' culture, such as the Tachi and the Kaweah. Each had distinct territories and language dialects. The Yokuts' culture was centered around the tule marshes and plains of the eastern valley floor. The annual flood cycle in the Central Valley created seasonal lakes and augmented prolific hunting and gathering grounds. The Yokuts maneuvered tule rafts with long poles to travel over the shallow lakes.

Like the Miwok, Monache, and Salinan peoples, all Yokuts are born into totemic moieties. Inherited through the father's side of the family, a moiety is symbolized by an animal. Every member of a Yokuts family regards the inherited totem's qualities as part of their character. Sometimes the totem animal was kept at the home. Each moiety group has a distinctive body-paint design that its members wear. Yokuts society also elaborated specific roles for individuals, such as the *winatum* (messenger), and even the *haiuta* (clown) who mocks behavior at ceremonies. The name "Yokuts" is derived from *Yokoch*—their word for "people." The prehistoric Yokuts population is thought to have reached 20,000.

Monache

The Monache language belongs to the Numic subgroup of the Uto-Aztecan family. Traditionally, the Monache (a.k.a. Western Mono) people inhabited southern slopes of the Sierra Nevada. Their foothill-based tribe is divided into six bands, one on each side of the Kings, Kaweah, and San Joaquin rivers. The Monache are closely related to the Tubatulabal people who are also a Shoshonean tribe. The name "Monache" is derived from *monachi*, the name applied to them by the Yokuts. The prehistoric Monache population is thought to have reached 2,000.

Tubatulabal

The Tubatulabal language belongs to the Tubatulabalic branch of the Uto-Aztecan family. Traditionally the Tubatulabal people inhabited the Kern River drainage. They spent summers in the high country gathering pine nuts, acorns, and berries, and hunting game that migrated from the hot valley floor after the grass had browned. During winter, seasonal camps were moved to lower elevations. *Tubatulabal* is a Shoshonean word meaning "pine-nut eaters." Relatively recent migrants to the Sierra, the Tubatulabal are a Shoshonean people related to tribes of the Great Basin and the Southwest. Their prehistoric population is estimated to have reached 500.

Modern changes in the Central Valley—both natural and manmade—have left few traces of the traditional Yokuts way of life. In prehistoric times, the Central Valley flooded each year, creating huge, shallow lakes, such as Buena Vista, Tulare, and Kern, which covered much of the bottomlands. *Pah-ah-su*, later known as Tulare Lake, swelled to several hundred square miles during the spring runoff. The Tulare Lake area was the homeland of the Tachi Yokuts. Neighboring peoples came to Pah-ah-su annually in late spring to trade and gather quantities of grass seeds, tule shoots, and wildflower bulbs. The Kern National Wildlife Refuge, a managed marsh whose floodwaters are diverted for use elsewhere in the state, is a small remnant of the former Tulare Lake.

Archaeological remains from Buena Vista and Tulare lakebeds suggest that the early culture of the Central Valley was contemporaneous with the San Dieguito culture in Southern California. At Buena Vista Lakebed near Bakersfield, a Clovis point and a chipped-stone crescent were found that radiocarbon-date to 5500 BC (Heizer and Elsasser, 1980). At the Tranquillity Site near Fresno, 1000 BC-era artifacts have been found among the fossilized remains of now-extinct Pleistocene camels, horses, and bison estimated to date back to 10000 BC. The Farmington Site near Stockton holds quantities of choppers and scrapers thought to be the work of early man. In the Owens Valley, artifacts from the Rose Spring Site radiocarbon-date back to around 2000 BC.

Unlike coastal archaeological sites, whose middens were whitened by shell fragments, those of the Sierra foothills have a dark, greasy soil resulting from an accumulation of animal bones and soot of ancient fires. According to archaeological surveys sponsored by the National Park Service, much of the Sierra Nevada was used seasonally by Native Californians, who spent most of the year at lower elevations. Campsites in the southern Sierra were first visited infrequently about 3,000 years ago, and then more regularly beginning 2,000 years ago. Many campsites have been documented along what is now the John Muir Trail. The annual journey of the Monache people to Mono Hot Springs is a tradition archaeologists believe dates back 5,000 years. Today, the Monache people come by car, but in prehistoric times, the springs was a stopover along the trade route leading over Mono Pass to the Great Basin.

Archaeological evidence of trade routes between the villages on the coast, those in the Central Valley, and those east of the Sierra Nevada has been documented in Great Basin sites containing Pacific Coast shell fragments, and from the Sierra Nevada obsidian found at village sites in the Central Valley. Regionally, the Monache traded acorns, baskets, arrowshafts, manzanita berries, shell-bead money, and deerskins with the Owens Valley Paiute for rabbitskin blankets, moccasins, rock salt, pine nuts, water baskets sealed with pitch, obsidian, and skins of the mountain sheep. The Yokuts obtained arrow points fashioned by the Monache out of obsidian that had been collected by the Owens Valley Paiute.

Natural Resources and Material Culture

An abundant food supply in the Central Valley promoted the evolution of a large prehistoric population with a rich material culture. Regional plant foods included acorns, grass seeds, and cattail roots from the seasonally receding lakeshores on the valley floor. Acorns were the dietary staple among people of the foothills. Fishing for trout, sucker, salmon, and eel was done from tule rafts with holes cut at the center floating on Tulare Lake. Duck decoys fashioned with woven bottoms and actual duck heads were used to lure mallards and Canada geese, which provided eggs. The Tachi hunted geese and ducks from behind blinds along the shore. Animal foods included salmon, deer, and waterfowl. Salt was obtained from *alit* (salt grass) and from salt deposits in low-lying areas. The Yokuts also gathered mushrooms.

While there were several styles of Yokuts dwellings in use, the most common in the valley was a *kawi*, with tule-mat walls and a steep, gabled roof. Multiple dwellings were built side by side and covered with a sunshade made of rushes. For a home in the hills, the Yokuts often constructed a *ho*, a cone-shaped house covered with tule mats or thatch. An earth-covered sweathouse had a central place in each village.

The Monache introduced a pottery known as Owens Valley brownware to the west side of the Sierra, where it was used by both the Monache and the Yokuts. In the alluvial plains, mortars were fashioned out of white oak, while in the foothills, mortars were made in the granite. Strings of shell disks known as *Keha* were used as money. A dependable string was made from the fibrous stalk of milkweed.

The Yokuts and the Tubatulabal still produce beautiful baskets. The "Tulare bottleneck," a jar-shaped basket with a flared neck and a fringe of mountain quail plumes, is renowned throughout the world. Yokuts baskets were made traditionally of closely sewn, bundled grass wrapped with the root fibers of sedge. While fern root was used to create black designs, redbud bark was used for red. The Yokuts, the Monache, and the Tubatulabal share similar styles of basketry.

Just as the Owens Valley is a center for petroglyphs, the Tulare foothills around Porterville are the center for a style of pictographs. Painted in red, white, yellow, and black, regional rock art is exemplified by the Tulare Painted Cave, the Rocky Hill pictographs near Porterville, and the art at Hospital Rock and Potwisha in Sequoia-Kings Canyon

National Parks. The monochrome pictographs of Hospital Rock are of the Great Basin style, linking them to the Monache people, while, less than 2 miles down the Kaweah River at Potwisha, the more colorful Tulare foothill style of pictographs clearly links them to the Yokuts.

Museums and Interpretive Sites

The **Kern County Museum** in Bakersfield features Yokuts baskets, among a world-class collection of artifacts, (805) 861-2132.

The **Sequoia-Kings Canyon National Parks Visitor Center** in Cedar Grove is a good place to acquaint yourself with the natural history in Kings Canyon, (209) 565-3134. (See also hike 48.)

The **Fort Miller Cultural Preserve** at the Table Mountain Rancheria east of Fresno maintains a native-plant garden. Exhibits include reconstructed fort buildings. The project is funded through profits from Indian gaming, (559) 822-2587.

The **Sierra Mono Museum** in North Fork is owned and operated by Native Americans. The museum features an extensive Mono (and others) basket collection, along with historical and cultural exhibits. The museum curates artifacts unearthed by the Forest Service and by the Pacific Gas and Electric Company. The museum is open Monday through Saturday from 9 A.M. until 4 P.M., (209) 877-2115. Indian Fair Days occur on the first weekend in August.

hike 46   Unal Trail

Roundtrip Distance	3 miles
Location	Mountain camp in Tubatulabal territory
Administration	Greenhorn Ranger District, Sequoia National Forest (760) 379-5646
Map	Unal Trail brochure

There are many places in Sequoia National Forest that remain as the Tubatulabal left them. Throughout the surrounding wilderness are 1,700-year-old fire rings left among the granite, marking the campsites of early hunting parties. The forest contains some of the drainage of the Kern River, which was the summer hunting and gathering grounds of the Tubatulabal. The name "Unal Peak" includes the Tubatulabal word for "bear." From the top of Unal Peak you can look west to the Yokuts homeland, and east to the Monache and the Tubatulabal lands. The local Native American community collaborated with the Forest Service in building the Unal Trail. The brochure, available at the trailhead, interprets the traditional ways of the Tubatulabal.

Trailhead

Go 8 miles west on Hwy. 155 from Wofford Heights on the west side of Lake Isabella, to Greenhorn Summit. Turn left on Rancheria Rd. (you'll see a sign for SHIRLEY SKI MEADOWS) and go several hundred feet south to the trailhead near the Greenhorn Fire Station, at the intersection of Forest Service Rd. 25S17 and Rancheria Rd.

On The Trail

The Unal Trail interprets the ethnobotany of the Tubatulabal people. The trail climbs Unal Peak and then descends through a village site with a reconstructed house and some grinding rocks. From the trailhead, ascend a switchback to signpost 1. Go left (south) at the loop intersection here and traverse the lower flank of Unal Peak through a forest of cedar, pine, fir, and oak to a water hole at 1.2 miles. In open areas you can identify gooseberry, elderberry, currant, thimbleberry, and chinquapin. The trail soon loops to climb toward Unal Peak, gaining views of the surrounding mountains. There are panoramic views from the summit at 2 miles. Descend north, along the edge of the forest to the village site. After exploring the exhibits, continue along the trail as it descends quickly east to the trailhead.

hike 47   Kaweah Oaks Preserve

Roundtrip Distance	2 miles
Location	Oak woodland in foothill Yokuts territory
Administration	Four Creeks Land Trust (209) 738-0211
Map	Kaweah Oaks Preserve

Kaweah Oaks Preserve is a 324-acre remnant of the former lush woodlands of the Central Valley, where dense groves of valley oak once covered the riverbanks. The largest woodland spread out from the delta of the Kaweah River, where 400 square miles of oak trees flourished. The preserve safeguards some 150-year-old valley oaks, among western sycamore, Fremont cottonwood, Oregon ash, and willow. The forest understory includes elderberry, blackberry, wild grape, and wild rye grass. The preserve very closely resembles the way it was when the Yukol Yokuts lived here. In the meadow near the entrance, surface ground water—due to the high water table—leaves a salt deposit as it evaporates. Consequently, salt grass, alkali sacaton, cone flower, and clustered field sedge flourish here. The salt was collected and used by the Yokuts in curing meat and as a trade commodity.

Trailhead

Go 7 miles east of Visalia on Hwy. 198 to Rd. 182. Turn left and go 0.4 mile to the preserve gate and trailhead parking on the left.

On The Trail

Take this walk either in the cooler months or in the morning, as the summer heat can be particularly intense where the trail leaves the forest canopy. Passing giant valley oaks along Deep Creek (a tributary of the Kaweah River), the Nature Trail Loop winds through a remnant of the former Central Valley landscape. From the trailhead, go through the gate and head down the ranch road to the picnic area at 0.3 mile. Interpretive signs here tell you about the preserve's flora and fauna. Walk through the picnic area and cross the weir to the Nature Trail Loop. Growing along the trail are coyote melon, once used in a game resembling soccer played by Yokuts children. The wild grapes once harvested by grizzly bears now attract over 125 species of birds to this natural oasis. Listen for woodpeckers at work on the tree trunks as you continue to the end of the loop at 1.7 miles. Then retrace your steps from the picnic area to the parking lot.

hike 48   Zumwalt Meadow Loop

Roundtrip Distance	1.5 miles
Location	Seasonal camp in mountain Monache territory
Administration	Sequoia-Kings Canyon National Parks (209) 565-3134
Map	Zumwalt Meadow brochure

The discovery of ancient campsites near the crest of the Sierra Nevada in Sequoia-Kings Canyon National Parks has provided important pieces of the archaeological record on prehistoric travel across the Sierra Nevada. An early obsidian-flaking workshop has been identified near Taboose Pass, at an elevation of more than 11,000 feet. The River Trail follows a prehistoric trade route along the Kings River and over Kearsarge Pass to the Owens Valley. A camp at Zumwalt Meadow along this route was used by early travelers.

Village sites are considerably lower, at or below 5,000 feet in elevation. A village site in Cedar Grove contained leaf-shaped arrow points that had become obsolete by AD 1450. Side-notched triangular arrow points replaced the leaf-shaped points in the upper level of the site. Steatite fragments from pots introduced to the region about AD 1300 imply that the site was occupied from about AD 1300 to 1700, before pottery was introduced. Because no pottery shards were found, it is assumed that the site was abandoned by AD 1700.

A boardwalk spans the wetland along the Kings River

Trailhead

To reach the trailhead, take Hwy. 180 east from Fresno 55 miles to the Big Stump entrance station (fee required) of Sequoia-Kings Canyon National Parks. From the entrance, go 37.5 miles northeast on Hwy. 180 through Cedar Grove to Zumwalt Meadow. The parking area is on the right, just before the ROADS END PERMIT STATION. (The highway in Kings Canyon is closed from October through May.)

On The Trail

The Zumwalt Meadow Loop visits the grounds of a Monache summer encampment along the former Kings River trade route. Acorns, grass seeds, pine nuts, yucca, manzanita berries, and chia seeds and roots were gathered here. Bedrock mortars can be seen along the creek. The excavation of another site near the west end of the valley indicates that trout were fished from the river. Structural supports for houses were fashioned from willows growing along the riverbank.

The trailhead is at the southeast end of the parking area. Follow the Zumwalt Meadow Loop along the South Fork of the Kings River, passing bedrock mortars along the trail. Cross over the footbridge at 0.1 mile and walk to the left. The loop begins at a fork in the trail. Go right, passing through a talus field at the foot of Grand Sentinel. White fir,

Along an ancient trade route in Zumwalt Meadow

alder, willow, cattail, cottonwood, and creek dogwood grow here sheltered by the canyon walls. Across the meadow is North Dome, whose 3,600-foot rise above the valley floor compares to that of Half Dome in Yosemite Valley. At the Roads End Trail junction, go left. Pass through a meadow of grasses and wildflowers to a boardwalk. Ferns grow waist-high here as the boardwalk crosses a wetland. At the loop's end, turn right and retrace your steps to the parking area.

hike 49   Potwisha to Hospital Rock

Roundtrip Distance	6 miles
Location	Rock-art sites in foothill Monache and Yokuts territories
Administration	Sequoia-Kings Canyon National Parks (209) 565-3134
Map	Sequoia-Kings Canyon National Parks

Excavations at Hospital Rock revealed a midden deposit averaging 6 feet in depth. Findings record extensive use of Owens Valley brownware, a pottery used no farther west than in the San Joaquin Valley villages of the Yokuts. Also found at the site were steatite pot fragments, beads, metates, manos, and obsidian blades. Quantities of freshwater mussel shells brought here from the Kaweah River suggest that this shellfish was a dietary staple. The lower level of the site contains a smaller range of objects, indicating habitation by an earlier culture.

Trailhead

Go 40 miles east of Visalia on Hwy. 198 to the Ash Mountain entrance station (fee required) of Sequoia-Kings Canyon National Parks, adjacent to the Foothills Visitor Center. Continue 3.9 miles east on Hwy. 198 to the POTWISHA CAMPGROUND sign. Turn right opposite the campground and continue to the signed trailhead parking area.

On The Trail

The chaparral-clad foothills here are known for hot summers and snow-free winters. The trail along the Kaweah River from Potwisha to Hospital Rock is an ancient one linking two large village sites. It is thought that Potwisha was inhabited by some Yokuts, while Hospital Rock was home to some Monache. From the parking area, the trail leads northeast. Within the first 0.1 mile, the trail passes grinding holes and pictographs. Then it meanders along the North Fork of the Kaweah River to cross Highway 198 at 1 mile. Continue east, traversing oak woodland above the river to the Monache exhibits and picnic area at Hospital Rock at 2.5 miles. Pass through the picnic area, crossing again to the east side of Highway 198 at the Buckeye Flat Campground road. Follow the campground road a short way to Hospital Rock on the left. The rock was named to honor a medicine man whose healing powers were well known to people in this region. Neighboring Yokuts called this rock *Pahdin*, or "place to go under," where "under" refers to the supernatural realm. The pictographs are painted in a crevice in the rock. Figures including a rattlesnake, a grizzly bear, and several human-like figures are colored in red pigment. Across the campground road on the right

Hospital Rock pictographs

are grinding rocks. A short, paved trail leads from the grinding rocks southeast to stairs accessing several inviting swimming holes along the river. When you're ready, retrace your steps to the parking area.

hike 50   Way of the Mono Trail

Roundtrip Distance	0.5 mile
Location	Summer village site in foothill Monache territory
Administration	Mariposa Ranger District, Sierra National Forest (209) 683-4665
Map	Way of the Mono Trail brochure

The Monache people traveled into the hills of what is now Sierra National Forest in the summer to hunt and to gather plant materials. They camped along Willow Creek in Crane Valley long before the dam that created Bass Lake was built. Bringing little with them, the Monache used the plant materials they found here for the things they needed. Houses were covered with incense cedar bark and sealed with ponderosa pine pitch. The black oak and coast live oak produced acorns, which were ground and made into bread. Acorns and seeds were prepared in grinding holes here atop a granite outcrop overlooking the valley. Brushes made from soaproot bulbs were used to keep the acorn grounds in the grinding hole. En route to the grinding rock, an ailment pile was set up for stones that relieved pains incurred by carrying loaded burden baskets. A suitable rock found along the route could be held to an injury to absorb the pain. With the ailment transferred to the rock, which was then discarded in the ailment pile, a person would continue more comfortably along their way.

Trailhead

Go 4 miles north of Oakhurst on Hwy. 41 to Rd. 222. Turn right and head 4 miles east to the signed trailhead on the right, across from the Denver Church Picnic Area (no fee).

On The Trail

The Way of the Mono Trail interprets the ethnobotany of the Monache people while you explore an area they inhabited for over 1,000 years. (The interpretive brochure is available at the trailhead.) Beginning at the east side of the parking area, the trail works its way north, along switchbacks that reveal specimens of cedar, pine, oak, and soaproot. From the ailment pile in 0.3 mile, continue north to the granite outcrop overlooking the Crane Valley. (Today much of what you'll see is Bass Lake.) Pause to enjoy the view, as the Monache women did while they processed acorns in the grinding rocks here. Continuing past labeled plants, the trail loops west and then descends to the parking area.

 # Guided Walks

The **Rocky Hill pictographs** situated among hillside rock shelters are an important rock-art site of the Wukchumni Yokuts. Guided group walks led by a member of the Wukchumni people are offered by the Archaeological Conservancy out of Sacramento, (916) 448-1892.

    Tulare Painted Cave is a representative Yokuts Tulare Foothills pictograph site. A lizard is painted at the entrance to the cave. Lizards were considered supernatural messengers because they move in and out of cracks in the rocks, which are thresholds of the spirit world. Guided walks are offered through the Tule River Reservation east of Porterville, (209) 782-2316.

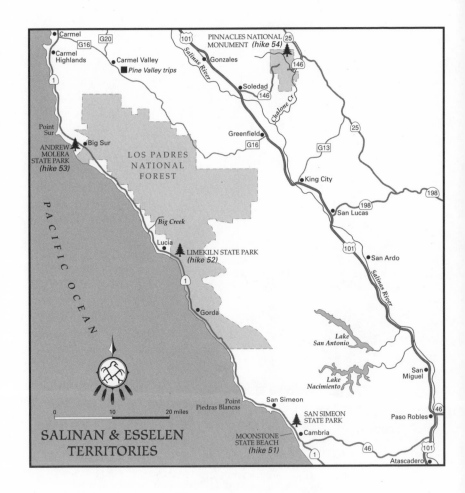

Carmel
G16 G20
Carmel
Highlands
Carmel Valley
Pine Valley trips

1

Point
Sur
ANDREW
MOLERA
STATE PARK
(hike 53)
Big Sur

PACIFIC OCEAN

Big Creek
Lucia
LIMEKILN STATE PARK
(hike 52)

1

Gorda

LOS PADRES
NATIONAL
FOREST

PINNACLES NATIONAL
MONUMENT (hike 54)
101
25
146

Gonzales

Soledad
146

Salinas River

Chalone Cr

Greenfield
G16
25

G13

King City

198
198

San Lucas
198

101
San Ardo

Salinas River

Lake
San Antonio

Lake
Nacimiento

San
Miguel

San Simeon

SAN SIMEON
STATE PARK

Paso Robles
46

Point
Piedras Blancas

MOONSTONE
STATE BEACH
(hike 51)

Cambria

46

1

46

101

Atascadero

0   10   20 miles

SALINAN & ESSELEN
TERRITORIES

Salinan & Esselen
Central Coast & Coast Ranges

Landscape and People

The Big Sur coast is the homeland of the Salinan and Esselen peoples. The Portola expedition described 10 villages along the route they traveled between San Luis Obispo and Monterey in 1769. Many of these were likely homes to these tribes. The terrain includes sea coast, Coast Range mountains, and the upper Salinas River Valley. Because the Santa Lucia Mountains here are steep and no river cuts a navigable channel through them, there was little interaction between the inland-valley people and those living along the coast. The Salinan were remote from the Esselen, and they considered the Ohlone—their distant neighbors to the north—an enemy people.

Salinan

The Salinan culture was centered around the upper drainage of the Salinas River. Of the Hokan language family, the Salinan language most closely resembles that of the Chumash. Dialects include Playano (along the coast), San Miguel (northern Salinas Valley), and San Antonio (southern Salinas Valley). From the Salinas Valley, the Salinan homeland extends east to the Yokuts lands in the Central Valley and west to the coast, running south from the Esselen border at Big Creek to the area of the Chumash in Morro Bay. There were four known Salinan villages along this stretch of coast. Archaeologists approximate their locations as follows: Tsilakak was near San Simeon; Ma'tihl'she was near Ragged Point; Lema was near Gorda; and Ehmahl was south of

Lucia. The prehistoric Salinan population is thought to have reached 3,000.

Esselen

The Esselen people lived exclusively along the Big Sur coast between Point Sur and Big Creek, and east to the crest of the Coast Range. They fished from river banks and from tule-balsa rafts in saltwater lagoons. Though the Esselen are Hokan speakers like the Salinan, very little is known about this people. Their language is almost perfectly a generic Hokan language, without the distinguishing characteristics of Chumash or Salinan. The Esselen are thought to be a remnant of the culture that existed before the Penutian-speaking people arrived in California—a time when Hokan speakers claimed Central California. The prehistoric population of the Esselen is thought to have reached 1,300.

Charcoal from an archaeological site at Post Ranch in Big Sur has been dated to 1000 BC. The site includes an arrow point of green Franciscan chert quarried from Cooper Point near the Big Sur River mouth. Slate's Hot Springs (now the Esalen Institute) and Tassajara Hot Springs have been used by the Esselen people for centuries. Descendants make an annual pilgrimage to Tassajara Hot Springs to celebrate their connection to the earth. Mortars and rock art remain in Pine Valley, which can be visited with Esselen guides.

The earliest-dated site in the Salinan region is from the Middle Horizon of the Central California Culture—a coastal site from around AD 50. Curved shell hooks and hopper mortars from the site indicate a Chumash influence. Evidence indicates that the Salinan people also traded with the Yokuts, journeying to Tulare Lake to market their shell beads.

Natural Resources and Material Culture

The ruggedness of the Big Sur coast was tempered by a generous variety of natural foods. Traditional plant foods of the region include yucca, acorns, pine nuts, clover greens, and the seeds of sage, chia, wild sunflower, and native grasses. The western slope of the Santa Lucia Mountains hosts majestic yucca plants, whose roots and fruit were roasted in earthen ovens. The roots were also used to make a soap. The Salinan made a wash of oak galls for use as an antiseptic. Seal, sea lion, and shellfish were hunted by the people living along the coast. In the interior, steelhead, sucker, and salmon were speared in the Salinas River. Protein from rabbit, deer, and bear meat was supplemented by snake, lizard, and larvae of the yellow jacket.

Traditional Salinan houses were square, made of poles covered with a thatch of rye grass or tule reeds. Shell beads were used for money. The Salinan manufactured abalone- and mussel-shell beads in three colors, of which blue was the most valuable, followed by pink and then white. Made of shells from a distant source, the blue beads held such value that possession of just two would equal wealth. Salinan baskets, which closely resemble those of the Yokuts, are coiled grass stems bound by a bunch-grass thread.

Museums and Interpretive Sites

Mission San Antonio de Padua in Jolon features Salinan baskets, (381) 385-4478

hike 51   Moonstone Beach

Roundtrip Distance	4.5 miles
Location	Coastal Salinan camp
Administration	San Simeon State Park (805) 927-2020
Map	San Simeon State Park

In winter the Salinan people set up seasonal camps along the coastal bluffs to harvest pine nuts and seafood. They left mortar holes in the sandstone bluffs overlooking Moonstone Beach. The bluffs stretch north from Santa Rosa Creek to San Simeon Creek, which is the approximate site of the village of Tsilakak. In summer the Salinan traveled inland to harvest acorns, seeds, and berries.

Trailhead

Exit Hwy. 1 at Moonstone Beach Dr. in Cambria and follow it to its south end at the Santa Rosa Beach parking area (fee required). (Check the Tidelog before taking this hike; the beach walk (second half) may not be possible at high tide.)

On The Trail

The Coastal Trail follows the exposed blufftop between Santa Rosa and San Simeon creeks. Watch for whales before descending in 1 mile to Moonstone Beach at Leffingwell Landing. Here, the trail crosses a beach of fine pebbles ("moonstones" are the smooth, milky ones) before passing through a picnic area as it ascends the northwest bluffs. Continue northwest, winding through buckwheat, Monterey pine, and cypress. At 1.4 miles the trail climbs to a vista point. From here, the prominent feature on the northwest horizon is Point Piedras Blancas, the site of another Salinan winter camp. At low tide the beach beyond here is passable. The trail descends the bluffs to the beach in several hundred yards. Follow the coastline to San Simeon Creek at 2.25 miles. The site of Tsilakak is thought to be in the vicinity of the creek mouth, near a stand of oak. Vernal pools here attract waterfowl and, as they evaporate, produce concentric rings of grasses and wildflowers through late spring. Now, retrace your steps to the parking area.

The bluffs of Moonstone Beach contain mortars left by the Salinan

hike 52 Redwood Trail

Roundtrip Distance	1 mile
Location	Coastal Salinan camp
Administration	Limekiln State Park/California Land Management
	(831) 667-2403
Map	Limekiln State Park

The Vizcaíno expedition recorded their encounters with native people navigating tule rafts along this stretch of coast in 1602. Archaeologists believe the village of Ehmahl was located just southeast of Lucia, near Limekiln Creek. Forming the steepest coastal slope in the continental United States, this watershed is part of the Man and the Biosphere Reserve System of the United Nations. The Santa Lucia Range rises from sea level to over 5,000 feet at the summit of Cone Peak in less than 3.5 miles. The resulting, diverse ecosystems provided the Salinan people with a rich variety of natural foods. There are 12 plant communities ranging from coastal strand to redwood forest. Within a short distance, they could gather abalone from the sea, acorns from the oaks in the canyons, and seeds from the grasses and sages of the coastal sage scrub and chaparral communities.

Trailhead

Go 2 miles south of Lucia on Hwy. 1 to the entrance to Limekiln State Park (fee required). Follow the road through the Redwood section of the campground to the signed Redwood trailhead at the road's end.

On The Trail

Although there are Salinan middens nearby, the beauty of their homeland is the most striking part of this walk. This canyon stays cool in summer, cut deeply into the limestone flank of Cone Peak, and blessed with redwood forest and the incredibly clear-running waters of Limekiln Creek. The trailhead is at the north end of the Redwood Campground, marked by a sign interpreting the canyon's redwoods. The forest was logged to provide fuel for limestone-reducing kilns up-canyon, but second-growth trees now tower over the canyon floor. Cross the footbridge and head upstream, past sorrel and maidenhair ferns growing in limestone seeps. Cross several additional footbridges as you climb within the shelter of the canyon walls. At the second footbridge an unmarked spur trail on the right leads to Limekiln Falls, which make a 120-foot plunge over a limestone cliff. The main trail reaches the historic limekilns at the base of a natural landslide in 0.5 mile. Lime was manufactured here during the late 1880s; much of it was shipped to San Francisco for use in cement construction. From here, the creekbed climbs steeply into chaparral. Explore the redwood forest as you retrace your steps to the parking area. Optionally, from the trailhead, you can boulder-hop downstream (or follow the camp road) to the beach. Oaks, bays, and willows are dominant in the lower portion of the canyon. From Limekiln Beach, you can view Cone Peak to the north and watch for sea otters in the often calm waters—thick with kelp beds—offshore.

hike 53 Headlands Trail

Roundtrip Distance	2.8 miles
Location	Coastal site in Esselen territory
Administration	Andrew Molera State Park (831) 667-2315
Map	Andrew Molera State Park

 Jojopan, the Esselen name for the Big Sur River, was important to the Esselen people. They fished along the riverbanks, and the riparian woodland provided tule, rush, and willow used in housing and raft construction. Acorns were harvested from the oaks in the fall. Seafood and shellfish were collected at the river mouth. Middens remain among the bluffs.

Trailhead

Exit Hwy. 1 at the entrance to Andrew Molera State Park 22 miles south of Carmel. Park near the campground (fee required).

On The Trail

The Headlands Trail explores the lower Big Sur River valley. The trail-head is at the northwest end of the parking area, marked by a sign to the campground. The trail meanders southwest along this designated Wild and Scenic River, joining an old ranch road in 0.3 mile to pass through the campground. Continuing past stately oaks and sycamores, the trail soon reaches Cooper's Cabin, where it slips into tule and willow growing along the river. Just short of 1 mile you pass over a footbridge to the Headlands Trail junction. Go right here and climb wooden stairs to reach the top of a low ridge. This route follows the ridge to a loop on Molera Point. From the headland, enjoy the views extending south along the coastline to Cooper Point and north to the promontory, Pico Blanco. An outcrop of green Franciscan chert at Cooper Point was quarried by the Esselen people and used in the manufacture of stone implements. The prominent, white-marble peak of 3,709-foot Pico Blanco is sacred to the Esselen. Indeed, many of the metamorphic rocks found in the Big Sur area, including marble, schist, and slate, hold religious significance throughout Native California. Returning to the stairs at the junction of the Headlands Trail, either retrace your steps to the parking area or bear right toward the beach, which can be hiked at low tide.

hike 54   High Peaks Loop

Roundtrip Distance	5.3 miles
Location	Seasonal camp in inland Salinan territory
Administration	Pinnacles National Monument (831) 389-4485
Map	Pinnacles National Monument

The inner Coast Range part of Pinnacles National Monument provided a hunting and gathering ground for Chalone, a major inland village of the Salinan people. In keeping with the Spanish custom of naming creeks after the native villages at their mouths, the village was likely situated where Chalone Creek enters the Salinas River. Though middens and mortar holes remain throughout Pinnacles National Monument, there were no permanent villages here. Archaeological investigation indicates that camps were used for several months here, during periods of high water along the Salinas River. The people of Chalone came here after the winter rains to hunt deer and rabbits attracted to the new chaparral growth, and to gather clover from grasslands, which was eaten as a green.

Trailhead

Northbound: Exit Hwy. 101 at Hwy. G13 in King City. Go northeast to Bitterwater and bear left on Hwy. 25 to Hwy. 146 (30 miles total). Go left for 4 miles to the East Entrance station (fee required). Continue 1.7 miles to park by the Bear Gulch Visitor Center. **Southbound:** Follow Hwy. 25 for 30 miles south of Hollister to Hwy. 146. Turn right and continue (as above) to the visitor center.

On The Trail

The High Peaks Loop takes in caves, creeks, and intriguing rock outcroppings. Follow the Condor Gulch Trail from the east end of the parking area (across the park road from the visitor center). The trail climbs for 1.7 miles along a ridge before reaching the High Peaks Trail. Watch for mariposa lilies here in the spring. Go left on the High Peaks Trail

Intriguing rock outcroppings along the High Peaks Trail

and head west. Soon the trail circles to ascend a ridge overlooking the Balconies Cliffs, and the jumbled-rock landscape extending beyond them along the San Andreas Fault. This landscape is what remains of a 23-million-year-old volcano, the other half of which lies 200 miles south along the fault. At 2.3 miles, take the Tunnel Trail. From here, railings and narrow passages direct you through the rock labyrinth to the 3-mile mark, from where the High Peaks Trail descends through juniper and sculpted rock to the Bear Gulch Trail at 5 miles. Go left and follow the Bear Gulch Trail back to the trailhead.

 # Guided Walks

Pine Valley trips, arranged through Ventana Ranch/Window to the West in Carmel Valley, visit land that never left Esselen stewardship. Guided pack trips and hikes throughout Ventana Wilderness are available. Guides are well versed in Native culture. Esselen guides lead the Esselen Cultural Expedition. Ventana Ranch offers three- and five-day trips to Pine Valley, which serves as a base camp in a large meadow backed by sandstone cliffs. Petroglyphs, a waterfall, and swimming holes here await your exploration, (831) 625-8664.

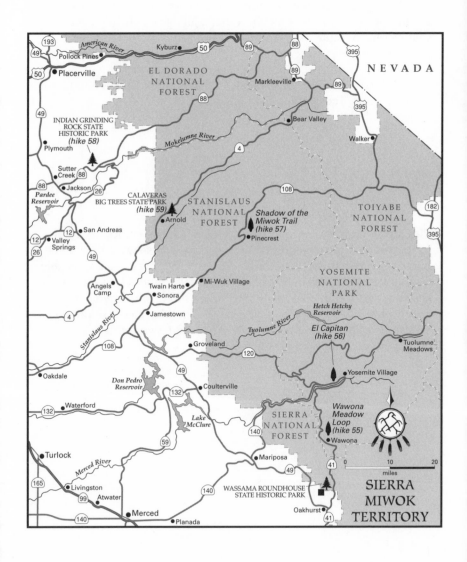

Sierra Miwok
Central Sierra Nevada

Landscape and People

The Sierra Miwok homeland extends south from present-day Amador County through Mariposa County, on the Sierra's west slope. Within an area bordered by the Consumnes River in the north and the Fresno River in the south, permanent villages lined the Mokelumne, Stanislaus, Calaveras, and Merced rivers throughout the foothills. The people traveled to seasonal Sierra camps at higher elevations in the heat of summer. Neighboring Plains Miwok villages flourished along the deltas of the Sacramento and San Joaquin rivers.

Speaking Penutian languages, the greatly dispersed Miwok peoples include the culturally distinct Coast, Lake, Plains, and Sierra Miwok. Each group modified its material culture in response to the physical attributes of its particular homeland. The name "Miwok" is derived from *miwu*, the Miwok word for "person." Sierra Miwok villages were politically autonomous, extended families governed by chiefs, many of whom were women. The prehistoric Sierra Miwok population is estimated to have reached 9,000.

As it remains today, the Yosemite Valley was a desirable destination renowned throughout prehistoric California. The valley had been visited by people from the Great Basin for 4,000 years. Later, the Miwok migrated to Yosemite from the Central Valley. Through the ages, this extraordinary landscape has inspired explanation. According to local myth, Yosemite Valley was formed by Tis-sa-ack and her husband Nangas, who sought to live there. As she traveled, Tis-sa-ack carried a burden basket of acorns and a baby carrier. Nangas followed with a bow, arrows, and a staff. Upon arriving in the valley, the two began to quarrel. Tis-sa-ack fled toward Mirror Lake. The Merced River was created from her path. The acorns that fell from her burden basket as she ran became magnificent oak trees. As the quarrel progressed, Tis-sa-ack threw down her baskets. The baby cradle landed against the north wall of the valley, its arched sunshade forming the Royal Arches. Having disrupted the peace—a breach of customary conduct—they were punished by the spirits. Tis-sa-ack became Half Dome as Nangas became Washington Column. There they remain forever, facing—yet separate— cliffs of granite.

Throughout the Sierra Nevada along streams near oak groves, thousands of mortars have been found in the granite. Petroglyphs remain along hunting paths. Many of the highways that cross the Sierra Crest originated as trade routes. Tuolumne Meadows was a camp along the trade route over Mono Pass to villages in the east. There are grinding holes in the granite of Lembert Dome, as well as along the Tuolumne River in Pate Valley. Through trade, the Sierra Miwok obtained salt, *ka-cha-vee* (brine fly pupae), *pe-aggi* (caterpillars of the Pandora moth), and pine nuts from the Mono Lake Paiute. Quality obsidian was also quarried near Mono Lake.

Archaeologists have recorded a series of chronologically related artifacts beginning around 1000 BC from the central western slope of the Sierra Nevada. Obsidian arrow points and shaping tools found here are crafted with a technology similar to the technologies of the Middle and Late Horizon Central California cultures. The Sierra Miwok, who arrived here around AD 1300, are apparently the most recent of several mountain cultures.

Natural Resources and Material Culture

Influenced by the regional availability of materials, Sierra Miwok foods, housing, and basketry varied. Dietary staples included black oak acorns, sugar pine nuts, trout, and deer. In winter, mushrooms were gathered and eaten with dried fish and stored acorns and pine nuts. The leaves of columbine were eaten as greens, and the seeds were used in a flour. A tea rich in vitamin C was made from the new growth of incense cedar. In summer, clover, squawroot, and brodiaea bulbs were gathered, along with meadow seeds and berries. Acorns were harvested in the fall. Fish could be brought to the surface by placing the pulp of toxic soaproot in a river pool. As the fish absorbed the toxin, they floated to the surface, where they were easily gathered.

In the mountains, the frames of conical summer dwellings were bound with fiber of wild grape vine and covered with cedar-bark slabs. Beds were made of pine needles, woven mats, and animal skins. Bows used in hunting were made of incense cedar, and strung with milkweed fiber. The southern Sierra Miwok basketry is made of grass, similar to that of the Yokuts. In the north, baskets are made of willow, sumac, strips of redbud bark, bracken fern, and bunch grass. Traditional currency included clam- and olivella-shell disk beads. Magnesite beads obtained through trade with the Pomo were rare and highly valued.

Museums and Interpretive Sites

The Visitor Center at **Calaveras Big Trees State Park** northeast of Arnold features clamshell disk beads, charmstones, arrow points of chert, obsidian, jasper, and shale, and a burden basket, (559) 795-2334. (See also hike 59.)

The **Yosemite Museum and Indian Village** in Yosemite Valley displays baskets and other artifacts and dioramas, and has Sierra Miwok crafts for sale. Outside, there is a reconstructed Sierra Miwok Village, (559) 372-0200. (See also hike 56.)

While many will want to spend more time viewing the extensive reconstructed village with mortars at **Indian Grinding Rock State Historic Park** north of Pine Grove, the Chaw'se Regional Indian Museum at the visitor center features Sierra Miwok artifacts. Besides periodic cultural demonstrations, an environmental camp provides an opportunity to spend the night in Miwok houses, (559) 296-7488. A Big Time Celebration is held annually in early August. (See also hike 58.)

Wassama Roundhouse State Historic Park, north of Oakhurst, consists of a sweathouse, a roundhouse, three bark dwellings, and some grinding rocks. Harvest celebrations and spiritual ceremonies are held in the roundhouse, while spiritual cleansing is done in the sweathouse. The site is used by the Sierra Miwok, so the buildings are not open to the public. The site may be viewed from 11 A.M. until 4 P.M. on Mondays, Wednesdays, and Saturdays, (559) 822-2332.

hike 55

Wawona Meadow Loop

Roundtrip Distance	3.5 miles
Location	Meadow camp in Sierra Miwok territory
Administration	Yosemite National Park (559) 372-0200
Map	Yosemite National Park

Highway 41 follows an early Miwok trail between Yosemite Valley and the foothills. Wawona Meadows was a campsite along this route. The Sierra Miwok people called this meadow *Pallahdun*, which means "resting place." The name "Wawona" was given to the meadow in historic times. *Woh-woh-nau* is a native name derived from the call of the owl, which is the spirit of the big trees to the Miwok. They camped at the meadow for centuries, gathering plant foods and materials for baskets.

Wawona Meadow was the site of Pallahdun, where basketry materials were gathered

Trailhead

From the Bay Area: Go 70 miles east of Merced on Hwy. 140 to the Arch Rock entrance station of Yosemite National Park (fee required). Follow Hwy. 140 about 6.5 miles east (first it becomes El Portal Rd., then Southside Dr. as it heads into Yosemite Valley) to Hwy. 41. Turn right and go 27 miles south to Wawona. The trailhead is across from the Wawona Visitor Center. **From Southern California:** Go 69 miles northeast of Fresno on Hwy. 41 to Wawona. The trailhead is across from the Wawona Visitor Center.

On The Trail

Having left the crowds behind in Yosemite Valley, you pass through the peaceful lands of Pallahdun on the Wawona Meadow Trail. From the parking areas at either the visitor center or the Wawona Hotel, cross Highway 41 and walk west beside the golf course to the signed trailhead. Go left along the Wawona Meadow Loop, passing through forest bordering the golf course, which soon gives way to wild meadowland. Following a split-rail fence, the trail circles the meadow. Watch for wildflowers and butterflies among the meadow grasses before returning to the parking area.

Along the loop you'll see willows lining the wet areas. Sierra Miwok women collected basketry materials here, including willow branches, fern roots, and bunch grass. In preparation for use, materials were either peeled, trimmed, and treated in cold water or boiling water, or buried in mud. A large, cone-shaped burden basket, worn on the back with a forehead support, was woven tightly and sealed with soap plant root, This sealant dried to a form a hard lining that retained even small seeds. Sierra Miwok women also wove a seed-beater for seed collection, a small, tightly woven basket for drinking water, and a mushbowl basket for serving acorn mush. Ceremonial baskets displayed intricate, precise designs woven of redbud or fern root boiled till it was black.

hike 56

El Capitan

Roundtrip Distance	7 miles
Location	Site of Sierra Miwok village in Yosemite Valley
Administration	Yosemite National Park (559) 372-0200
Map	Yosemite National Park

The Sierra Miwok people lived in villages along the Merced River in Yosemite Valley. "Yosemite" is derived from the Sierra Miwok word *uzumati* (grizzly bear). The Miwok called the Yosemite Valley *Ah-wah-nee*, meaning "place of a gaping mouth," in reference to the granite walls rising dramatically from the valley floor.

The legend explaining the origin of El Capitan involves two bear cubs who fell asleep on a huge rock boulder along the river. During their slumber, the rock rose to its present height of 7,569 feet. After a sharp-eyed crane discovered them atop the newly formed pinnacle, several of the animals attempted to climb the slick rock and rescue the cubs. None succeeded until a tiny worm tried. To the sneers of the others, he began to climb, all

Yosemite Village roundhouse

the while chanting his faith. He ultimately made it to the top and guided the bears safely down. The Miwok called the great rock *To-tokan-oo-lah* in his honor.

Trailhead

From the Bay Area: Go 70 miles east of Merced on Hwy. 140 to the Arch Rock entrance station of Yosemite National Park (fee required). Follow Hwy. 140 east. First it becomes El Portal Rd., then Southside Dr. as it heads into Yosemite Valley. Follow the signs for Yosemite Museum and Park Headquarters. Park here in the designated day-use lot. **From Southern California:** Go 95 miles northeast of Fresno on Hwy. 41 to the trailhead. Follow the directions above in Yosemite Valley.

On The Trail

Though you could cover this ground in a car or a shuttle-bus, one advantage of walking is that you can look up at the towering cliffs without a vehicle's roof impeding your view. The trail along the valley floor includes a visit to a reconstructed village site, then follows the Merced River downstream to the foot of El Capitan. From the Yosemite Museum and Indian Village, follow the park road to Northside Drive (the main road leading out of the valley) and go right on the wheelchair-accessible path that leads southwest beside it. Pass the junction with the Yosemite Falls Trail at 1 mile, and continue through Sunnyside Walk-in Campground. The background buzz gets much quieter a short distance from this hub. Continue as the trail crosses Northside Drive to meander along the Merced River. In prehistoric times this area was burned regularly to maintain an open meadow for hunting. The trail continues beside the river before crossing Northside Drive again near the base of El Capitan at 3.5 miles. Recall the story of To-tokan-oo-lah as you gaze at the extraordinary granite cliff of El Capitan. If you can linger, you might see the cliffs aglow with the hues of sunset. Return via the shuttle or retrace your steps to the parking area.

hike 57   Shadow of the Miwok Trail

Roundtrip Distance	0.25 mile
Location	Seasonal camp in Sierra Miwok territory
Administration	Summit Ranger Station, Stanislaus National Forest (559) 965-3434
Map	Shadow of the Miwok Prehistoric Trail

The northern Sierra Miwok visited the Pinecrest area during the summer months, coming up from foothill villages to harvest acorns and hunt the deer herds migrating into the cooler high country. Nearby, Highway 108 follows an early trade route leading east over Sonora Pass and south to the village sites of the Owens Valley. A traditional Sierra Miwok village has been reconstructed at Pinecrest by local Miwok tribal members. Miwok consultants prepared the interpretive trail and its brochure.

Trailhead

Go about 30 miles northeast of Sonora on Hwy. 108 to Pinecrest Lake Rd. Turn right and almost immediately find the Summit Ranger Station on the left. Park there (no fee) and cross the road to the Miwok village.

On The Trail

The Shadow of the Miwok Trail visits a reconstructed Sierra Miwok village. Walk through the village, where exhibits include both the frame of a dwelling and a completed one, a sweathouse, some bedrock mortars, and a granary. Houses here were traditionally covered with the bark of incense cedar. Beyond the village, the trail passes a meadow stream with a clearing encircled by ponderosa and sugar pines and incense cedar. Sierra Miwok legend depicts the water spirit Hushepi inhabiting mountain streams such as this one, her long hair flowing over the streambed. Enjoy this intimate meadow at your leisure. When the trail returns you to the village, retrace your steps to the parking area.

hike 58 Chaw'se South Nature Trail

Roundtrip Distance	0.75 mile
Location	Foothill village in Sierra Miwok territory
Administration	Indian Grinding Rock State Historic Park (559) 296-7488
Map	Chaw'se State Park Bountiful Land brochure

Chaw'se is the Miwok word for "grinding rocks." With 1,185 bedrock mortars, this is the largest grouping found in North America. Chaw'se is also noteworthy because the mortars are inscribed with petroglyphs, a tradition almost unique to California. Petroglyphs here depict concentric circles, radials, animal and human tracks, abstract human figures, and parallel wavy lines. Some are thought to have been worked into the marble 2,000–3,000 years ago.

The Sierra Miwok women harvested acorns and other seeds here in autumn, then dried and stored them in *cha'ka* (pole-frames interwoven to form large baskets) granaries lined with pest-repelling pine needles and wormwood. Acorns were cracked and shelled as needed, and the nuts were ground to a fine meal in bedrock mortars. To prepare acorn soup, first hot then cold water was poured over the meal to leach out tannin, and then the meal was placed in a watertight cooking basket. Water was added to produce the desired consistency, and then fire-heated rocks were inserted to cook the soup until it was done.

Chaw'se also offers an environmental camp experience at *U'macha'tam'ma'* (bark houses to the north). There, seven bark-clad houses, each holding up to 6 people, may be reserved for overnight stays. Contact the park for more information and to make reservations. (See "Museums and Interpretive Sites" above.)

Trailhead

Go about 10 miles east of Jackson on Hwy. 88 to the Pine Grove-Volcano Rd. Turn left and continue 1.5 miles northeast to the Indian

Grinding Rock State Historic Park entrance (fee required). Park by the museum.

On The Trail

The South Nature Trail lets you examine the ethnobotany of the Sierra Miwok while touring the grinding rocks and the reconstructed village. The trail begins at the rear of the Chaw'se Regional Indian Museum. Walk west along the paved, wheelchair-accessible path, passing the mortar and petroglyph site. Continue past the dwellings and the round-house to the beginning of the numbered signposts (and the end of the pavement) at 0.2 mile. The numbers correspond to numbered descriptions in the Bountiful Land brochure (available from the museum). Continue past the reconstructed Miwok village at 0.25 mile, near the junction with the North Loop. Bearing left, the South Nature Trail crosses the creek several times as it passes plant specimens. Ecosystems that the trail explores are riparian oak woodland, meadow, and conifer forest. Labeled specimens include milkweed, coffeeberry, valley oak, soap plant, western chokecherry, snowberry, and horsetail. The intriguing and explicit plant-use descriptions were written with the help of the local Native American community and the Amador Tribal Council. Take a moment to consider what you've learned. Where the loop ends near the roundhouse, follow the trail to the right, back to the parking area.

hike 59   Calaveras Big Trees North Grove

Roundtrip Distance	1 mile
Location	Seasonal camp in Sierra Miwok territory
Administration	Calaveras Big Trees State Park (559) 795-2334
Map	Calaveras Big Trees State Park, North Grove Trail brochure

During the hot, summer months at lower foothill elevations, some bands of Sierra Miwok camped higher—in that part of the Sierra now protected as Calaveras Big Trees State Park. Sacred to the Sierra Miwok, the sequoia trees here are some of the oldest and largest (in girth) of all the earth's trees. The oldest Sierra redwood has lived for 3,200 years. The trail brochure boasts that several of these trees were possibly growing here before the birth of Christ. Indeed, several may well have been alive when the early people associated with the Middle Horizon of the Central California Culture migrated here around 1000 BC, and certainly by the time the Sierra Miwok arrived, around AD 1300. Besides sequoias, this lower montane forest includes sugar pine, white fir, incense cedar, ponderosa pine, black oak, and chinquapin. Early cultures harvested the acorn of the black oak and fished for trout in Big Tree Creek. Sugar pine nuts were harvested as an ingredient for pinole. The bark of the incense cedar was used both as an insulation in moccasins and as an exterior covering for Sierra Miwok *u'machas* (dwellings).

The big trees

Trailhead

Exit Hwy. 4 at the entrance to Calaveras Big Trees State Park northeast of Arnold, approximately 26 miles east of Hwy. 49 in the Sierra foothills. Park by the visitor center. (There is skiable snow along this trail in winter.)

On The Trail

With its interpretive brochure, the North Grove Trail gives you information on the ethnobotany of the Sierra Miwok within the redwood grove where they camped in summer. From behind the visitor center, a short spur trail leads east to the North Grove Trail. Turn right (south) and follow a split-rail fence to the beginning of the interpretive trail. The brochure (available at the visitor center) interprets the signed specimens along the trail, focusing particularly on the redwoods. Head right, along the North Grove Trail, and wander along the north bank of Big Tree Creek. Along the creek massive redwoods tower to 300 feet. Watch for the colorful flash of plumage from red-breasted sapsuckers in flight, birds that drill holes in the tall redwoods.

Growing among the redwoods are mountain dogwood, hazelnut, and sugar pine. Mountain dogwood produces showy spring flowers and summer fruit. Dried sugar pine sap was used by the Miwok as both a glue and a chewing gum. Hazelnut was used in basketry. The abrasive stems of horsetails growing along the creek were used to polish arrowshafts. In 0.5 mile the trail crosses Big Tree Creek and loops back via the south bank near the edge of the sequoia grove. Look for mortars scoured in the granite along the creek before you return to the parking area.

courtesy National Park Service   **Gathering acorns in Yosemite Valley**

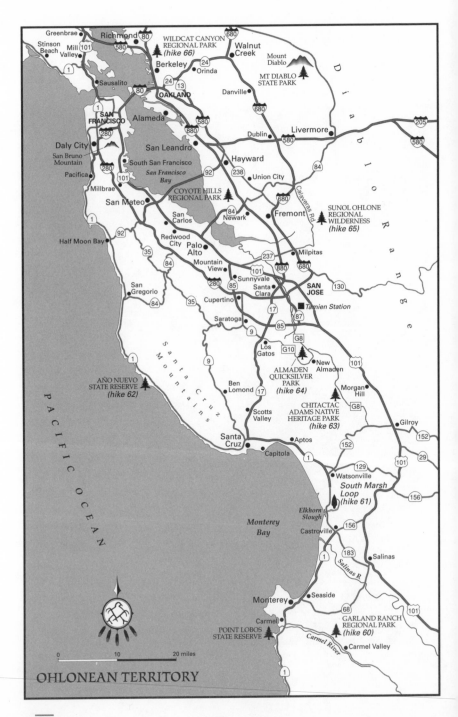

OHLONEAN TERRITORY

Ohlone
Central Coast & Coast Ranges

Landscape and People

The Ohlone homeland extends from the San Francisco Bay Area south through the Monterey Peninsula to Point Sur. Living in one of the most food-rich regions in California—a land brimming with prolific oak groves and seed meadows at the edge of the Pacific Ocean's bounty—the Ohlone people had all they needed. The terrain was sea coast, alluvial plains, and coastal mountains. Villages dotted the bays and rivers. Though they traded and intermarried with other groups, the Ohlone traditionally lived as separate tribelets. They did not consider themselves a unified people.

Before European contact, there were 40 Ohlone tribelets, each of perhaps 250 people, having a distinct language and a clearly delineated territory. The people living in what we now call the San Francisco Peninsula spoke Ramaytush. Those in the South Bay spoke Tamyen. Those in the East Bay spoke Chochenyo. Those along the southern shore of the Carquinez Strait spoke Karkin. Rumsen was spoken in Monterey, while those living near San Juan Bautista spoke Mutson. Within some tribelets there were 12 distinct dialects. "Ohlone" is a corruption of *Oljone*, once a village along the San Mateo coast. The name "Costanoan" (coast-dwellers) was later applied by the Spanish.

Each territory developed a major village as a trading center, and several smaller villages in the interior as seasonal harvest camps. The Ohlone languages are of the Penutian family. Other Penutian speakers include Tsimshian in British Columbia, Nez Perce, Chinook, Klamath, Modoc, and Central American Maya. Penutian speaking groups may have arrived from the north and settled near the San Francisco Bay 4,500 years ago, displacing Hokan speakers who had previously lived there. From these people evolved the separate Ohlone groups. The prehistoric Ohlone population is thought to have reached 10,000.

Visualize for a moment the San Francisco Bay Area without urbanization, and the river valleys to the south without agriculture. This is the world the Ohlone people knew. Before the Bay was diked, thousands of acres of marshland ringed its shore. Native bunchgrass carpeted the meadowlands. Oak and bay forest covered the hills. Animal life was prolific. Ducks, geese, and shorebirds filled the marshes, large herds of pronghorn antelopes grazed the hills, and bald eagles and condors patrolled the skies. Grizzly bears might be seen feeding on a whale washed ashore. Salmon and sea otters thrived in the Bay and along the coast amid beds of mussels, clams, abalone, and oysters. Since the water table was much closer to the surface in prehistoric times, many areas that are now dry were brimming with seeps and springs. After winter rains, the Carmel, Salinas, and Pajaro rivers and Alameda and Coyote creeks inundated their canyons to their outlets.

The modern landscape is still intimately linked to its Ohlone past. During the construction of the Caltrain/Amtrak station near San Jose, remnants of Tamien village were unearthed. Implements of Franciscan chert, obsidian, and bone were found among bowl mortars and over 35,000 olivella-shell beads. To educate the multitudes passing through the station about the people of Tamien, Caltrans planned a permanent exhibit to display artifacts, with sketches and a narrative describing the archaeological recovery of artifacts. A history of the Ohlone people was written by tribal consultants. While Tamien Station now commemorates the ancient village on the Caltrain line, the administrators did not ultimately accept responsibility for the exhibit's care. It awaits a home. At Hayward's Dry Creek Regional Park near Jordan Pond a lone tree marks the grinding rock of an Ohlone village. Oakland's Lake Temescal is named for a Juchiyunes sweathouse built near the banks of Temescal Creek. On the Peninsula, Portola recorded having camped below a village on what is now Pedro Point in Pacifica. San Bruno Mountain contains village sites of the Awashtes tribelet. Another village site is at Twin Pines Park in Belmont. The village of Orysom in the South Bay was later chosen as the site of Mission San Jose.

In this region, archaeological evidence comes mainly from bedrock milling stations, seasonal camps, special task sites, and the shellmounds of major villages. A special task site, such as the bulb-roasting site (Ala-342) at the foot of the East Bay hills in Alameda County, might include ovens and storage pits (Fentress, 1994). Along the Bay Area Ridge Trail on the flanks of Mission Peak are prehistoric stone walls that may predate the Ohlone. At Mussel Rock near Daly City, a village site excavation offered another view of the archaeological record.

The shellmounds of the San Francisco Bay shore are among the richest in the state, on a par with those of the Chumash found on the Channel Islands. There are over 425 shellmounds throughout the Bay Area, with hundreds more scattered along the coast to the south. The Ohlone shellmounds are typically large ones, indicating a long or intensive period of use. The Emeryville Mound is 270 feet in diameter and 30 feet deep. Within its layers are recorded significant changes in tools and the introduction of the bow and arrow, which occurred around AD 500.

The antiquity of human settlement in this region has been measured through obsidian hydration-dating of a Castro Valley site to about 5530 BC. Another (Ala-60), though not precisely dated, is thought to date back 8,000 years. This milling site contains 25 conical mortars used in processing grass seed, which predates acorns as the Native Californian food staple. At the same site are 44 bedrock mortars dating back 4,500 years. Within the site's top layer, six bowl mortars were found, which suggests a more recent habitation, perhaps extending into the historic period.

The Ohlone traded mainly with the Miwok and the Yokuts. Much as Interstate 580 does today, a main trade route to the Central Valley crossed Altamont Pass. The Jones Trail (which passes through St. Joseph's Hill Open Space Preserve) is a segment of a former route along Los Gatos Creek across the Santa Clara Valley. The shore at Carquinez Strait was a meeting ground of the Patwin (southern Wintun), Miwok, and Ohlone peoples. Linked to the trade are several nearby archaeological sites in Carquinez Regional Shoreline, and east of Vallejo near Sulphur Springs Mountain. Salt, beads, pine nuts, obsidian, and abalone shells were the most sought after trade goods.

In the Ohlone creation story, Mount Diablo was at first an island surrounded by flood water. Standing at its summit, Coyote, with the advice of Eagle and Hummingbird, decided to father the human race. Coyote taught humans how to sustain themselves and, in his passing, relinquished the world to the Ohlone people. Mount Diablo, actually in Miwok territory, was named "Devil" by the Spanish because the Ohlone maintained it is inhabited by *puh* (spirits). Mount Diablo is one of four Bay Area peaks particularly revered by the Ohlone. Mount Umunhum in Santa Clara County is considered the resting place of Hummingbird. The peak retains its Ohlone name. Of the remaining prominent features on the Bay Area horizon, Mount Tamalpais and Mount Hamilton are also sacred in Ohlone tradition. The Ohlone creation story is similar to that of the Yokuts and that of the Maidu in that water covers most of the world in the sacred time before creation in each culture. In the Monterey Bay area, the island rising from the water in the creation of the world is Pico Blanco.

Natural Resources and Material Culture

Acutely attuned to the natural world, the Ohlone knew well how to make use of the region's abundant food supply. Acorns and grass seeds were the staples, to which were added rabbits, seals, sea otters, salmon, smelt, sea urchins, abalone, mussels, clams, oysters, and meat of an occasional beached whale. The Karkin tribelet fished the formerly great salmon runs in the Carquinez Strait from tule boats. Tribelets living near the marshes relied upon the massive spring and fall migrations along the Pacific Flyway for waterfowl and their eggs. Duck skins stuffed with tule were used as hunting decoys. Clover greens and flower seeds were delicacies. The people traveled inland annually, where acorns, brodiaea bulbs, and grass seed abounded. Large trout were also fished from inland streams.

Though seasonal foods varied, acorns were stored for year-round use. The acorn harvest marked the beginning of the new year. That most acorn milling sites in the region contain five or fewer mortar holes implies a seasonal use. Each tribelet's territory provided access from the main village to marshes, rivers, meadows, and forests in order to harvest the ripening foods. Houses were dome-shaped and covered with tule thatch. Stone blades were made of chert and obsidian. A double arrow (a single shaft with a second arrow point affixed below) used throughout Central California was crafted by the Ohlone.

Of the rock-art sites found in Ohlone territory, most are cupules (depressions in rocks that resemble small mortar holes). A common form of rock art found worldwide, cupules are used both in processing acorns and in ritual. Cupules were made by women to enhance fertility, and by shamans to influence weather. They are usually found near bedrock mortars, waterways, and other petroglyphs. Some are found on ridges near prominent overlooks. Other regional rock art consists of small, oval or curved incisions with raised centers. The incisions, termed Pecked Curvilinear Nucleated (PCN) petroglyphs, were carved in chlorite schist boulders near watercourses. Along with cupules, PCNs mark boulders that may have been considered local sources of spiritual power.

The Ohlone developed an accomplished material culture, as exemplified in their basketry. Often made of willow shoots, sedge roots, and bracken fern, these baskets are paragons in their craft. Ohlone baskets are on display at the Santa Cruz City Museum, the Los Altos Public

Library, and Mission San Juan Bautista. Since the Ohlone gained status through generosity rather than material accumulation, the wealthy might give prodigiously during feasts and burn the most exceptional baskets at a funeral.

Museums and Interpretive Sites

Coyote Hills Regional Park in Newark includes a reconstructed village at one of the park's four midden sites, and a reconstructed tule boat displayed among interpretive exhibits and artifacts in the visitor center. Among the staff are members of the Ohlone Tribe, (510) 795-9385.

Daniels Nature Center at Skyline Ridge Preserve in the Santa Cruz Mountains features exhibits and bowl mortars. Outside, there are mortars in a rock outcrop near the dam at Alpine Pond, (650) 949-5270.

Santa Teresa Springs, at **Santa Teresa County Park** south of San Jose, is the site of a large Muwekma village that archaeological evidence suggests was inhabited for over 3,000 years. Ohlone legend credits a female spirit with creating the springs in order to free the village from disease. Interpretive panels offering a timeline of California history are planned for the park, (408) 225-0225.

The **Presidio of Monterey** offers a self-guiding walking tour of its grounds that include Rumsen archaeological sites. For more information, call either (831) 242-5000 for Presidio Public Affairs or (831) 646-3991 for the Presidio of Monterey Museum, which is scheduled to open in the fall of 2000.

hike 60   Rumsen Grinding Rocks

Roundtrip Distance	2 miles
Location	Rumsen village site in the Carmel River Valley
Administration	Garland Ranch Regional Park (831) 659-6062
Map	Garland Ranch Regional Park

The Rumsen are a tribelet of the Ohlone traditionally centered in the Carmel River Valley. The main village here, also called Rumsen, was inland from the coast, along the river's south bank. Sites of Rumsen habitation remain throughout Garland Ranch Regional Park. Though many early traces have been covered by activities of the park's ranching days, a grinding rock can be seen here along the Mesa Trail. Running year-round, the Carmel River passes through grassland often brimming with wildflowers. The Rumsen people traveled frequently down river to hunt sea lion and gather seafood from the mineral-rich coastal waters off Point Lobos. Their middens have been found among the bluffs there. The Rumsen found a highly varied landscape in the Carmel Valley, including live oak woodlands, redwood groves, fern canyons, meadowlands, and slopes of coastal sage scrub.

Rumsen women maintained family-owned seed meadows in the grasslands where they would go in the spring bringing willow seedbeaters and large burden baskets to collect bromegrass, chia, evening primrose, and clarkia. Back at the village grinding rocks, they processed seeds in a mortar to crack the hulls, and winnowed them in a basket to separate the grain. Flower seed might be blended with the grass seed, roasted in a shallow basket with hot coals, and served. With the seed harvest complete, the vegetation would then be burned for optimal plant succession the following year.

Trailhead

Exit Hwy. 1 at Carmel Valley Rd. in Carmel. Go 0.6 mile east to the parking area at Garland Ranch Regional Park (no fee). The trailhead is across the river by the visitor center.

On The Trail

From the parking area, cross the footbridge over the Carmel River. Note that the river floods its banks in the wet season, making exploration more challenging. From the visitor center, follow the Lupine Loop to the left, through the open meadow. Continue to the junction of the Mesa Trail in 0.6 mile, just past a bench. Go left on the Mesa Trail for several steps, beyond the intersection of the Waterfall Trail, to an unsigned spur trail on the left leading within several yards to the grinding rock. The Rumsen Grinding Rock is explained by an interpretive panel. As you pause here, imagine what bustle this quiet spot must have known 250 years ago, with the grinding and hammering of pestles as women processed acorns and seeds for the daily meal. From the grinding rock, retrace your steps back to the Lupine Loop. Go left to continue along the loop and explore the west side of the valley. Here, cottonwood and sycamore stands dot the large, open floodplain. The route soon returns to the willow-lined Carmel River. Explore the visitor center before crossing the river to the parking area.

hike 61   South Marsh Loop

Roundtrip Distance	3 miles
Location	Coastal gathering site in Ensen territory
Administration	Elkhorn Slough National Estuarine Reserve (831) 728-2822
Map	Not necessary

The bounty of Elkhorn Slough sustained the Ohlone village of *Kalintaruc* (ocean at houses). The people hunted tule elk and duck, fished, and gathered seafood here. The slough is lined with midden sites—some dating back 5,000 years. Archaeologists unearthed a string of beads made from over 3,000 local olivella shells at the village site near the mouth of the slough. Situated just east of the Monterey Bay Submarine Canyon, Elkhorn Slough benefits from an abundant supply of fish and shellfish that wash in with the tide. Shorebirds winter here, and waterfowl stop over on migration. Upland are marine terraces covered by a coast live oak woodland. This is one place where you should bring a bird-watching guide.

Trailhead

Exit Hwy. 1 at Dolan Rd. in Moss Landing. Head 3.5 miles east to Elkhorn Rd. Turn left (north) and go 2 miles to the reserve entrance. The Elkhorn Slough National Estuarine Reserve is open from Wednesday through Sunday each week.

On The Trail

Beginning at the visitor center, the South Marsh Loop meanders through a meadow down to the slough. Pass through a field of lupine, blue dicks, and mustard to the Elkhorn Dairy building, which overlooks the slough. From there, the trail descends toward the salt marsh. At the marsh, head south along the trail through the pickleweed. The trail soon bears left, descending slightly to the main channel of the slough. Elkhorn Slough is an estuary filling an abandoned channel of the Salinas River. Here fresh water meets salt, creating one of richest concentrations of biodiversity imaginable. Watch for wildlife before retracing your steps to the parking area.

hike 62   Año Nuevo Point Trail

Roundtrip Distance	3.2 miles
Location	Coastal Oljone camp
Administration	Año Nuevo State Reserve (650) 879-0227
Map	Año Nuevo State Reserve

Before European contact, the Año Nuevo area sustained a large community. Throughout the dunes stretching from Año Nuevo Point to Gazos Creek, middens have been documented. This is the land of the Oljone tribelet, thought to be the namesake of the Ohlone people. The area was a center for hunting marine mammals, fishing, and gathering abalone and mussels. Tule rafts were used to fish the offshore waters. Chert quarried from the beach at Año Nuevo was traded throughout the Coast Range and east into the Central Valley. Preliminary stone flaking from rock quarried here was done here, though spear points, knives, scrapers, and arrowheads were completed elsewhere. Long associated with a prolific marine mammal population, Año Nuevo Point is one of the main elephant seal breeding grounds along the California coast. It is also a rookery for sea lions and harbor seals, and there are members of each species here year-round.

Trailhead

To reach the trailhead 20 miles north of Santa Cruz, exit Highway 1 at the entrance to Año Nuevo State Reserve (fee required) on the west side of the road. Park near the visitor center.

On The Trail

The Año Nuevo Point Trail traverses a headland covered with coastal sage scrub to Año Nuevo Point, where the Oljone people harvested a rich bounty from the sea. A massive sand dune on the point provides enough height for sweeping views over the coastal waters. The trail begins at the southwest end of the parking area, near the visitor center. Walk west to the junction of the Cove Beach Trail. Turn right, following signs to the WILDLIFE AREA TRAILHEAD and AÑO NUEVO POINT. Continue to the staging area at 0.9 mile. Pass by the interpretive display and pick up a permit to enter the Wildlife Area before continuing along a boardwalk through the dunes. Beyond the staging area the Año Nuevo Point Trail is bordered by wire-cable fencing. Beach strawberries and dune grass cover the sands. Several spur trails afford opportunities for quick scenic overlooks. All trails soon reconnect to cross a series of seeps and climb the dunes to the overlook. Naturalists are usually available here to help you interpret the sights. During the elephant seal breeding season from December through March, this hike can be made by guided walk only. (Call the park for more information, or to make reservations.) This is when the largest males come ashore. Off-season, you are still likely to see females and juveniles, and far fewer visitors. Keep a respectful distance as you share the trail with the resting elephant seals. When you're ready, retrace your steps to the parking area.

hike 63   Chitactac Adams Native Heritage Park

Roundtrip Distance   0.25 mile

Location   Mutson village site in Santa Clara Valley

Administration   Mount Madonna Ranger Office, Santa Clara County Parks (408) 842-2341

Map   Chitactac Adams Native Heritage Park

Chitactac was a Mutson village along what is now Uvas Creek. The village flourished for over 2,000 years in this sheltered valley just uphill from the once marshy, food-rich bottomland of the Santa Clara Valley. Soapstone, charcoal, olivella- and clamshell beads excavated here have been dated to 700 BC. Over 75 bedrock mortars have been found throughout the park, a large number by regional standards. A group of mortars and cupules remain in an outcrop overlooking the creek at the Food Processing Station. Petroglyphs along the creek include both cupules and concentric circles with concave centers.

Trailhead

Exit Hwy. 101 at Tennant Rd. in Morgan Hill. Go 1 mile west to Monterey Hwy. Turn left and go 0.5 mile to Watsonville Rd. Turn right and proceed 5.5 miles to the park entrance (no fee) on the right. The park is closed on weekdays.

On The Trail

The best part about this site is its presentation. All traces of the Mutson village here are informed by interpretive panels. At the trailhead, interpretive panels depict the petroglyphs here, as well as the buildings composing the Mutson village. Accompanying text also details Ohlone social structure, their plant use, the network of trade routes, and their culture. The wheelchair-accessible trail begins at the interpretive shelter. Follow the trail to the right, around an outcrop to the site of Chitactac village. The trail gradually descends switchbacks to an interpretive panel on Ohlone buildings. A spur trail leads down several steps toward the creek to a panel depicting the nearby rock art. This vantage allows for a view of the petroglyphs in the boulders along the creek. Easiest to see in bright light, the cupules and concentric circles are thought to be associated with rituals influencing hunting and fishing, the weather, astrono-

Chitactac was the Mutson village along Uvas Creek

my, and other shamanistic endeavors. Climb the steps and continue along the trail to grinding holes in a sunlit outcrop above the river, with an interpretive panel on food processing. Another interpretive panel farther along the trail details the resources that were available at Uvas Creek, and their uses by the people of Chitactac. Subsequent interpretive panels along the trail focus on the Ohlone in historic times. Your trail loops around the park's southern boundary and east, ascending a few steps to the parking area.

hike 64   New Almaden Mine

Roundtrip Distance	3.3 miles
Location	Cinnabar mine in Quiroste territory
Administration,	Almaden Quicksilver Park, Santa Clara County Parks (408) 268-3884
Map	Almaden Quicksilver Park

The Ohlone traveled here via Los Alamitos Creek to gather cinnabar, which was traded throughout the state for use as a pigment. Native Californians would travel great distances to trade for it. Controlled by the Quiroste tribelet, the Almaden mine was the principal source of this mineral. To mine the cinnabar, a 100-foot-long tunnel was constructed underground, large enough for one man to comfortably work inside. Rounded streambed cobbles functioned as hammers, picks, and mauls. Skeletons and stone implements found near the working face of the tunnel indicate that there once was an untimely cave-in. Unlike specialized Pomo chert drill makers or Gabrieleño soapstone pot designers, no specialized miners class developed among the Quiroste working here. Instead, the cinnabar mines were probably worked over a long period of time by many different people. Just as the Pomo salt wars resulted from the Potter Valley Pomo's failure to offer the Stonyford Pomo gifts before taking salt, battles occurred here when the Yokuts attempted to gather cinnabar without first acknowledging the resident Quiroste. During historic times, Almaden developed into the richest quicksilver (mercury) mines in California, with shafts extending 2,300 feet below the ground. The mines closed in 1972 in response to the discovery of mercury's toxicity.

Trailhead

Exit Hwy 85 at Almaden Expwy. (G8) in San Jose. Follow Almaden Expwy. 4.2 miles southeast to Almaden Rd. Continue 2.9 miles on Almaden Rd. through the town of New Almaden to the Almaden Quicksilver County Park staging area on the right, next to the ranger station and the Almaden Museum.

On The Trail

The Mine Hill Trail traverses the hills, passing signs of both prehistoric and historic mining activity in the park. From the parking area, follow the Mine Hill Trail up-canyon along Los Alamitos Creek, paralleling the former Ohlone route. The trail begins to switchback as it climbs northeast among chaparral, intermittently broken by serpentine outcroppings. Cinnabar forms under unique conditions where serpentine rock is geothermally transformed. The trail ascends higher as it switchbacks to the top of Capehorn Pass. At 1,000 feet above sea level, the pass offers you a panoramic view of the San Francisco Bay and of the Ohlone ancestral homelands. Your view extends north from the cities of the South Bay to the East Bay hills. Where the Mine Hill Trail ascends via a hard left from Capehorn Pass, instead take an easier left on the Randol Trail, which follows a middle trail fork northwest. Seasonal wildflowers may carpet the ridgetop above you as the Randol Trail traverses several ravines to the picnic area at Day Tunnel. Now sealed, this was the original entrance to the mines. When you're through exploring the site and enjoying the view, retrace your steps to the parking area.

hike 65   Indian Joe Creek Trail

Roundtrip Distance	1 mile
Location	Seasonal camp in Tuibun territory
Administration	Sunol Ohlone Regional Wilderness (925) 862-2601
Map	Sunol Ohlone Regional Wilderness, Indian Joe Creek booklet

This part of the Ohlone homeland has remained near-wilderness, very much like it was in prehistoric times. The Sunol Ohlone Regional Wilderness provides a glimpse of what lies along the Ohlone Wilderness Trail, which connects Mission Peak (above Fremont) to Del Valle Regional Park (south of Livermore) through Sunol. In its entirety, the Ohlone Wilderness Trail runs 25 miles through their former territory.

Sunol is the homeland of the Tuibun tribelet of the Ohlone people. Indian Joe Creek was named for the last Native American known to have lived here. His ancestors had lived in the area for 3,000 years. They camped here while harvesting acorns along Alameda Creek, and hunting tule elk, which still roam the hills. Shaded by alder, willow, and sycamore, Alameda Creek and its tributaries nurture many plants that were gathered by the Tuibun. They would follow the creek from the bay shore to reach these hills. Uphill is a woodland of blue oak, prized for its flavorful acorns. The acorns were pounded into flour in mortars; the flour was rinsed in the cold creek water to remove the bitter taste, and then cooked into soup or mush. Mortars can still be seen in a boulder along the creek near the visitor center.

Trailhead

Exit I-680 at Hwy. 84 at Scotts Corner in Sunol. Go 4 miles south on Calaveras Rd. to Geary Rd. Turn left and go 1.5 miles to the park entrance (fee required.) Park by the visitor center.

On The Trail

The Indian Joe Creek Trail booklet available at the visitor center describes the plants along the route. The trail begins at the north side of the parking area to the right of the visitor center. Cross the footbridge over Alameda Creek and turn right, heading upstream on the Indian Joe Nature Trail. Plant materials found along the creek include willow, which was used in basketry, and white alder, whose bark was used to make an orange dye. The route bears left onto Indian Joe Creek Trail in 0.1 mile, and climbs steeply through a canopy of oak along the creek. The leaves of the bay trees growing here were used to repel pests at the village site, or burned to create smoke that masked the human scent of hunters. The leaves of sticky monkey flower were eaten both raw and cooked. Toyon berries were crushed to make a drink, or parched in a fire before eating. As you complete the climb at 0.4 mile, you'll find a bench provided for a quiet rest. When you're ready, the trail descends from here along an old ranch road. Try to identify the plants composing the grassland and chaparral as the route takes you back to the visitor center and parking area.

hike 66   Wildcat Creek Trail

Roundtrip Distance	9.6 miles
Location	Canyon in Huchiun Ohlone territory
Administration	East Bay Regional Park District (510) 635-0138
Map	Wildcat Canyon Regional Park

Wildcat Creek was the home of the Huchiun tribelet of the Ohlone people. The main village was located at the mouth of Wildcat Creek. Where the creek entered the tidal marshland around the former bayshore, middens have been found. Near the creek in Richmond's Alvarado Park, there's an oval depression (a Pecked Curvilinear Nucleated petroglyph) carved among cupules in a boulder. This kind of petroglyph is thought to mark schist rock believed to hold spiritual power. The Huchiun traveled up Wildcat Creek to hunt game and to

trade shell beads at the site now named Indian Camp—
near the picnic area and parking lot of the
Environmental Education Center in Tilden Nature Area.
Pictographs of an adult's and a child's red hematite
handprints can be found along the way in the cliff face
near Wildcat Peak. A prehistoric hematite quarry isn't far
away.

Trailhead

Exit I-80 at University Ave. in Berkeley. Go 2.1 miles east to Oxford St.
Turn left and go 0.7 mile north to Rose St. Turn right and go one block
to Spruce Street. Turn left and go 1.8 miles to an intersection with
Grizzly Peak Blvd. and Wildcat Canyon Rd. Cross the intersection and
immediately turn left from Wildcat Canyon Rd. onto Canon Dr. There
is a sign here for nature area, pony ride, wildcat canyon. Go downhill to
a junction with Central Park Dr. Turn left and go 0.1 mile to the parking lot at Tilden Park Nature Area.

On The Trail

The Wildcat Creek Trail follows a former Ohlone route between inland
hunting and trading camps along Wildcat Creek and the village near the
bay. The trail begins at the Environmental Education Center in Tilden
Park Nature Area, and follows Wildcat Creek 4.8 miles downstream to

The Ohlone route through Wildcat Canyon

where the creek entered the bay in prehistoric times. Along the creek, the route passes under a canopy of willow, creek dogwood, bay, and alder. While this woodland runs the length of Wildcat Creek, it is particularly interesting at 0.3 mile as the boardwalk explores the environs of Jewel Lake. Bay, live oak, and large leaf maples cover the steep, west slope. Views appear down-canyon as you walk. You pass the junctions of the Havey Canyon Trail at 2 miles, the Mezue Trail at 2.25 miles, and the Belgum Trail at 4 miles, before reaching Alvarado Park. Native bunch grass grows on the rolling hillsides of the lower canyon. From the chaparral on the higher slopes, women from the village would gather elderberry, blackberry, snowberry, bracken fern, and coyote brush. Father Juan Crespi traveled this route in 1772, camping with his party along the creek. He traded glass beads with the Huchiun for food and tools. At the northern terminus of this walk in Alvarado Park, cupules and PCNs can be found in a boulder along the creek. Though it is now several miles away from the bay, this was the bayshore approximately 2,000 years ago. This was the vicinity of the village, and several middens remain both up- and downstream. When you're ready, retrace your steps to the parking area.

 # Guided Walks

Coyote Hills Regional Park offers guided walks to a reconstructed Ohlone village at an archaeological site (Ala-328) that saw 2,000 years of habitation. An archaeological dig displays a cross section of one of the park's four middens. The staff includes Ohlone tribal members. Call the visitor center at (510) 795-9385 for dates and times of the guided walks. At the San Francisco Bay's edge, the Coyote Hills rise above the surrounding marshland. During high tides about 2,000 years ago, the hills became islands in the bay. The visitor center displays an Ohlone tule boat among its artifacts and exhibits on Ohlone culture. Trails and boardwalks explore the park, which is open Tuesdays through Sundays, from 9:30 A.M. to 5 P.M.

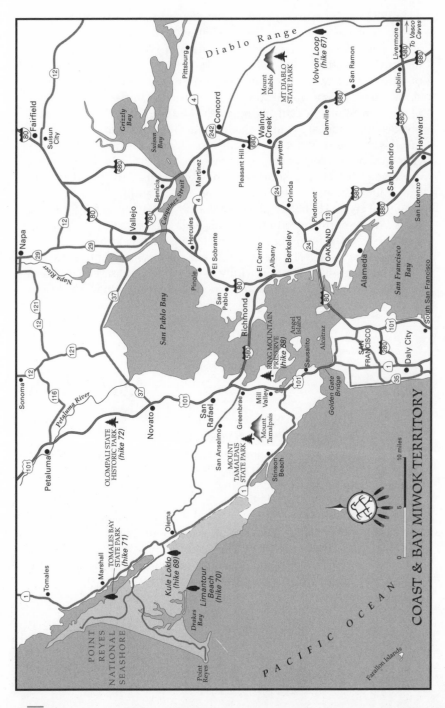

COAST & BAY MIWOK TERRITORY

Coast & Bay Miwok
North Coast & Coast Ranges

Landscape and People

Marin and southern Sonoma counties compose the homeland of the Coast Miwok people. Much of the terrain is the rugged coast and coastal mountains, from the Marin Headlands to Bodega Head, as well as the San Francisco Bay shore and the Petaluma River inland to Petaluma. Mount Diablo was an enclave of the Bay Miwok surrounded entirely by Ohlone territory. The prehistoric population of the Coast Miwok is thought to have reached 3,000.

Like the Ohlone, the Coast Miwok are Penutian speakers. Their dialects are Bodega Bay Coast Miwok, spoken around Bodega, and Southern Coast Miwok, spoken in Marin County. The Coast Miwok are one of five groups tracing their ancestry to the Miwok people. The Coast, Bay, Lake, Plains, and Sierra Miwok people adapted culturally to the particular lands they settled.

The name "Miwok" is derived from *miwu*, the Sierra Miwok word for "person." (The Coast Miwok word is *mitcha*.) The Coast Miwok referred to themselves by the name of their home village. There are over 600 known, permanent and seasonal Coast Miwok village sites. A Coast Miwok village might include from 75 to several hundred people. Villages were on or near waterways, usually no more than a half mile from a shore. Many archaeological sites have been found along the shores of Tomales Bay. Early ethnographers documented the larger villages of Sakloki near Tomales and Echa-kolum near Marshall. There are over 100 Coast Miwok sites within Point Reyes National Seashore, many clustered around Drakes Estero and the adjacent Limantour and Drakes beaches. A larger permanent village was *Olema-loke* (Coyote Pass) near Olema. Farther south, the name "Bolinas" is thought to derive from the name of a Gualen village, whose territory extended from Bolinas Lagoon to the north shore of the Golden Gate.

Archaeologists uncovered a site on the McClure Ranch in Point Reyes National Seashore that by itself defines the McClure Phase of the Middle Horizon of Central California, dating 1000–500 BC. Artifacts found here include granite mortars weighing up to 100 pounds, fishnet stone sinkers, and large obsidian blades for *atlatls* (throwing sticks used before the bow and arrow was introduced). Intricate bone ornaments decorated with beads were found here, along with perforated charm-stones and quartz crystals with pitch on one end. Very early sites are thought to be submarine, since the sea was lower 10,000 years ago, possibly permitting overland access to the Farallon Islands.

The village of Olompali, on the San Francisco Bay side of Marin, is one of the largest known Coast Miwok village sites. The people of Olompali fashioned charmstones of basalt and schist that may have been used for hunting or fishing; these have been recovered here. Part of the ethnographic record comes from Sir Francis Drake, who landed along the shore in Coast Miwok territory in 1579. Whether Drake sailed his ship, The Golden Hind, into Drakes Bay near Point Reyes or into San Francisco Bay near Olompali for repairs is still controversial. Wherever the ship anchored, the crew remained ashore for five weeks. The diary of the ship's chaplain transcribed Coast Miwok words and described housing, boats, clothing, and ceremonial practices. An old English coin found at Olompali may have originated from Drake's expedition. Through excavations at Limantour Beach, archaeologists have been trying to ascertain the location of Drake's landing. Though they haven't settled on a definite location, their excavations have uncovered Chinese porcelain that had been modified into Miwok disk beads.

The Coast Miwok traded with the Southern Pomo and Wappo for obsidian either from a quarry located in present-day Annadel State Park near Santa Rosa or from the vicinity of Glass Mountain in Napa County. A yellow body paint came from an area around The Geysers in the Mayacmas Mountains. Many basketry materials were obtained near Healdsburg. In trade, the Coast Miwok offered stone implements of chert quarried near Pacheco Valley, disk beads, abalone, kelp, and fish.

Natural Resources and Material Culture

Food sources along the coastline were abundant. Regional plant foods included tanbark oak acorns, the most prolific trees of which were privately owned. Seeds of flowering plants such as tidytips, goldfields, buttercups, clarkia, fiddleneck, and checker bloom were gathered in baskets and ground into flour. Blackberries, gooseberries, thimbleberries, and elderberries were gathered in late summer. Brodiaea root, wild clover, and hazelnuts were gathered from the grasslands and forests. Deer, elk, and grizzly bear were hunted. Traditional seafoods included eel, octopus, fish, seals, and sea lions. Edible seaweed, kelp, and shellfish such as rock scallops, bay shrimp, sea urchins, mussels, and abalone were gathered along the shoreline. Sand dollars were collected for good luck. People of inland villages traveled to the lands of the Coast Miwok to fish, and paid for the opportunity in *pispi* (clamshell beads). During the Middle and Late Horizons, beads were made from the olivella shell. Sometime after AD 1200, the clamshell took its place as the material of choice for money.

Kotcha, the Miwok house, was constructed either of dome-shaped willow frames tied with willow bark and covered with bundled bunch grass or tule, or of longer-lasting conical-shaped fir frames covered with redwood bark slabs. Rope was made from either tule or lupine root. *Saka*, a tule canoe maneuvered by a double paddle, was used in West Marin lagoons and in the San Francisco Bay. Basket materials included willow, sedge, and hazelnut. Obsidian was used in arrow points, while local chert was used for drill bits, scrapers, and choppers.

Female baked-clay figures have been recorded at archaeological sites in Marin County dating to 1000 BC. While similar figures in smaller numbers have been unearthed at sites along Humboldt Bay and in northern San Diego County, Marin County was a center of clay figurine manufacture. Thought to be related to fertility, some of these figurines suggest pregnancy.

Museums and Interpretive Sites

The **Marin Museum of the American Indian** in Novato is located near a Miwok village site (see hike 72). The museum displays Miwok baskets and other cultural implements. Members of the regional Native American community demonstrate skills for visitors. There are also hiking trails and a lecture series, (415) 897-4064.

The **Jesse Peters Native American Art Museum** in Santa Rosa contains extensive resources on Coast Miwok culture. The Under the Oaks celebration held here the first week in May features Native American dancing and foods. The museum is open Mondays through Fridays from 12 P.M. until 4 P.M., (707) 527-4479.

The **Bear Valley Visitor Center** in Point Reyes National Seashore displays a diorama of a Coast Miwok village and has programs at the Kule Loklo village exhibit, (415) 663-1092.

hike 67

Volvon Loop

Roundtrip Distance	5.5 miles
Location	East Bay Volvon territory
Administration	East Bay Regional Park District, Morgan Territory Regional Preserve (510) 757-2620
Map	Morgan Territory Regional Preserve

M organ Territory Regional Preserve lies within the homeland of the Volvon Miwok people, one of five Bay Miwok tribelets in the Mount Diablo area. On a high ridge in the shadow of this prominent mountain, the preserve contains several archaeological sites. According to Volvon tradition, Tuyshtak (either Mount Diablo or by some accounts, Sonoma Mountain) was the birthplace of the world. In its incipient stage, Coyote came from the west across the sea and stood on the summit of the mountain, then an island rising above floodwaters. To dry them, Coyote shook his tule belt toward the north, south, east, and then the west. As he shook his belt, the waters began to recede. Where the land gradually appeared Coyote planted food-bearing trees, shrubs, and grasses.

The First People arrived after the flood. They do not appear as humans, and are known by the animals their personalities reflect, such as Frog, Falcon, and Hummingbird. Coyote created humans from feathers he threw into the wind for distribution. Where the feathers landed, there stood people. Ultimately, the First People were transformed into animals, plants, rocks, weather, and stars. Bay Miwok stories are told of the First People in a manner that reflects the characteristics of the particular animals. For example, because Hummingbird was swift, Coyote sent him east to steal fire from the rising sun. Hummingbird was successful, darting to get a bit of flame as the sun came up over the horizon; he fled swiftly with stolen fire. He returned to the mountain, carrying the fire under his chin. Hummingbird is credited with having brought cooking fire to the Miwok people. We know hummingbirds for their swiftness, and now we know why we see a flash of brilliant, fire-like color on a hummingbird's throat. The First People are commemorated by trail names here at Morgan Territory such as Hummingbird, Condor, Prairie Falcon, and Eagle.

Trailhead

Exit I-580 at North Livermore Ave. in Livermore. Go 4.1 miles north to Morgan Territory Rd. Turn right and go 5.5 miles to the Morgan Territory Regional Preserve parking area (no fee), and the trailhead for the Volvon Loop.

On The Trail

Far enough inland to be fog-free and high enough to avoid smog, Morgan Territory offers some great views. The Volvon Trail dips and climbs among rolling hills dotted with majestic oaks to a ridgetop overlook. From the trailhead, follow the Volvon Trail east, through the picnic area. Pass through a cattle gate and continue over a knoll topped by a massive oak tree growing among boulders. The route continues down between the hills to a junction with a dirt road. Turn left on the dirt road at the sign for VOLVON TRAIL, and continue through the valley to the junction of the Blue Oak Trail, at 0.6 mile. Bear left here, leaving the dirt road, but staying on the Volvon Trail. Continue north near the ridgetop, passing the Condor, Prairie Falcon, and Hummingbird trail junctions, to the Volvon Loop Trail intersection at 2 miles. Go right and climb gradually to a ridgetop affording impressive views northwest to Mount Diablo, to distinctive Mount St. Helena crowning the Napa Valley to the north, and—on clear days—east across the Central Valley to the Sierra Crest under the apex of the sky. In Miwok tradition, the sky is a dome set upon the earth with openings to north, south, east, and west. Because the sky apertures are continually opening and closing in rapid succession, only the swiftest creatures are able to pass through. Birds fly north through the opening to their northern nesting grounds in the spring, and return in the fall, once their young are agile enough to enter. When you're ready, descend along the Volvon Trail to the junction of the Coyote Trail at 3.3 miles. Go right on the Coyote Trail and continue where it leaves the multi-use route at 4 miles, follows a footpath along a shady creekbed, and climbs back to the Condor Trail at 5.5 miles. This is a great area for spring wildflowers. Bear right on the Condor Trail and head several hundred yards southwest to the trailhead.

hike 68

Ring Mountain Preserve

Roundtrip Distance	2 miles
Location	Hilltop view of Mount Tamalpais in Coast Miwok territory
Administration	The Nature Conservancy (415) 435-6465
Map	none needed

Circular petroglyphs cut into a stone outcrop near the top of Ring Mountain are thought to date back 2,000 years. Elsewhere, well-worn mortars have been found among the mountain's outcrops. Ring Mountain is a serpentine-rock wonderland overlooking San Francisco Bay. Many of the plants living here are serpentine-endemic, and exist in no other region. Bunches of native grasses grow on the hillsides, while in drainages, oak and bay woodlands are nourished by springs and seeps. From the top, Mount Tamalpais and Mount Diablo, both sacred to the region's Native cultures, are visible.

With its impressive views of Mount Tamalpais, the top of Ring Mountain is a good place to consider the myth of the sleeping maiden, Tamalpa, for which that mountain is named. With a discerning eye, the mountain appears as Tamalpa's silhouette from here, with her feet toward the sea and her long hair flowing toward the bay. A Coast Miwok legend tells that the people living below the mountain never ventured to climb it for fear of Ah-shawn-nee, a spirit guarding the peak with dark powers. The spirit directed illness and death on the village until the Great Spirit intervened, offering a healing herb to anyone who would climb the mountain to pick it. Piautyuma, son of a Coast Miwok chief, set out to climb for the much needed herb. He was met by Tamalpa, Ah-shawn-nee's daughter, who had been sent to lure him to the mountain's edge, where he might fall and die. Instead, the two fell in love. The angry Ah-shawn-nee threatened that whoever reached the top first would turn to stone. In an attempt to save Piautyuma, Tamalpa rushed toward the summit, got there first and, as she was lying down to rest, turned to stone. Ah-shawn-nee's spell immediately brought about her loss of power, and benevolence returned to the mountain where Tamalpa rests in stone.

Trailhead

Exit Hwy 101 at Paradise Dr. in Corte Madera. Follow Paradise Dr. 1.4 miles southeast, passing Westward Dr., to the signed trailhead (no fee) at the preserve gate on the right side of the road.

On The Trail

Climbing among springs and seeps, forests of oak and bay, and hillsides of native grasses, you reach the stone outcrops atop Ring Mountain. Your trailhead is at the gated fire road on Paradise Drive. Go through the preserve gate, cross the footbridge, and climb the railroad tie steps along the signed PHYLLIS ELLMAN TRAIL. At 0.1 mile, cross a seasonal stream and turn left (southeast) onto the Loop Trail. Climb southeast, bearing left at trail junctions and streambed crossings until the Loop Trail reaches a **T**-junction in 0.75 mile. Turn right, passing an ancient oak growing out of a stone jumble before ascending the summit. The route is marked with an arrow near signpost 10. (Though there are several unmarked choices along the climb, all ascending trails ultimately lead to the top.) Soon the trail enters the moss-covered oak forest with

Looking south at the San Francisco Bayshore from Ring Mountain

rock outcroppings that surmount Ring Mountain. Just ahead is signpost 11, and a view of the Bay Area below. When you're ready, the trail descends to the right, down to a saddle. It then climbs to the right, to the junction of the Phyllis Ellman Trail, and then descends along switchbacks marked with arrows, past signpost 16 to the beginning of the Loop Trail. From here, retrace your steps to the parking area.

hike 69 — Kule Loklo

Roundtrip Distance	0.8 mile
Location	Coast Miwok interpretive exhibit
Administration	Point Reyes National Seashore (415) 663-1092
Map	Point Reyes National Seashore

Overseen by Pomo and Miwok tribal members and by cultural historians, the Coast Miwok village at *Kule Loklo* (Bear Valley) was built by the Miwok Archaeological Preserve of Marin, volunteers, and National Park Service rangers. A good place to witness the revival of Native California cultures, the re-created village is the site of the Strawberry Festival in the spring and the Acorn Harvest Festival in the fall. Kule Loklo celebrations feature Point Arena Pomo, Kashaya Pomo, Miwok, and Maidu dancers. At the summer celebration in August, acorn mush is served. There are also basket-weaving and fire-making demonstrations. Any Kule Loklo festival is a world-class cultural event. The Miwok Archaeological Preserve of Marin (call Sylvia Thalman at (415) 479-3281, or write for list of classes to 2255 Las Gallinas, San Rafael, CA 94903) offers classes in traditional skills here as well. Or come on an off-day, and enjoy the peaceful setting in the rolling hills of West Marin.

Trailhead

Exit Hwy. 101 at Sir Francis Drake Blvd. in Larkspur. Go 21 miles west on Sir Francis Drake Blvd. to Hwy. 1 in Olema. Turn right (north) and go 0.2 mile to Bear Valley Rd. (be alert or you'll miss it). Turn left and proceed 0.8 mile to the signed NATIONAL SEASHORE HEADQUARTERS AND VISITOR CENTER road. Turn left and follow the park road uphill to the parking area by the visitor center (no fee).

On The Trail

The Kule Loklo Trail takes you to the re-created Coast Miwok village, where interpretive panels describe some of their culture. While Kule Loklo is not an original village site, its exhibits include a ceremonial roundhouse, both tule and bark houses, and a subterranean sweathouse. Although the houses are always accessible to the public, the roundhouse and sweathouse are open only on ceremonial days. There is an acorn granary and a sunshade over the picnic area.

The signed trailhead is just north of the visitor center, by the corner of the pasture. Follow the Kule Loklo Trail northwest along the fence perimeter. Continue walking beside a eucalyptus grove to the first interpretive sign for the village at 0.3 mile. The trail turns right here, passing a series of panels describing Coast Miwok life before reaching the village. Explore the buildings and the native plant garden before retracing your steps to the parking area.

hike 70   Limantour Beach

Roundtrip Distance	5 miles
Location	Coast Miwok bead-making facility
Administration	Point Reyes National Seashore (415) 663-1092
Map	Point Reyes National Seashore

A prolific bed of Washington clams led to a Coast Miwok bead-making facility at Limantour Beach. An archaeological dig here uncovered both finished and unfinished beads of clamshell, soapstone, and magnesite; triangular abalone-shell pendants; and flaked stone drill bits. Bones of shorebirds were fashioned into intricate ear ornaments and whistles with incised diamond shapes, crosshatching, and bands. Tar from beach seeps that was stored in clamshells was used as an adhesive.

From remnants in the middens it is evident that the Miwok found a variety of game nearby. Deer, elk, sea otter, seal, and sea lion remains also provide evidence that butchering and preserving of the meat were done here. Driftwood was the fuel used to preserve meats and heat tar. Acorns were brought here to be ground, as evidenced by remaining bowl mortars.

Trailhead

Exit Hwy. 101 at Sir Francis Drake Blvd. in Larkspur. Go 21 miles west to Hwy. 1 in Olema. Turn right (north) and go 0.2 mile to Bear Valley Rd. (be alert or you'll miss it). Turn left and go 2 miles, passing the road for the National Seashore Headquarters and Visitor Center, to Limantour Rd. Turn left and go 7 miles west to the road's end at the Limantour Beach parking area (no fee).

On The Trail

Distant from any permanent village, the Limantour sandspit provided a site both to harvest needed goods and to process them. The trailhead is at the west end of the parking area at Limantour Beach. Cross a levee over the marshy end of the Limantour Estero, and walk through the dunes and out to the shoreline. The Coast Miwok once worked near here, beside burning hearths in the sand. Walk to the right along the shoreline. Partly clad in dune grass, the dunes rise steeply behind the beach, obscuring views of Limantour and Drakes esteros on the other side. Instead, the sandspit walk offers the panoramic view of sheer Drakes Bay cliffs—arching out from the estero to Chimney Rock. Continue to the end of the sandspit for 2.5 miles to see the tidal mouth of the esteros. Some believe this is the landing site of Sir Francis Drake, who upon his arrival was met by the Coast Miwok tribe bearing generous gifts. When you are ready, retrace your steps to the parking area.

hike 71   Indian Beach

Roundtrip Distance	1.5 miles
Location	Coast Miwok village site
Administration	Tomales Bay State Park (415) 669-1140
Map	Tomales Bay State Park

Eleven seasonal village sites, as well as a manufacturing site of chert tools, lie within Tomales Bay State Park. Middens here include shells of clams, cockles, and bay mussels; fishnet sinker stones; and fired clay balls used in a sling to hunt waterfowl. Since the shores are protected from ocean winds by the Point Reyes Peninsula, the climate is often comfortable here when it is foggy or windy elsewhere. Given the climate and abundant food supplied by the bay, it is not surprising that there are over 100 documented seasonal sites along the shores of Tomales Bay. The woods provided staples associated with oak, bay, willow, and pine trees. Salmonberry, gooseberry, thimbleberry, and elderberry could be found in the woods in late summer. On this shore, ferns grow downslope to the beaches, while bishop pines grace the upper slopes.

Trailhead

Turn west onto Bear Valley Rd. from Hwy. 1 just north of Olema. Go 2.5 miles west to Sir Francis Drake Blvd. Bear left (really straight) and follow Sir Francis Drake Blvd. 7 miles north to Pierce Point Rd. Turn right and go about 2 miles to Tomales Bay State Park (fee required) on the right. After passing the entrance kiosk you follow the park road east toward the bay. Park at the Hearts Desire Beach parking area.

On The Trail

Through its interpretive panels, the Nature Trail describes the ethnobotany of the Coast Miwok on your way to reconstructed bark houses at Indian Beach. The trailhead is at the northwest corner of the parking area near the restrooms. Pass an interpretive sign on the Miwok and follow the Nature Trail northwest through a tunnel of brush. Bear left at the Loop Trail junction, and continue northwest to the intersection of a gravel road in 0.2 mile. Turn right onto the gravel road, which for now is the Loop Trail, and follow it 0.75 mile through the woods to the lagoon at Indian Beach. Walk to the right along the beach to explore the bark houses. Like Bolinas Lagoon farther south, Tomales Bay is an ocean estuary along the San Andreas fault. At low tide, you can return to your car by following this beautiful shoreline south to Hearts Desire Beach. Otherwise, retrace your steps to the parking area.

hike 72 Olompali Loop

Roundtrip Distance	2.5 miles
Location	Bayside village site in Coast Miwok territory
Administration	Olompali State Historic Park (415) 892-3383
Map	Olompali State Historic Park

During the 1970s, Charles Slaymaker's archaeological dig at what is now Olompali State Historic Park uncovered one of the major Coast Miwok village sites in Marin County—the continuous occupation of which lasted 4,000 years. About 2,000 years ago, the bay shoreline was higher, near the present-day Highway 101 corridor. The village was tucked uphill from shore along Olompali Creek. *Olompali* is thought to mean "South Mountain." By AD 1300, Olompali was a major Miwok trading center.

During historic times, Olompali was granted to Camilo Ynitia, an Olompali Miwok who ran a cattle ranch here in the 1840s. He exported hides and tallow to the East Coast, Mexico, and South America for the manufacture of candles and leather goods. Ynitia was one of the only Native Americans in Northern California to be granted land during the early 19th Century. An important site yielding significant information on the Coast Miwok, Olompali is both a state historic landmark and an entry on the National Register of Historic Places.

Tens of thousands of Coast Miwok artifacts have been recovered within the park by archaeologists. One Elizabethan silver sixpence was unearthed from a soil layer dating to around AD 1600, which corresponds to the landing of Sir Francis Drake. The coin is part of the Bancroft Library's collection at the University of California at Berkeley. From sorted and processed soils and from midden deposits, archaeologists determined the compacted floor areas of dwellings and ceremonial structures. Olivella- and clamshell beads, as well as beads of slate, steatite, and magnesite, have been found among arrow points, stone pendant charms, and charm-stones of basalt and schist. While there are other village sites in the vicinity, none are as large as the main village at Olompali.

Reconstructed dwelling at Olompali

Trailhead

Leave Hwy. 101 from the southbound lanes at the OLOMPALI STATE HIS-TORIC PARK exit just north of Novato, 2.5 miles south of San Antonio Rd. Park by the visitor center in the estate grounds (fee required). (Since there is no northbound exit, northbound traffic should make a U-turn at San Antonio Rd.)

On The Trail

The Loop Trail makes a wide circuit of the park, touring the outskirts of the former village of Olompali. Along the way are grinding rocks and a reconstructed Coast Miwok village. Foregoing the estate grounds for now, your route begins at the gated fire road leading west into the hills. Climb to the junction with the Loop Trail within several hundred yards. Go right, crossing a bridge and passing the ruins of a barn, to join the dirt road signed LOOP TRAIL leading to the left. Follow this uphill along Olompali Creek to the reconstructed village dwellings.

Grinding holes at "kitchen rock"

The trail continues northwest, traversing a grassland dotted with oak and bay trees. The trail soon veers west into woodland and climbs past a tiny reservoir surrounded by ferns and moss. Continue above the earthen dam constructed in historic times to a fork in the trail at 0.75 mile. Bear left here staying on the Loop Trail, and climb to a bench at 1 mile. At yet another junction, keep left on the Loop Trail. You traverse a wooded hillside, with intermittent bay views, to a second bench in a fern-covered drainage at 1.5 miles. Descend via switchbacks, pausing to appreciate the cool, smooth trunks of the madrones here, to the last bench on a knoll overlooking the estate grounds. Explore the grounds. Next to the Burdell barns, along the dirt road running through the grounds, is "kitchen rock," with its mortars of various sizes that were used in the preparation of acorn meal. View the artifacts at the visitor center before returning to the parking area.

Guided Walks

Pictographs of abstract figures in red, yellow, and black can be seen at **Vasco Caves Regional Park** near Altamont Pass. In addition, there are bedrock mortars, a midden, and excavations that perhaps once served as floors of dwellings. Guided walks are available through the East Bay Regional Park District, (510) 635-0135.

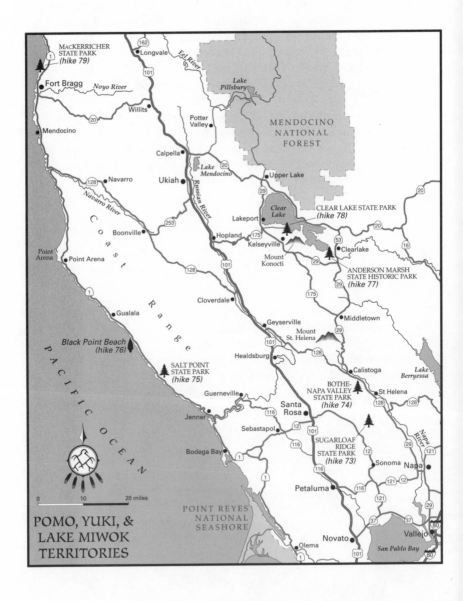

POMO, YUKI, &
LAKE MIWOK
TERRITORIES

Pomo, Yuki, &
Lake Miwok
North Coast & Coast Ranges

Landscape and People

The homeland of the Pomo, Yuki, and Lake Miwok peoples blankets present-day Napa, Sonoma, Mendocino, and Lake counties. The terrain includes the coastline from the Russian River mouth to Westport (north of Fort Bragg), and the Russian River watershed inland. Although these groups' territories stretched east through what is now Mendocino National Forest to the crest of the inner Coast Range, regional settlement was centered around the Clear Lake Basin. This temperate region sustained one of California's earliest, and ultimately largest, Native populations.

Pomo

Within the Pomo language-family territory, major settlements ringed Clear Lake, with many more along the Russian River from the coast inland to *Balo-kai* (wild oat valley), now known as Potter Valley. A village bearing the name "Pomo," located in lower Potter Valley, is thought to be the namesake of these people. When discussing a large group of villages, the people also attach the word "pomo" as a suffix. There are actually seven distinct languages of the Pomo language family in the Hokan stock. Dispersed throughout California, Hokan-speaking people continue one of the oldest residencies in the state. The prehistoric population of the Pomo is thought to have reached 21,000.

Yuki

North and southeast of the Pomo were the lands of the Yuki. Unlike those of most Native California languages, the Yukian dialects are not related to any other North American language family. It may be that Yukian-speaking people were the original Californians. Their settlements lined the Napa and Eel river watersheds, and a small portion of the northern Mendocino coast. The four Yukian dialects include *Wappo* (the name is derived from the Spanish word for "brave") of the Napa River Valley; Yuki of the upper Eel River watershed; *Huchnom* (people out of the valley) along the lower South Fork of the Eel River; and Coast Yuki, or *Ukoht-ontilka* (beside big water) along the California coast between Cleone and Rockport. The prehistoric population of the Yuki people is thought to have reached 2,000.

Lake Miwok

Between Pomo and Wappo lands, the Lake Miwok lived along streams near the south end of Clear Lake. They also lived in Coyote Valley, which is now flooded by the waters of Lake Mendocino. Since their language is in the Penutian family, the Lake Miwok people probably share cultural heritage with Coast, Bay, Plains, and Sierra Miwok peoples, as well as—to a lesser degree—several other Central California Penutian-speaking tribelets. The prehistoric Lake Miwok population is estimated to have reached 500.

Though they did not speak a common language, the Pomo, Yuki, and Lake Miwok peoples shared many similar customs. They traded with one another and shared in feasts and ceremonies. The Yuki would bring bear skins and red woodpecker feathers south to trade with the Pomo for magnesite beads, seashells, baskets, and black obsidian from Mount Konocti. The Wappo were permitted to pass through Pomo territory to the sea to gather fish and seaweed. Kabel, now known as Rocky Point on Clear Lake, was an important fishing site once shared by the neighboring tribes. People would travel great distances to fish there.

Archaeological evidence suggests that an earlier people inhabited the Clear Lake region before the Pomo. At Borax Lake, immediately east of Clear Lake, Clovis points, fluted-stone projectile points, and stone crescents of local obsidian have been found dating from 8,500 to 4,000 years ago. This culture coincided with that of the San Dieguito culture in Southern California. A more recently excavated site near Willits contained Mendocino Complex artifacts that radiocarbon-date to 1800 BC. The Mendocino Complex includes milling stones and bowl mortars similar to those of the Middle Horizon Central California culture.

Natural Resources and Material Culture

A prolific food supply provided a varied diet for the Native cultures here. Regional plant foods included acorns, chia seeds, and pine nuts. Brodiaea bulbs, yellow pond lily roots and seeds, miner's lettuce, cow parsnip shoots, clover, and mallow flowers were harvested as vegetables. Berries of toyon, manzanita, and those ripened on the vine were gathered in late summer. Regional seafoods were mussel, turban snail, ruffled purple rockweed, octopus, crab, sea anemone, sea urchin, sea lion, salmon, and steelhead. Traditional mammal foods included elk, deer, bear, and mountain lion.

Cooking salt was collected from a salt spring in Bakamtati Pomo territory near what is now Stonyford, from a spring near North Yolla Bolly Mountain in Mendocino National Forest, and from Salt Point on the coast. In preparation for the salt journey, carriers were mended, and baskets were fitted with latticework trays to carry salt in layers. A month-long journey was made with plans to arrive in the salt country near Yolla Bolly Mountain at the time of the full moon. Salt was gathered from crystalline crusts blanketing the ground at the spring by moonlight, to avoid those claiming the territory. Enough salt was gathered to last a year.

Beads used in trade were fashioned from Washington clamshells collected at Bodega Bay and from magnesite quarried east of Clear Lake. Materials were cut into disks, drilled, and strung. Cylindrical beads of magnesite were heated to bright hues of red and yellow, polished, and then hand-rubbed over many years to increase their value. Obsidian was quarried from an outcrop in what is now Annadel State Park near Santa Rosa and from outcrops at Borax Lake near Clear Lake's east shore and at Mount Konocti.

The region is best known for basketry. Pomo baskets include some of the greatest variety of shapes and weaves in California. Among the sturdier baskets made were fish traps, seedbeaters, baby baskets, mortar baskets, and burden baskets. They were woven from willow, the bark of redbud, and the roots of sedge, bulrush, digger pine, fir, and grapevine. Ceremonial feather baskets made of nutmeg root were brilliantly decorated with green feathers of the mallard, red feathers of the acorn wood-pecker, yellow feathers of the western meadowlark, and black feathers of the California quail. Though simpler, the baskets of neighboring tribes reflect the methods and styles of the Pomo basket-makers.

Museums and Interpretive Sites

The **Salt Point State Park Visitor Center** north of Jenner includes exhibits on flora and fauna and artifacts from the prehistoric cultures here, such as arrowheads. There are publications about the Pomo for sale. The visitor center is open weekends, (707) 847-3221. (See also hike 75.)

The **Lake County Museum** in Lakeport contains exhibits on the cultures of the Pomo, Wappo, and Lake Miwok peoples. There are Pomo baskets and stone implements on display, (707) 263-4555.

The **Pomo Cultural Center** at the visitor center on Lake Mendocino in Ukiah features baskets, games, and exhibits of native flora and fauna. The visitor center is open in summer, (707) 462-7581.

The Sonoma Coast State Beaches' **Jenner Visitor Center** overlooks Penny Island in the Russian River delta once inhabited by the Pomo people. A tribal member provides interpretive information. The visitor center is open weekends, (707) 875-3483.

The Bo-Cah' Ama Council is working on the **Pomo Demonstration Village and Museum** on the Buldam village site at Brewery Gulch, just south of the town of Mendocino. The site, named *Ya-Ka-Ama Bo-cah'* (Our Land by the Big Water), includes a flat area where annual Pomo events are open to the public. The council hopes to construct a visitor center at the site displaying baskets and other artifacts with all-Native American docents. The Mendocino Area Parks Association (MAPA) has information about this exhibit at the Ford House here, (707) 937-5397.

The **Fort Ross State Historic Park Visitor Center** south of Gualala displays Pomo baskets and has exhibits describing Native life at this Russian colony in the 1800s, (707) 847-3437.

hike 73   Creekside Nature Trail

Roundtrip Distance	1 mile
Location	Mountain village in Wappo territory
Administration	Sugarloaf Ridge State Park (707) 833-5712
Map	Sugarloaf Ridge State Park

At the headwaters of Sonoma Creek in Sugarloaf Ridge State Park is the village site of Wilikos. Home to the Wappo people for thousands of years, the village supported about 100 people in 40 dwellings along the creek. The houses at Wilikos were made of curved willow branches covered with grass thatch and ranged up to 40 feet in length. There was a sweathouse at the center of the village. The Wappo also used willow found along the banks of Sonoma Creek in basketry. Branches of coyote bush were used to make arrow shafts. The Wappo ground acorns of the coast live oak into flour. The omnipresent poison oak, to which the Wappo people were largely immune, furnished a black dye used in basketry. They traveled to the sea for abalone, clamshells, and fish. They went north to Clear Lake to trade, fish, and acquire obsidian.

Trailhead

Exit Hwy. 12 at Adobe Canyon Rd. 17 miles east of Santa Rosa. Follow Adobe Canyon Rd. 3 miles east to the park entrance (fee required). Park in the first lot on the left after the entrance kiosk.

On The Trail

The Creekside Nature Trail interprets the ethnobotany of the Wappo people. Numbered signposts along the trail correspond to descriptions of flora found on the park map. The trail begins across the road from the parking area, near the bathrooms. Your route passes quickly into the bay and oak woods lining Sonoma Creek and follows its north bank to an open meadow. Walk through the Campfire Center, and continue through the meadow along the creek. At 0.3 mile a spur trail leads a short distance up to a bench atop a hillock offering a great view of the surrounding Mayacmas Mountains. From this vantage point, the site of Wilikos lies north, tucked behind the flank of Red Mountain. This is also a good place to observe butterflies. Back on the nature trail, continue southeast between the meadow and the streamside woods to cross Sonoma Creek at 0.5 mile. Circling back toward the trailhead, the Creekside Nature Trail climbs through the oaks before crossing seasonal Rattlesnake Creek and reaching the park road at the trail's end. Follow the park road left, down into the campground. Watch for a trail signed *campfire center* on the right at 0.8 mile that passes between campsites. Follow it across the bridge over Sonoma Creek to the Creekside Nature Trail junction at the Campfire Center. Go left on the trail to return to the parking lot.

The meadowlands along Sonoma Creek

hike 74   Ritchey Creek Loop

Roundtrip Distance	4.5 miles
Location	Canyon Wappo village sites
Administration	Bothe-Napa Valley State Park (707) 942-4575
Map	Bothe-Napa Valley State Park

The homeland of the *Koliholmanok* (woods people) Wappo ranges south from Calistoga, through Bothe-Napa Valley State Park, to Rutherford. Villages along Ritchey and Mill creeks were home to these people for thousands of years. Their dome-shaped houses were made of willow frames covered with grass thatch. Their artifacts include fashioned tools of bone, wood, and stone, as well as rounded stones that were propelled from slings when hunting small game.

The Wappo harvested black oak acorns, hazelnuts, pine nuts and bay nuts as dietary staples. Pacific rush was used to string the clamshell beads used for currency. Sedge, redbud, and willow were materials used in basketry. Manzanita wood was whittled into fishhooks and harpoon heads. Under the direction of Wappo elder Laura Fish Somersal, a Native American Garden containing these species and others was planted near the visitor center at Bothe-Napa Valley State Park. Specimen labels include the Native names and plant uses.

Trailhead

Exit Hwy. 29/128 at the Bothe-Napa Valley State Park entrance on the west side of the highway halfway between St. Helena and Calistoga. Follow the park road through the entrance kiosk (fee required) and park by the visitor center.

On The Trail

The Ritchey Creek loop takes in the ethnobotany of the Wappo people. This hike begins easily at the visitor center, and tours the adjacent, native plant garden. From the garden, follow the park road over Ritchey Creek to the signed trailhead near the creek on the right. Follow the

RITCHIE CREEK TRAIL upstream along the south bank until it becomes a dirt road and crosses the creek in 0.25 mile. Bear left here, following the Redwood Trail upstream to the junction of the Coyote Peak Trail at 0.75 mile. Go left, following the Coyote Peak Trail as it climbs more than 500 feet within 0.75 mile to the summit for a view of the canyons and the Napa Valley below. When you're ready, continue to the South Fork Trail at 2 miles. Go right here, descending to the creek. Cross the bridge and take the immediate right onto the Redwood Trail. Fording the stream again, follow the creek back to the parking area.

hike 75   Salt Point Coast Trail

Roundtrip Distance	3 miles
Location	Seasonal coastal village in Kashaya Pomo territory
Administration	Salt Point State Park (707) 847-3221
Map	Salt Point State Park

Named for the salt collected from crevices in the rock here, Salt Point was a seasonal home to the Kashaya Pomo and the Coast Yuki peoples. From ridgeline villages, the people came down to the water to fish and gather shellfish; while here, they camped in the shelter of trees lining Warren Creek. They cooked their harvest beside leeward rocks at the point, discarding refuse in middens that remain today. Tide pools and sheltered sandy coves here are rich in marine life. Stump Beach Cove (just a name, no tree stumps here) provides an opportunity to picnic and observe—seasonally—the breeding of pelagic cormorants.

Trailhead

Exit Hwy. 1 at the Salt Point State Park Gerstle Cove entrance (fee required) 15.5 miles north of Jenner. The turnoff for the park is on the left. Leave your car at the Salt Point day-use parking area.

On The Trail

Salt Point State Park is listed as an Archaeological District on the National Register of Historic Places. The blufftop walk along the Coast Trail from Gerstle Cove to Stump Beach surveys the former Pomo and Yuki gathering grounds. From the trailhead at Salt Point, your route heads north along the bluff, crossing Warren Creek at 0.25 mile. The cove at the mouth of Warren Creek can be accessed via a spur trail leading down to the shoreline. Abalone and kelp were gathered there by the Kashaya Pomo and the Coast Yuki. Farther upstream, Warren Creek once supported the summer settlement known as *Melhom-i'ikem* (surf fish). The trail continues north along the bluff, which is an ancient marine terrace of exposed sandstone outcrops supporting coyote bush and lupine. As you approach Stump Beach in 1.25 miles, the trail veers away from the steep coastal cliffs and descends the bluffs tapering off toward Miller Creek. The creek crossing here is wet in the winter. Enjoy the sights from the sheltered sandy cove at Stump Beach, before retracing your steps to the parking lot.

hike 76 · Black Point Beach

Roundtrip Distance	0.6 mile
Location	Coastal Pomo village site
Administration	Sonoma County Regional Parks (707) 785-2377
Map	Not necessary

B lack Point was once the site of Kowishal, a major Pomo village along the Sonoma coast. With hooks made of shell and bone, the people of the village fished in the Gualala River for salmon and in the ocean for surf fish. They gathered abalone, mussels, sea palms, kelp, and ruffled purple rockweed along the shore. From submarine caves, octopuses were brought to the surface with the placement of buckeye or soap plant root poison in the water.

Hawks soar here at human eye level, quartering the ground for prey. Pomo tradition credits Hawk with bringing light to the world. In the very beginning, the world was always dark. Coyote and Hawk grew tired of bumping into each other in the darkness. Coyote gathered a heap of rushes and rolled them into a ball. He handed it to Hawk, who flew to the sky, carrying the ball of rushes and some flints. High above the land, Hawk rubbed the flints together to spark a fire, and then lit the sphere, bringing light and heat to the world. Below Black Point is an inviting black sand beach. The visitor center at the adjacent Gualala Point Regional Park interprets the area.

Trailhead

Go 29 miles north of Jenner on Hwy. 1 and exit at Black Point Shoreline Access (fee required) near milepost 50.80, just north of the Sea Ranch Lodge.

On The Trail

The Black Point Beach Trail visits the former gathering grounds of Kowishal. The trail begins at the west end of the parking area. Follow the trail through a wet, grassy meadow to a private Sea Ranch road. Cross the road and continue toward the sheared cypress near the bluff. You also cross a private trail before arriving at the top of the cliffs. Black Point Beach is accessible from the Blufftop Trail via a spur trail's many descending stairs. The pebbly black-sand beach extends north for 0.5 mile. For farther wandering, the Blufftop Trail extends several miles on the bluffs in both directions. The grass-covered bluffs carry masses of

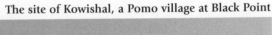

The site of Kowishal, a Pomo village at Black Point

fragrant, yellow bush lupine in spring. Blufftop views are endless, and there is good wildlife watching. When you're ready, retrace your steps to the parking lot.

hike 77   Marsh Loop

Roundtrip Distance	2.2 miles
Location	Reconstructed Pomo village and archaeological sites
Administration	Anderson Marsh State Historic Park (707) 944-0688
Map	Anderson Marsh State Historic Park

Anderson Marsh is an ancient hunting and gathering ground at the southeast end of Clear Lake. Because of the importance to the Pomo people of the land within what is now Anderson Marsh State Historic Park, it is has been listed as an Archaeological District on the National Register of Historic Places. Archaeological sites within the park date back more than 10,000 years. The main Pomo village just offshore on present-day Indian Island once sheltered 1,000 people. Lake travel was done in tule boats. The marsh was important to several local cultures occupying the central California coastal highlands. Near neighbors to the Pomo, the Lake Miwok lived downstream from the marsh along Cache Creek. Because of the abundance of resources here, people from distant tribes came to fish, trade, and quarry obsidian. Within the park are petroglyphs, middens, and bedrock mortars.

Trailhead

Exit Hwy. 29 onto Hwy. 53 in Lower Lake. Go 2 miles north to Anderson Ranch Pkwy. and turn left. Take the immediate right to the Anderson Marsh State Historic Park entrance (fee required), and continue to the ranch buildings and trailhead parking. The visitor center is open Wednesdays through Sundays.

On The Trail

The marsh loop begins at the west end of the parking area next to the park headquarters and visitor center. Walk west along the Anderson Flats Trail toward the marsh. At the junction with the Ridge Trail in 0.25 mile, take the Ridge Trail left along the fence and into the hills. The trail climbs to a reconstructed Pomo village below the ridgeline. Deer and small game were hunted; acorns, clover, roots, bulbs, fruits, and berries were gathered here. Just beyond the village is the McVicar Trail intersection at 0.5 mile. Turn left on the McVicar Trail and go 0.1 mile to the Marsh Trail. Turn right here, heading north as the trail skirts the marsh. The marsh provided tule, sedge root, and willow for use in basketry. An extract from the soap plant found nearby was used in fishing. When it was added to the water, soap plant extract produced a toxicity that brought the stunned fish to the surface, where they could be collected. Continue along the Marsh Trail to Ridge Point. Here, the trail bears east to the intersection of the Cache Creek Nature Trail at 1.1 mile. Turn left on the nature trail, following interpretive panels through the riparian woodland along Cache Creek, and back to the trailhead at 2.2 miles.

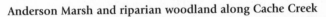

Anderson Marsh and riparian woodland along Cache Creek

Indian Nature Trail

Roundtrip Distance	0.5 mile
Location	Lakeside village in Pomo territory
Administration	Clear Lake State Park (707) 279-4293
Map	Clear Lake State Park

Evidence of human habitation along the south shore of Clear Lake in Clear Lake State Park dates back more than 10,000 years. The area was an important hunting and fishing encampment between the shores of *Ba-Tin*, the Pomo name for Clear Lake, and Mount Konocti, which still bears the Pomo name. With its abundant foods and resources, Clear Lake supported many large Native societies with elaborate material cultures. In tule boats, the Pomo people traveled throughout the lake basin. Clear Lake remains important to the Pomo living here. Fish and tule reeds are still harvested from the lake; acorns and manzanita berries growing along the shore remain a part of the diet. To the west is Mount Konocti, a 4,200-foot active volcanic dome long considered sacred. Pomo stories depict a hollow chamber under the mountain filled with a huge subterranean lake where blind fish swim.

Trailhead

Exit Hwy. 29 at Soda Bay Rd. just south of Lakeport. Head 6 miles east on Soda Bay Rd., skirting Kelseyville, to the Clear Lake State Park entrance (fee required) on the left. The visitor center features Pomo games and artifacts, and is open Saturdays.

On The Trail

The Indian Nature Trail is an interpretive loop that passes through a village site. Highlights include a grinding rock, local obsidian, and plants used by the Pomo people for food, medicine, and building materials. The trail begins several hundred yards north of the park entrance station on the right (east) side of the park road. Take the loop's right fork and climb southeast through oak (and poison oak) woodland along switchbacks. Climb past rock outcrops and sun-splashed chaparral to a signed spur trail to the overlook. Follow this trail a short distance to the right where a bench offers views of the scenic meadow below and the summit of Mount Konocti above. From the overlook, retrace your steps to the loop trail. Bear right at the loop junction, and continue to traverse the wooded hillside. The trail soon bends west, passing an obsidian sample and a stone mortar as it descends to the beginning of the loop. While the interpretive brochure has been discontinued due to vandalism, it is not difficult to imagine Pomo lifeways as you pass through this ancient woodland. Bear right at the junction to return the park road, and retrace your steps to the parking area.

hike 79   Laguna Point Trail

Roundtrip Distance	0.5 mile
Location	Coastal camp in Yuki territory
Administration	MacKerricher State Park (707) 937-5804
Map	MacKerricher State Park

A seasonal camp for over 2,000 years, Laguna Point is on the former boundary between the territories of the Pomo and the Coast Yuki. The tidepools have long provided important sources of abalone, clams, sea anemones, and surf fish. Mussels were the most common food collected here. Chiton and barnacles were cooked in hot coals and sun dried. A tool made of elkhorn was used to pry abalone from the rocks; then, the innards were tenderized and cooked. Harpoons of bone were used in hunting seals and sea lions. Salmon and surf fish were caught in nets. The Yuki, Pomo, and Kato peoples have used this area for centuries, often traveling great distances to trade and harvest seafood. Tribal members still honor this coastal access as a major area for gathering natural resources used in traditional foods and ceremonies.

Trailhead

Exit Hwy. 1 at Mill Creek Rd. in Cleone, 3 miles north of Fort Bragg. Head west following Mill Creek Rd. past Lake Cleone, and through the tunnel under the Haul Road that runs along the coast here. Leave your car in the Laguna parking area (no fee required) at the road's end.

On The Trail

The Laguna Point Trail takes you to a coastal observation deck near the former Pomo camp, and gives you an opportunity to view the prolific tidepools at Laguna Point. The trailhead is on the northwest corner of the parking area. Follow the wheelchair-accessible boardwalk through an opening in the fence and continue west through a cypress grove. An interpretive panel here explains Pomo lifeways along this coast. Follow the boardwalk through the headland vegetation. At 0.2 mile, the boardwalk veers slightly south, reaching the seal-watching station at 0.3 mile. South of the observation deck, the blufftop trail circles the point. Wander among the native flowering plants along the headlands. The trail overlooks the tidepools here. If you're interested, the footpath continues along the bluff for a mile farther, or you can walk along the Haul Road in either direction for many miles. Enjoy ever-changing views of the powerful surf breaking on the rocky coastline before you return to the parking lot.

The headland overlooks prolific tidepools

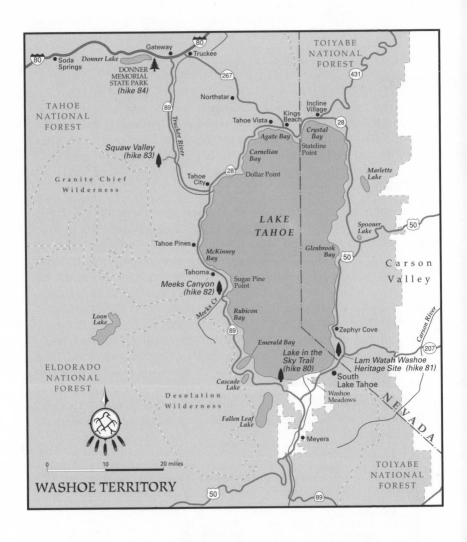

WASHOE TERRITORY

Washoe

Tahoe Sierra Nevada

Landscape and People

Centered in the Carson Valley, the Tahoe Basin, and along the upper Truckee and Carson rivers, the Washoe lands spanned the eastern slope of the Sierra north to Honey Lake and southeast to Topaz Lake. The Washoe language belongs to the Hokan family. As the only Hokan speakers east of the Sierra Crest, the Washoe may have settled here when Hokan speakers first arrived in California, or may have been displaced here after the Penutian speakers' migration to the Central Valley. Their prehistoric population is thought to have reached 500.

The Lake Tahoe Basin is important to the Washoe culture. Before European contact, the Washoe came seasonally to this important fishing ground during the spawning run in the lake's tributaries of native cutthroat trout. Washoe summer fishing camps and seed milling sites were located along the lakeshore and at the mouths of creeks.

In a Washoe creation story, the Lake Tahoe setting is the result of a great wave sent across the continent by the Great Spirit. The violent quakes and eruptions that followed ultimately formed the Sierra Nevada. The Great Spirit sheltered the few surviving people in a lakeside cavern. As in Shoshonean tradition, Washoe myth holds that the lake is home to Water Babies, the spirits of lakes and streams. Throughout the Great Basin, a vision of a Water Baby, who might appear as an old male dwarf with the long hair of a young girl, carries immense power. Because a Water Baby becomes malicious when disturbed, the Washoe believe that anyone upsetting its home risks retaliation, causing harm to all the world's people. *Da ow a ga*, the Washoe word for "lake," is the origin of the name "Tahoe."

Archaeologists have estimated that the prehistoric cultures on the eastern slope of the Sierra Nevada date back 8,000 years. The Martis Archaeological Complex comprises sites attributed to people who lived between Nevada's Pine Nut Mountains and the Sierra between 2000 BC and AD 500. The Martis culture is considered an early precursor of the Washoe. The King's Beach Complex contains relics of a changing Washoe culture, which dates from AD 500 to 1800. During this period, the Washoe had separated from other Hokan-speaking peoples and migrated here.

Tahoe areas near Emerald Bay, Cascade Lake, Meeks Bay, Echo Lake, and Fallen Leaf Lake were the more populous ones in prehistoric times. Many Washoe place names reflect their geographic setting. The tale of the Weasel Brothers helps explain one. On a seasonal journey from the Washoe winter home in the Pine Nut Mountains to Lake Tahoe, the smaller of the Weasels attacked a Water Baby. The battle ended at *Debelelek* (a place smeared red) near the mouth of Little Tallac Creek. Here, where the blood was shed—where the Water Baby was killed—there is a deposit of red clay. The Washoe name for the Truckee River's outlet is *Dabayo duwe* (flowing away over the edge). Appropriate for what is shaped like a long bag opening eastward, the Washoe for Emerald Bay is *Salita's* (sunshine coming in).

The Washoe traded with Maidu and Sierra Miwok villages in the Sierra and Paiute villages to the east. Medicinal herbs were obtained from the Pyramid Lake Paiute. The Washoe traversed their summer highlands north to south along a path which later became part of the California (Emigrant) Trail. The Rubicon Trail as well as those leading over Echo Summit and Emigrant Pass began as trade routes between Washoe villages and hunting grounds and those of Central California. There, offering pine nuts and other barter items, the Washoe obtained the bulk of their acorn supply. The Sierra Miwok acknowledged Washoe rights to hunting grounds along the Stanislaus River as far west as present-day Calaveras Big Trees State Park and along the American and Consumnes rivers. The Washoe route from Carson Valley to Lake Tahoe led up the West Fork of the Carson River, then over Luther Pass, and finally, down the upper Truckee River to the south shore of Lake Tahoe. To reach the Central Valley, the Washoe followed the South Fork of the American River, much as Highway 50 does today. The Weasel Brothers also follow this route in Washoe tales.

Natural Resources and Material Culture

Though the Washoe moved seasonally between winter and summer villages—a pattern which typically limited heavy or bulky material culture—they are renowned for their basketry. Traditionally, food, basketry, and medicinal materials were harvested from over 170 varieties of plants. Dietary staples included pine nuts and seeds of grasses and flowering plants.

The pine nut crop in the Eastern Sierra varies greatly each year, and hunting and gathering camps were moved to where pickings were best. The tastiest pine nuts are those of the single-needled pinyon, the needles of which, unlike those of other pines, do not grow in bundles. Traditionally, cones were harvested green and roasted in an open fire to burn the pitch. The nuts were then extracted and dried for both food and trade. Other parts of the pinyon pine were also used medicinally.

Other Washoe plant foods included wild onion, chokecherry, cow parsnip, and meadow rue. Some former campsites can be identified here by healthy chokecherry bushes that began from seeds of berries brought to camp long ago. The Washoe gathered grass seeds along the eastern shore of Lake Tahoe in spring. In summer, when trout migrated upstream, the Washoe followed to fish and gather ripening berries. The Pandora moth larvae gathered among groves of yellow pine were a delicacy.

The winter house (galis dangl) was a 15'-diameter, cone-shaped structure made of poles tied with willow fibers and covered in slabs of bark. A fireplace was set in the center underneath a smoke hole. The door faced east. Also a dome-shaped building, the summer house (gadu), was covered in willow boughs. Washoe basketry utilized a frame of willow and rosewood, with fern roots and redbud—barter from the west—used to create designs in black and red.

Museums and Interpretive Sites

The Marion Steinbach Indian Basket collection within **Gatekeepers Museum** in Tahoe City displays an extensive collection of Native Californian baskets. The museum has many Washoe cultural exhibits, located in William B. Layton Park near the site of the Washoe camp, Dabayo duwe, (530) 583-1762.

The Washoe Exhibit at the **Baldwin Estate Museum** features Washoe cultural exhibits and a native plant garden cared for by the Washoe Tribe. Located at the Tallac Historic Site, the museum is open Memorial Day through Labor Day, but is closed on Tuesdays, (530) 541-5227. Watch for the opening of the Washoe Cultural Center across Highway 89 from the Tallac Historic Site. (See also hike 80.)

The **Emigrant Trail Museum** at Donner Memorial State Park presents prehistoric artifacts, cultural exhibits, and displays of the region's petroglyphs, (530) 582-7892. (See also hike 84.)

hike 80

Lake in the Sky Trail

Roundtrip Distance	2 miles
Location	Lakeside Washoe village site
Administration	Tallac Historic Site (530) 541-5227 and Taylor Creek Visitor Center (530) 573-2674
Map	Lake in the Sky Trail, Washoe Garden brochure

The seasonal Washoe village of Dawgasasiwa was located at the mouth of Taylor Creek, while smaller encampments extended east to what is now Camp Richardson. Located on the low-lying isthmus between Fallen Leaf Lake and Lake Tahoe, Dawgasasiwa occupied a rich and desirable gathering area in the Basin. The Washoe Garden at the Tallac Historic Site here provides an introduction to some of the 170 plants used for food, medicine, and basketry by the Washoe. With examples of both Washoe winter and summer dwellings, the garden is branching out as well as expanding. Labeled specimens include wild onion, sage, bitterbrush, wild rose, corn lily, mule ears, pines, Indian rhubarb, and chinquapin. The garden and the Washoe exhibit in the Baldwin Estate Museum were created by the Washoe Tribe of Nevada and California.

Washoe dwelling at the Tallac Historic Site

Trailhead

Exit Hwy. 89 at the Taylor Creek Visitor Center turnoff, 3 miles west of the Hwy. 50 "Y" in South Lake Tahoe. Park in the lot (no fee) at the visitor center. The Baldwin Estate Museum and the Washoe Garden are open daily from Memorial Day through Labor Day. (Watch for the reopening of the Washoe Trail here. Destroyed by a winter storm, it is only temporarily out of commission.)

On The Trail

The Lake in the Sky Trail (also a ski route in the winter) skirts Taylor Creek marsh heading toward the lakeshore, and then follows the Tahoe shoreline to the Tallac Historic Site. From the trailhead behind the visitor center, follow the paved path through a woodland. Interpretive panels along the route depict both the history and prehistory of the area. The first one introduces the Washoe people. The trail weaves northwest, passing through a meadow to a viewing deck over Taylor Creek marsh, before arriving at Tallac Point. The pleasant beach here is the site of *Dawgasasiwa*, which means "clear water." West of the Taylor Creek outlet is a bald eagle wintering area, which is a good year-round place to watch for fishing eagles. From Tallac Point, this trail follows the shoreline east to the Tallac Historic Site. Under the cover of willow and pine, the beach walk offers panoramic lake views and picturesque resting places. You reach the Tallac Historic Site in 1 mile, and can pass through the fence opening. Continue east for several hundred yards, following signs to the BALDWIN ESTATE MUSEUM. The Washoe Garden is just west of the museum. When you're done here, take the Tallac Historic Site Trail beyond the parking area and through the woods to return to the Taylor Creek Visitor Center parking area.

hike 81   Lam Watah Washoe Heritage Site

Roundtrip Distance	1 mile
Location	Lakeside Washoe village site
Administration	USFS Lake Tahoe Basin (530) 573-2600.
Map	Not necessary

Along the southeastern shore of Lake Tahoe, the Washoe spent summers fishing and gathering grass seeds near this creekside camp. The men fished from behind blinds made of willow boughs. Besides masking the fishermen, a blind's shadow on the creek attracted fish to where they might be trapped in a cone-shaped basket or skewered with a bone-tipped spear. The fish, usually trout or suckers, were wrapped in sunflower leaves and cooked over hot coals. Once cooked, they were dried on *biali* (wooden racks) to preserve them for winter. Only the male fish were taken, leaving the females to spawn and ensure future harvests. To the Washoe, this place is *Lam Watah* (mortars creek). Washoe women once ground their harvested seeds in the many bedrock mortars that you see here.

Trailhead

Exit Hwy. 50 in Stateline, Nevada, at Kahle Dr. Turn west on Kahle Dr. and within 50 feet park in the small lot on the right (no fee) near the USDA FOREST SERVICE TAHOE BASIN sign. (The area can be snow covered through late spring.)

On The Trail

The trail traverses an open meadow watered by creeks and springs to Nevada Beach. The route is often skiable in winter. From the trailhead, walk west through the meadow. Interpretive panels along the way explain the points of interest. Boulders along the way contain mortar holes. Intermittent boardwalks keep you dry over the wet areas. Seasonally, this is a fine meadow for wildflowers. Soon you skirt a pine forest, a likely spot to encounter Clark's nutcrackers. In 0.5 mile you reach Nevada Beach. Pass through the campground and explore the lakeshore. Though Stateline is nearby, the bustle is muffled by the forest, and you can view the lake in peace. When you're ready, retrace your steps to the parking area.

According to a Washoe legend, an evil spirit routinely troubled one man so that he chose to flee west over the Sierra. Along his journey, the evil spirit badgered him at every turn. Then, a good spirit offered him a branch of leaves, and said that when he dropped a leaf a lake would rise between himself and the evil spirit. As the man fled, he saw the evil spirit getting closer, and he was scared. Fumbling, he dropped much of the branch; from his feet spread Lake Tahoe, in all its vast breadth and depth. Assured, he continued west, dropping a remaining leaf when the evil spirit came in sight. Along his path, the waters of Lily, Grass, Heather, and all of the lakes of Desolation Valley rose to distance him from evil. In this way he soon reached the safety of Central California. One lake commemorates this event in its name—Fallen Leaf Lake.

hike 82   Meeks Canyon

Roundtrip Distance	9 miles
Location	Lakeside Washoe village site
Administration	El Dorado National Forest (530) 573-2674
Map	Desolation Wilderness

Near the mouth of Meeks Creek is the site of the Washoe summer encampment that they called *Mayala* (soda springs). Before European contact, this was one of the more populous areas along the lakeshore. Seeds were gathered and processed in the meadow near the lakeshore. When food supplies dwindled here, the Washoe traveled up Meeks Creek into the canyon, gathering ripening berries and other plant foods and fishing cutthroat trout that migrated upstream to spawn. Taking advantage of later harvest seasons at higher altitudes, Washoe women sought plant materials from several botanical zones. After a short climb, currants and thimbleberries could be found growing along the creek. In higher canyon meadows, seeds and leaves of mule ears were gathered. The late-retreating snows bring spring to the highest mountain canyons last. Here, lodgepole and Jeffrey pine and white fir are displaced by red fir and western white pine. The Washoe came here in late summer in search of game, to fish for trout in the high mountain lakes, and to gather the last of the harvest before returning to the Carson Valley in the autumn.

Trailhead

The trailhead is near the south end of Meeks Bay, 11 miles south of Tahoe City on the west side of Highway 89. Park in the lot near the old stables by the Desolation Wilderness trailhead parking sign (no fee) in El Dorado National Forest. (The area is snow covered through late spring.)

On The Trail

The signed DESOLATION WILDERNESS TRAILHEAD is at the west edge of the parking area, near the stables. Follow the trail (which is Forest Service Rd. 14N42) west, through the meadow along the north side of Meeks Creek. Seasonally, you may pass impressive tiger lilies and columbine en route to the Tahoe-Yosemite Trail in 1.3 miles. Go right here, beginning your climb into Meeks Canyon. You leave creek and meadow to ascend a glacial moraine until 1.6 miles. Soon, berries and monkeyflowers appear among ferns, alders, and willows as you rejoin Meeks Creek. Continue along the flats, alternating between the forest cover and open meadows of lupine and mule ears, whose large, soft leaves were used by the Washoe to diaper the young. Continuing to climb along Meeks Creek through higher forested canyon, you reach Lake Genevieve in 4.5 miles. This is the first of several lakes within Meeks Creek canyon, making it a popular backpacking route. (The next, Crag Lake, is at 4.9 miles.) Select a lakeside spot to enjoy before you retrace your steps to the parking lot.

hike 83   Squaw Valley

Roundtrip Distance	1.5 miles via tram (or 12 miles via Shirley Canyon)
Location	Washoe trail over Sierra Crest
Administration	Truckee Ranger District, Tahoe National Forest (530) 587-3558, and Squaw Valley USA (530) 583-6955
Map	Squaw Valley Hiking Trails

Not only does riding the tram to High Camp ensure your chances of completing the ascent to Emigrant Pass, but it also provides a bird's-eye view of the jumbled rocks of Broken Arrow, plus eye-level views of 8,000-foot-plus Emigrant, Squaw, and KT-22 peaks, together forming a majestic backdrop on the Sierra Crest. The meadow at Squaw Valley was a summer encampment of the Washoe people. From there, a well-worn Washoe trade route leads west over the Sierra into Central California. Most of the efficient routes over the Sierra were based upon early Native Californian trails, as is the case with the Emigrant Trail. This was the route taken to trade with Sierra Miwok villages and make use of their hunting grounds. This Washoe-established route became the Placer County Emigrant Route (later known as the Old Ridge Route), used by miners and emigrants en route to Sacramento. From Emigrant Pass you can see Granite Chief Wilderness, with the headwaters of the American River's Middle and North forks.

Trailhead

Exit Hwy. 89 at Squaw Valley Rd., 5 miles west of Tahoe City. Head 2.2 miles west to the parking area of Squaw Valley USA (no fee). From the lot, you can ride the tram to High Camp for the short option. Otherwise, drive back (east) along the road—across the bridge to the Squaw Valley Fire Station—and park by the side of the road at the Granite Chief/Shirley Canyon trailhead. (The area is snow covered through late spring.)

On The Trail

From an elevation of over 8,700 feet, the views from the Sierra Crest at the Watson Monument/Emigrant Pass marker are awe-inspiring, but the perch is exposed and often windy. There are several ways to reach the pass. The easiest is to first ride the tram to High Camp. From there, only a 500-foot climb over a series of snow-cat tracks remains. Walk to the right along the High Camp Loop, to Ridge Road. Turn right on Ridge Road and climb to the Siberian Ridge Road/Emigrant Trail junction. Go right on the Emigrant Trail to the saddle near the top of Emigrant chairlift. The Watson Monument is just left of the top of the lift. (For longer hikes, the Pacific Crest Trail passing nearby can be used.)

For the strenuous 12-mile option, the Shirley Canyon Trail offers a scenic hike via Shirley Lake, with wildflowers in season and waterfalls. From the Shirley Canyon trailhead, the trail climbs west, along the south bank of Squaw Creek. Along the route, there are several trail options. In sections there are no paths, and the route requires bushwhacking and clambering over steep granite boulders. Above all, parallel the creek, keeping it on your right. From the south side of Shirley Lake, find the Shirley Lake Road and follow it to High Camp at Squaw Valley. From here, follow the trail (described above) to the Watson Monument. Both the 12-mile hike through Shirley Canyon and the 1.5-mile walk from High Camp get you there. Enjoy panoramic views east to the impressive Tahoe Basin, and west over the Sierra Crest along forested ridges and watersheds the Washoe once traveled. Then, retrace your steps to the parking area.

Following a Washoe route west of the Sierra Crest

hike 84 Donner Lake Interpretive Trail

Roundtrip Distance	2 miles
Location	Lakeside village site in Washoe territory
Administration	Donner Memorial State Park (530) 582-7892
Map	Donner Memorial State Park

B efore the Washoe, an earlier people known as the Martis culture camped at Donner Lake, harvesting the freshwater clams and trout found there. Summer encampments, which were sheltered by the Jeffrey and lodgepole pine forest, were set up along the east shore of Donner Lake. Basalt flakes remaining from tool manufacturing here date back 8,000 years. The view west takes in the seasonal, migratory path of antelope and deer over Donner Pass. Along the Old Donner Pass Road, there are prehistoric carvings in the granite between China Wall and Rainbow Bridge. Concentric circles, ovals with parallel lines running through them, and zigzag lines with circles at one end are some of the petroglyph designs found in the sloping granite bedrock. Similar to petroglyphs found throughout the Great Basin, the geometric patterns here may be the work of shamans. The petroglyphs have not been dated, and their meaning is only speculative. One theory holds that the concentric circles record migratory patterns, each circle recording a one-way trip. Since it takes four trips to constitute a migratory pattern, any concentric-circle motif with less than four circles represents a migration based on chance rather than a pattern. The ancient Hopi of the Southwest left similar markings to record migrations.

Trailhead

Exit I-80 at Hwy. 89 just west of Truckee and go 0.1 mile south to Donner Pass Rd. Take Donner Pass Rd. 1.4 miles west to the Donner Memorial State Park entrance (fee required). Park in the lot at the end of the road, near the visitor center. (The area is snow free by late spring.)

On The Trail

The Lakeside Interpretive Trail offers a walk (or a winter's ski) along Donner Lake with successive interpretive panels on the flora and fauna and the cultural history here. From the parking area at the visitor center, follow the park road west along Donner Creek for several hundred yards to the signed trailhead for the LAKESIDE INTERPRETIVE TRAIL on the right. Walk west along the trail, following the lakeshore from the lagoon to China Cove at 1 mile. As you come out of the tree cover, there are views of Donner Lake, Mount Judah, Donner Peak, and the dramatic granite ramparts above Donner Pass. While the exposed trail is within earshot of Highway 80 here, you can focus instead on kingfishers and Steller's jays in the lodgepole pines. Soon, you reach the pebble beach at China Cove, where an interpretive panel depicts the prehistoric cultures here. Nearby is the site of a seasonal village. In the summer you can swim at China Cove before retracing your steps to the parking area.

If you wish to view the petroglyphs, a ranger will direct you to the site, which is snow free by summer. The best times to view the rock art are early morning and late afternoon, since intense reflection of the midday sun off the granite surface tends to further obscure the already-faint glyphs.

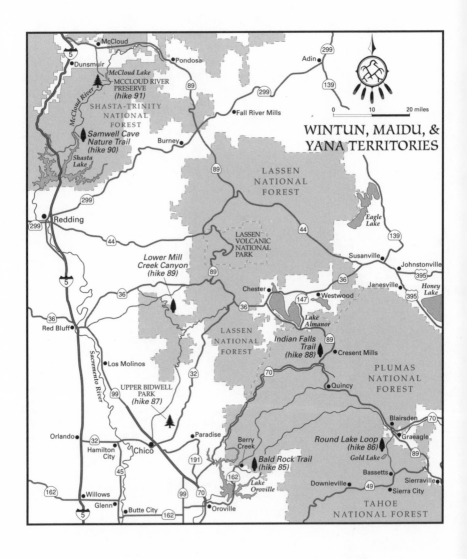

WINTUN, MAIDU, &
YANA TERRITORIES

Wintun, Maidu, & Yana

Sacramento Valley & Northern Sierra Nevada

Landscape and People

The present-day Sacramento Valley and adjacent foothills are home-lands of the Wintun, the Maidu, and the Yana peoples. North of the Sacramento/San Joaquin Delta, the terrain varies along with the rising Sacramento Valley floor—up tributary watersheds within deep canyons of the Coast Range, the Sierra Nevada, and the southern Cascades. Along an extensive network of major rivers once thick with salmon, this region—much like the San Joaquin Valley and its foothills—sustained one of the largest prehistoric populations in California.

Wintun

The Wintun were the largest language group in northern California prior to European contact. In their language the name *Wintun* means "Great People"; the use of this name was a source of pride. The large Wintun homeland stretched south from what is now southern Shasta County to the northern shore of Suisun and San Pablo bays in the Sacramento/San Joaquin Delta. Within this long north-south belt, Wintun villages were located along the west side of the Sacramento Valley to the Coast Range. The four Wintun languages include the Wintu in the north, the Nomlaki in the middle, and the Hill and the River Patwin in the south. Wintun is a Penutian language family, which, as a group, encompasses much of the west coast of North America from northern British Columbia to southern Mexico. The prehistoric Wintun population is thought to have reached 12,000.

Large groupings of *kewe*, or dome-shaped, earth-covered houses with doors facing east, were built on low hills along the rivers. Temporary shelters erected for the summer harvest had rectangular roofs covered with brush. Tule rafts were used in river and delta navigation. The delta of the San Joaquin and Sacramento rivers offered prolific salmon runs, and large populations of waterfowl passed through on their seasonal migration along the Pacific Flyway. Colorful, intricately constructed decoys were used to lure ducks into Wintun nets.

Maidu

Traditionally, the Maidu lived along the eastern Sacramento Valley floor and in the Sierra foothills from the Yuba and Sacramento rivers north to Big Chico Creek. While Maidu summer villages dotted the Northern Sierra, their territory was centered around the lower Yuba and Feather river watersheds. *Maidu*, which means "people," was later applied by ethnographers. The Maidu speak a Penutian language, like the neighboring Wintun, Modoc, Miwok, Yokuts, and Ohlone. The Maidu language was divided among three dialects including Maidu in the northeast, Concow in the northwest, and Nisenan in the south. The prehistoric Maidu population was estimated to have reached 9,000.

Maidu territory spanned what is now Eldorado, Placer, Nevada, Yuba, Butte, Plumas, and southern Lassen counties. Homeland terrain includes large, flat-bottomed drainages of the northern Sierra from Big Meadow and Honey Lake valleys in the north, through Indian, Genesee, and American valleys, to higher-elevation, summer hunting grounds in Sierra and Mohawk valleys. Winter villages were located on the higher ground surrounding the meadows. If you take Highway 89 north from Quincy through Indian Valley, skirt Lake Almanor along Highway 147, and then head northeast along Highway 36 to Susanville, you follow an important Maidu trail—so important, in fact, that it was Worldmaker's Path. After a great flood, Worldmaker formed meadows and otherwise prepared for the coming of the Maidu. Big Meadows (now flooded by waters of Lake Almanor) was said by Worldmaker to be the best place for the Maidu to live; a large settlement later existed here for thousands of years. Likewise, Worldmaker made Mountain Meadows (since flooded by Mountain Meadows Reservoir) an ideal root-gathering spot that Coyote would stock. Full of Maidu lore, Worldmaker's Path became the major prehistoric route through the region. Along the way: salt licks cover rocks where salt was gathered, and deer attracted by it were hunted; ancient fishing camps line the rivers; bear grass on Whitegrass Mountain was gathered for basketry; and Split Rocks is the place where the wind begins.

Yana

The Yana homeland is the foothill country of Butte, Tehama, and southern Shasta counties. The Yana language family is part of the Hokan stock, the oldest in California, which also includes speakers of Pomo, Chumash, Karok, Chimariko, Washoe, and Shasta languages. Among the Yana, men and women spoke differently, in that women omitted the suffixes of certain words that men pronounced. The Yana group includes the Northern, Central, and Southern Yana, the Karok in western Siskiyou County, the Chimariko in Trinity County, and the Yahi.

The *Yahi*, whose name in their language means "people," occupied lands extending in a wedge from the Mill and Deer creek drainages (now protected as the Ishi Wilderness of Lassen National Forest) to the summit of Lassen Peak. The Yahi lived in the caves characteristic of their volcanic tableland, and in brush shelters. Masked by antlers and deerskin, the Yahi hunted deer among the herds.

More is known about the Yahi than most of the California Native cultures because of Ishi. In 1911, Ishi walked from his homeland to what are now the outskirts of Oroville, entering the modern world as the last survivor of his people. After Ishi's emergence into modern American culture, he spent his days at the University of California at Berkeley's Museum of Anthropology, where he demonstrated Yahi traditions. He ultimately brought the ethnographer Alfred L. Kroeber to his homeland and explained Yahi life there. He drew a detailed cultural map for Kroeber, which included a main village led by a female chief. Ishi had traveled throughout the region, and knew many words and traditions of the neighboring Maidu, Wintun, and Atsugewi. He contributed unprecedented amounts of information to the written cultural history of his people. From 1911 until Ishi's death in 1916 from tuberculosis, the world was enamored of this 50-year-old ambassador of a largely unknown way of life. The prehistoric Yana population is thought to have reached 2,000, of which the Yahi accounted for about 500.

Some archaeologists believe that the Early Horizon people in this region were Hokan speakers, such as the Yana, who were displaced by Penutian speakers around 1000 BC. Archaeological sites north of the Sacramento/San Joaquin Delta of possible Hokan affiliation date back to 2500 BC, suggesting that speakers of Wintun and Maidu, both Penutian languages, were not the first peoples in Central California. Perhaps referring to the upheaval of displacement, the Yana were also known as *No' zi*, which means "whale pursued by swordfish." The similarity of Pomo and Yana languages suggests that their territories may have originally been adjacent, and were later separated by the arrival of the Wintun.

Natural Resources and Material Culture

As in the Central Valley to the south, a prolific food supply sustained a large population in this region. Traditional food staples included principally acorns and salmon. These were supplemented by seeds, such as Indian pond lily and birch seed, from which a pinole was made. Mussels and fish were collected from the slow-moving Central Valley rivers, while antelope, elk, and deer were hunted on the plains. Salmon ran the Sacramento River and its tributaries as far upstream as the Feather River. Along the northern rivers spear fishing was done from scaffolding built out over the water. In the mountainous east, where acorns and salmon were not readily available, people hunted rabbits and deer and gathered grass seeds, and roots. Greens included clover, water cress, yellow dock, and dandelion.

For barter, the Wintu (the northernmost group of Wintun) offered obsidian, dried salmon, clams, shell money, salt, and pine nuts in exchange for Maidu bows and arrows, deerskins, and sugar pine nuts. The Maidu chert mine at Table Mountain (now overlooking Chico) was its principal source in the region. Chert from it was fashioned into drill bits and blades. To conserve the resource, Maidu chert miners limited removal of stone to the amount which they could dislodge with one strike of the hammer. Obsidian was obtained from the Wintu, who quarried it at Glass Mountain in the Modoc homeland. To remove quantities from the source, the Wintu built fires against the desired outcrop, causing it to fracture in blocks. The Maidu traded wild tobacco growing in Honey Lake Valley to all neighboring tribes.

The Yana of Deer Creek collected quartz crystals as charms. Hard black basalt was used for knives. Besides obsidian and chert, jasper was used for arrow points. For money, the Wintu, Maidu, and Yahi used both the dentalia shells of the Pacific Northwest tribes and the shell-disk beads of the Pomo. Maidu baskets were constructed of willow and maple shoots with designs such as flying geese worked in redbud and the stems of maidenhair fern.

Museums and Interpretive Sites

A Highway 49 roadside interpretive plaque describes the 4,000-year-old Nisenan (southern band of Maidu) culture along the North Fork of the Yuba River at Indian Valley Recreation Area. Another attraction of the **49 Miles along Highway 49** tour is the Indian Rock Picnic Area in Tahoe National Forest, where a former Maidu encampment left bedrock mortars.

The **Plumas County Museum** in Quincy exhibits a reconstructed Maidu house and a period diorama, as well as mortars, baskets, and other Maidu artifacts. The museum is open daily from May to mid-October, and weekdays in the winter, (530) 283-6320.

The **Lake Oroville State Park Visitor Center** in Oroville displays regional artifacts and books and offers a video on Ishi. Their Chaparral Trail takes in grinding rocks and a native plant garden. The museum is open daily, (530) 538-2219.

The **Hearst Museum of Anthropology** at the University of California at Berkeley retains Ishi's belongings and has a permanent exhibit on him. This is where he acted as a docent from 1911 until 1916. The museum is open Wednesday through Sunday, (510) 643-7648.

The **Rush Ranch Visitor Center** near Fairfield displays Native Californian obsidian blades and basketry among exhibits to help you identify resident birds and plants. Along the marsh outside are a reconstructed Patwin (southern group of Wintun) house and nearby mortar holes, (707) 421-1351.

hike 85

Bald Rock Trail

Roundtrip Distance	0.5 mile
Location	Foothills overlook and Maidu spirit home
Administration	Plumas National Forest (530) 283-2050
Map	Plumas National Forest

From a vantage point high atop Bald Rock, the Maidu spirit Uino guarded the Middle Fork of the Feather River. For the Maidu, such spirits concentrated the power of the land. These *ku'kini* lived at prominent geographical features such as peaks, crags, rapids, and waterfalls. Maidu shamans would go to such places to fast and experience visions. Indeed, Bald Rock offers a broad vista over what is now Plumas National Forest and the Sacramento River Valley. There are well-worn holes in the granite here where the Maidu milled harvested seeds.

Trailhead

Exit Hwy. 70 at Oroville Dam Blvd. (Hwy. 162) in Oroville. Head 1.5 miles northeast to Olive Hwy. (still Hwy. 162) and turn right. Continue

Uino guarded the Maidu from his perch atop Bald Rock

17 miles on Hwy. 162 to Bald Rock Rd. Turn right and go 7.2 miles into Plumas National Forest to the BALD ROCK TRAILHEAD sign on the left (no fee).

On The Trail

The Bald Rock Trail takes you to Uino's granite perch guarding Maidu territory, overlooking the Middle Fork of the Feather River's watershed and much of the Sacramento Valley. Your trailhead is at the northwest side of the parking area, near a large cedar. Walk northwest across a bridge and follow a seasonal creek as you climb through a woodland of cedar, western yew, oak, and bay. In 0.25 mile, the tree cover thins and rock outcrops become frequent. Soon, the delineated trail disappears on bedrock granite. Walk west on the granite, past the intriguing rock formations, picking your own route for a gradual climb to the top. Watch for sudden drop-offs, as some are abrupt. Find a perch for yourself in the granite to enjoy the view before retracing your steps to the parking area.

hike 86   Round Lake Loop

Roundtrip Distance	3.75 miles (or 6.75 miles with Pauley Creek option)
Location	Lakeside seasonal encampment in Maidu territory
Administration	Beckworth Ranger District, Plumas National Forest (530) 836-2575
Map	Lakes Basin Recreation Area

Under snow cover much of the year, the Lakes Basin was used by the Maidu as a summer hunting and fishing grounds. Maidu encampments each with several *K'um*, or temporary summer homes made of cedar bark, once were clustered along the shores of Gold Lake and many of the smaller lakes nearby. Fire rings and remnants from tool manufacturing remain at a site along the trail to Round Lake. Farther west along this trail—just beyond Snake Lake—the rock along Pauley Creek bears early petroglyphs. The Maidu do not claim rock art found within the Lakes Basin as that of their ancestors, perhaps implying that an earlier group first used the area.

Trailhead

Exit Hwy. 49 at Gold Lake Forest Hwy. in Bassetts. Follow it 7.5 miles north to the ROUND LAKE TRAILHEAD sign on the west side of the highway in the Lakes Basin Recreation Area (no fee). (This area is snow free by summer.)

On The Trail

The Round Lake Loop Trail is one of the more popular in the Gold Lakes Basin because of the many mountain lake vistas it provides. The trail climbs west from the parking area, with plentiful wildflowers along the trail in the summer. Ascending a ridgeline, the trail affords continual views of both near and distant lakes. You reach an abandoned mine overlooking Round Lake in 1.4 miles. As you reach 6,700 feet in elevation, there are good views of the Gold Lakes Basin. Without descending as far as the shore of Round Lake, the trail soon reaches a junction. The Round Lake Loop bears right (north) here toward Silver Lake. (If you're up for an optional 3-mile extension, go left at the junction and head another 1.5 miles west, passing an intersection with the Pacific Crest Trail, and continuing beyond Snake Lake to the stone carvings along the Pauley Creek outlet. Retrace your steps to the Round Lake Loop and

A rest stop along the Round Lake Loop Trail

bear left (north) to reach Silver Lake.) The view from Silver Lake may be the best one on the hike. From here, the trail descends east toward the trailhead, passing Cub, Little Bear, and Big Bear lakes. Enjoy a lakeside spot of your choice before returning to the parking area.

hike 87 Yahi Trail

Roundtrip Distance	7 miles (add several miles for cave option)
Location	River canyon at the Yahi/Maidu border
Administration	Upper Bidwell Park (530) 891-4671
Map	Yahi Trail brochure

Upper Bidwell Park is now essentially Chico's backyard wilderness on the banks of Big Chico Creek, which once demarcated the homelands and hunting grounds of the Yahi from those of the Maidu. Along the trail you'll discover traces of the Maidu culture with ethnobotany of the Yahi, whose villages lay just to the north, in Deer and Mill creek canyons. The park encompasses a lush riparian woodland along the creek bottom with foothill chaparral upslope. You'll see specimens of foothill gray pine (the trail guide urges you to try a pine nut) and blue oak, whose acorns were harvested by the Maidu. Specimens of redbud and deer grass used in basketry grow here. The park brochure reasons that the deep grinding holes along the creek were left by Maidu rather than Yahi, because the Yahi gathered grass seed here, and to grind it they would have worn only shallow-grooved mortars in the rock. Beside the creekside mortars, a cave among the canyon walls here has a floor pitted with grinding holes.

Trailhead

Exit Hwy. 99 at East 8th Ave. in Chico. Go 1.5 miles east to Chico Canyon Road. Turn left and follow Chico Canyon Rd. (which becomes Manzanita Rd.) to Upper Park Rd. Follow Upper Park Rd. 1.75 miles to the trailhead at Parking Area E (no fee) by Horseshoe Lake. (The Chico Creek Nature Center is in Lower Bidwell Park.)

On The Trail

The Yahi Trail, winding along Big Chico Creek's banks in its canyon, offers both an educational and a scenic introduction to the plants used by the Maidu and the Yahi. Interspersed along the trail are numbered signposts that correspond to descriptions provided in the Yahi Trail brochure (available at the trailhead). From the trailhead, walk east along the signed YAHI TRAIL through grassland to cross Upper Park Road at 0.1 mile. From there, the trail continues along the creek, bending northeast at 0.75 mile. Grinding holes can be seen along the creek upstream from Day Camp at 1 mile. (The cave with grinding holes in the floor occupies a niche in the canyon's north rim. You can access it from a steep spur trail at 1.25 miles near Parking Area I.) The Yahi Trail continues along Big Chico Creek, passing a fish ladder at 2 miles and many more plant specimens. In the warm summer months, swimming holes may prove irresistible along the creek. From the trail's end at 3.5 miles, retrace your steps to the parking area.

Maidu grinding rocks along Big Chico Creek

hike 88   Indian Falls Trail

Roundtrip Distance	0.5 mile
Location	Waterfall and pool informed by Maidu stories
Administration	Plumas National Forest (530) 283-2050
Map	Plumas National Forest

O ne Maidu story tells that their Thundering Falls (now known as Indian Falls) was once much higher. A spirit woman sat on a rock above the falls with her long, roiling hair mimicking the water's tumbling motions over the edge. She sang a beguiling song that enticed those coming close enough to hear it. So many were the lives wrecked at Thundering Falls that Worldmaker, stopping here along his journey, reduced their height to better preserve the Maidu people. Worldmaker is credited with all that is comfortable about the Maidu lands.

When describing difficulties caused by their rugged, mountain terrain, the stories often blame Coyote. For example, the pool at the foot of Indian Falls was once thick with salmon. Worldmaker had intended to place this fishing paradise at a lower elevation, where it would be convenient to Maidu winter villages. Yet Coyote foiled these plans, and the falls were placed up in the narrow canyon where the Maidu would reach them only after much effort.

Trailhead

Take Hwy. 70 north of Quincy to Hwy. 89. Follow Hwy. 89 north for 2 miles to the parking area (no fee) on the east side of Hwy. 89, which is several hundred yards north of the intersection with Indian Falls Rd.

On The Trail

Indian Falls Trail descends to the ancient Maidu fishing hole at the foot of the waterfall. A small sign marks the trailhead at the northwest corner of the parking area, which is maintained by the Friends of Indian Falls. You descend north, through oak woodland to a shaded picnic area overlooking the falls in 0.25 mile. From here, the trail continues to the south bank of Indian Creek, where you may want to swim on hot days. Or you may want to walk farther on swimmers' informal creekside trails, dodging the occasional sunbather. When you're ready, retrace your steps to the parking area.

Indian Falls—
"her long, roiling hair mimicking the water's tumbling motions"

hike 89 Lower Mill Creek Canyon

Roundtrip Distance	Up to 13 miles
Location	Foothill canyons of Yahi homeland
Administration	Almanor Ranger District, Lassen National Forest (530) 258-2141
Map	Ishi Wilderness

From Table Mountain in the south, across Deer and Mill creeks and up the canyons to the southern border of Lassen National Park, the Ishi Wilderness protects the former Yahi lands. Deep, stream-cut canyons with steep basalt walls and pillars, and exposed hillsides broken by only occasional caves, make this is a seldom-visited land. The Yahi lived in these canyons for 3,000 years. While it's pleasant in spring, the summer turns hot and dry. Prior to European contact, the Yahi caught salmon in Mill Creek, hunted deer among the foothills, and collected pine nuts, redbud, and other useful plant materials near the water source. Years later, *Ishi*, whose name was the Yahi word for "man," and members of his family hid in these canyons for decades while the modern world gradually encroached. By 1911, Ishi was alone here. He was discovered near a house on the outskirts of Oroville. Ishi soon joined Alfred L. Kroeber, an anthropologist from the University of California at Berkeley, and spent the remainder of his life interpreting the traditional lifeways of the Yahi people.

Trailhead

Exit I-5 at Hwy. 36 in Red Bluff, and drive east to Paynes Creek Rd. Turn right (south) and follow signs to BLACK ROCK and MILL CREEK. Continue 0.3 mile to Plum Creek Rd. Turn right and go 8 miles to Ponderosa Way. Turn right (south) and follow the occasionally rough (two-wheel-drive-passable) Ponderosa Way for 20 miles—across Antelope Creek to Black Rock Campground and the Mill Creek trailhead (no fee). (After wet weather, call the Almanor Ranger District for road conditions.)

On The Trail

The Lower Mill Creek Canyon Trail follows the ancient path the Yahi traveled along the north side of Mill Creek, heading downstream for 6.5 miles to Papes Place. The trail begins on the west side of Black Rock Campground and climbs to a gated dirt road leading several hundred yards through spring-fed meadows. Beyond a ranch here lies the wilderness, where the trail passes through open, rolling woodland. Along the way are both inviting swimming holes and deep canyon vistas. Despite cliffs towering up to 1,000 feet above a meadowland of grasses, oaks, and wildflowers, the trail is relatively flat. Chaparral carpets the south-facing slope, while live oak and ponderosa pine provide cover on the other side of the canyon. A lush riparian woodland with Indian rhubarb and wild grape lines Mill Creek. Three miles in, the trail passes through more cow pasture before crossing Avery Creek. The trail continues, intersecting the Rancheria Trail before reaching Papes Place. When you are ready, retrace your steps to the parking area.

Yahi canyon country

hike 90

Samwel Cave Nature Trail

Roundtrip Distance	1.5 miles
Location	Cave in Wintu homeland
Administration	Shasta Lake Ranger District, Shasta-Trinity Natioinal Forest (530) 275-1587
Map	A Spelunker's Guide to Samwel Cave

S amwel is a corruption of the Wintu word for "holy place." Subterranean pools within the limestone recesses of Samwel Cave have long been a source of healing powers for Wintu shamans and the subject of Wintu stories. The cave is also an important archaeological site for early human settlement in northern California. Deep within the cave—beyond its gated antechamber—are artifacts left by a culture so old that it predates the Wintun. The interpretive-trail signposts provide background on the local Wintu legend, as well as the archaeological finds. Wintu legend depicts a woman who sought the water's healing powers within the cave pools. Attempting to reach them without the assistance of a shaman, the woman slipped and fell into a deep pit. It may have been her skeleton that was found there—many years later—by University of California archaeologists.

Trailhead

Exit I-5 at Gilman Rd., 18 miles north of Redding. Drive 16 miles east to the McCloud River Bridge, where the road becomes gravel. Cross the bridge and continue 2.8 miles on Fenders Ferry Rd. to a turnout on the right on the second of a pair of ridges leading down to the lake (no fee.) The site is interpreted at Shasta Lake Ranger District's Visitor Information Center in Mountain Gate.

On The Trail

The Samwel Cave Nature Trail's interpretive signs tell a story that begins at the shoreline and ends within the cave. A steep access trail takes you from the parking area along Fenders Ferry Road down to a junction with the interpretive trail just before it enters the cave. Built for hikers arriving by boat, the interpretive trail actually begins 0.5 mile away at the lakeshore. Walk down to the shore for the view, but also to read the signs on your way back up. From the lakeshore, walk southeast up toward the cave's main entrance in a limestone cliff. Before it was inundated beneath Lake Shasta, this was the McCloud River Canyon. The original Wintu name for the cave translates as "molded acorn, " a reference to the effect its dampness has on an oak tree at the entrance. The sunlit antechamber of the cave contains signs that explain the archaeological findings within the gated inner rooms. The first chamber is spacious, and can be explored without a flashlight. When you're ready, retrace your steps to the parking area.

hike 91   McCloud River Trail

Roundtrip Distance	5 miles
Location	McCloud River Wintu village site
Administration	McCloud River Preserve (530) 926-4366
Map	Not necessary

McCloud River Preserve provides a glimpse of the river as it might have been 150 years ago, when the Wintu lived in houses along its banks, trapping salmon and steelhead here, and gathering acorns and pine nuts nearby. This was one of the richest and most populous of Wintu lands. People came here seasonally in large numbers to fish. Because of their river thick with fish, their mountains full of bear and other game, the Wintu regularly hosted great festivals in celebration. Bark houses lined both banks of the McCloud and lower Pit rivers—wherever a flat occurred. Situated between two other mighty rivers, the Sacramento and the Pit, the McCloud was to the Wintu, *Wenem-mem* (in the middle).

Native fishery in the McCloud River has been adversely affected by the Shasta and McCloud dams and is the subject of a restoration effort. While ascending salmon and steelhead are now stopped below Shasta

Dam, the Shasta rainbow here at the preserve are descendants of those fish much prized by the Wintu. Their line remains wild, having never been bred with hatchery fish. The Wintu knew this section of river as the "place where water runs shallow and swift." Here, the elevation loss and a rugged riverbed create rapids. With the boulder-lined pools making an ideal habitat for trout, the river remains a fishing paradise. Redbud, white alder, and Indian rhubarb line the river. The steep, river-cut canyon fosters a comfortable microclimate hosting oak and pine that further insulate it from temperature extremes in the surrounding mountains.

Trailhead

Exit I-5 at Hwy. 89 about 10 miles north of Dunsmuir. Head 12 miles east on Hwy. 89 to McCloud. Turn right (south) on Squaw Valley Road and go 5 miles. Squaw Valley Rd. becomes Forest Service Rd. 11. Continue to FS Rd. 38N53 (the Ah-Di-Na Road) at Lake McCloud. Turn right on 38N53 and go 7 miles, passing Ah-Di-Na Campground, to the road's end at the McCLOUD RIVER PRESERVE sign. Park beside the road (no fee).

The prolific fish brought the Wintu to the McCloud River

On The Trail

Best done in the summer after the spring runoff has subsided, the self-guiding nature trail provides details about the resources used by the Wintu, here in this beautiful, natural setting. From the parking area, walk southwest across the bridge over Wheelbarrow Creek, and past the NATURE CONSERVANCY PRESERVE sign. Continue southwest, down to the north bank of the McCloud River. The trail closely follows the river for 0.5 mile to the headquarters at the preserve boundary. In season, fragrant white azaleas and leopard lilies line the river, and large leaves of Indian rhubarb bob at the water's edge. Walking can be rough when the river is high, because the route then gets pushed up among poison oak along jagged, canyon walls. From headquarters, the trail follows the river for 2 miles into the preserve. The route is shaded by Douglas-fir and western yew, from which the Wintu once made bows. From the trail's end at the preserve's southwestern boundary, retrace your steps to the parking area.

 # Guided Walks

Dye Creek Preserve was a home of the Yana people. Well-preserved artifacts left by their culture have contributed significant archaeological evidence about California's prehistory. The preserve is situated in the foothills southeast of Red Bluff. Guided walks are offered in spring and fall, (530) 449-2850.

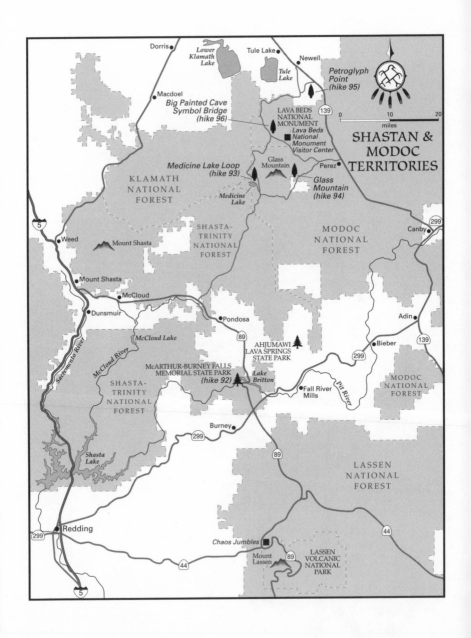

SHASTAN & MODOC TERRITORIES

Dorris

Lower Klamath Lake

Tule Lake

Newell

Tule Lake

Petroglyph Point (hike 95)

Macdoel

Big Painted Cave Symbol Bridge (hike 96)

LAVA BEDS NATIONAL MONUMENT

Lava Beds National Monument Visitor Center

Medicine Lake Loop (hike 93)

Glass Mountain

Perez

Glass Mountain (hike 94)

KLAMATH NATIONAL FOREST

Medicine Lake

SHASTA-TRINITY NATIONAL FOREST

MODOC NATIONAL FOREST

Canby

Weed

Mount Shasta

Mount Shasta

McCloud

Dunsmuir

Pondosa

Adin

Bieber

McCloud Lake

McCloud River

AHJUMAWI LAVA SPRINGS STATE PARK

MODOC NATIONAL FOREST

Sacramento River

McARTHUR-BURNEY FALLS MEMORIAL STATE PARK (hike 92)

Lake Britton

Fall River Mills

Pit River

SHASTA-TRINITY NATIONAL FOREST

Burney

Shasta Lake

LASSEN NATIONAL FOREST

Redding

Chaos Jumbles

Mount Lassen

LASSEN VOLCANIC NATIONAL PARK

miles

0   10   20

Shastan & Modoc

Cascade Range & Modoc Plateau

Landscape and People

The northeastern corner of California is the homeland of the Shastan and the Modoc peoples. The region is composed of rugged mountains and vast lava fields—mostly snow-clad until late spring. The terrain features the southernmost volcanoes of the Cascade Range, and the adjacent tableland of the Columbia (known in California as the Modoc) Plateau. Lassen Peak, Mount Shasta, and the Medicine Lake volcano dominate the landscape. While these geologically active volcanoes harbor powerful spirits, the people living here did not fear them. Hunting and fishing parties regularly journeyed up their flanks in summer, making use of the medicinal hot springs.

Shastan

The Shastan people occupied the upper reaches of the Sacramento Valley and the southern section of the Modoc Plateau. Shastan territory included much of present-day Siskiyou and Shasta counties, between the headwaters of the Klamath, Scott, Shasta, and Pit rivers. There are six major dialects of the Shastan language divided among its Sastean and Palaihnihan groups. The Sastean group includes the New River Shasta, the Okwanuchu, and the Konomihu (Kroeber, 1976). The Okwanuchu people once occupied the upper reaches of the Sacramento and McCloud rivers, an area that was later held by the Wintu. The Konomihu occupied part of the Salmon River drainage in what is now Siskiyou County, a territory later held by the Karok. The New River Shasta inhabited the upper Salmon and New river watersheds in central Siskiyou County. Unlike many California groups that exhibited decentralized, quasi-democratic leadership, the Shasta people had very powerful chiefs. "Shasta" is thought to originate from the name of a great leader called *Sasti*, who controlled Scott Valley at the foot of the Marble Mountains.

The Palaihnihan group includes the Achomawi (also known as the Pit River People) and the Atsugewi (also known as the Hat River People). The Achomawi occupied the Pit River watershed, from Montgomery Creek to Goose Lake. This river gained its name from the Achomawi practice of trapping deer within 9-foot-deep pits obscured by a layer of branches. The neighboring Atsugewi tribe inhabited the drainages of Burney, Hat, and Horse creeks, as well as part of the high country forming a triangle between Lassen Peak, Mount Shasta, and Medicine Lake. The Shastan people are the northernmost of the Hokan language stock, which is the oldest in California. Taken together, the pre-historic Shastan population is thought to have reached 4,000, of which 3,000 were comprised of Achomawi and Atsugewi peoples.

Modoc

The Modoc homeland spans much of the northern Modoc Plateau—particularly the shores of Tule and Lower Klamath lakes—into Oregon. Modoc lands extended south as far as the Pit River, and included what are now Modoc and eastern Siskiyou counties. Traditionally, the Modoc lived as a number of bands. They constructed subterranean lodges in perhaps 20 villages beside Tule and Lower Klamath lakes and along the Lost River. In summer they traveled to the mountains in accordance with the harvest patterns, living in temporary wickiups of poles and mats.

The Modoc language is part of the Penutian family, whose speakers once migrated south through western North America from British Columbia to Mexico. The Modoc were considered fierce by their neighbors—the Shasta, the Yana, and the Achomawi—who were occasionally raided for items used in trade. Though the Klamath tribe is the closest relative of the Modoc, the Klamath are a classic Pacific Northwest culture, while the Modoc way of life evolved with their California neighbors. "Modoc" is derived from *MoAdok MaKlak*, words used by the Klamath to refer to "people from the south." The prehistoric Modoc population is thought to have reached 700, divided equally between California and Oregon. Today, the Modoc people live on either the Quapaw Reservation in Oklahoma or the Klamath Reservation in Oregon. The National Park Service hosted a reunion of Oklahoma and Oregon Modoc at Lava Beds National Monument in 1990. Since then, the Modoc have returned annually to celebrate their reunion.

Throughout the region villages were located along lakes and rivers, with interior lava fields and flanks of the Lassen, Shasta, and Medicine Lake volcanoes used for hunting game and gathering supplies. Without fear, the Native cultures nevertheless approached the volcanoes with an attitude of respect. According to an Atsugewi oral history, one quaking shook the earth so violently that it made the people sick, and though an old women pounded two rocks together in prayer that the shaking would stop, by the time it did, the people living in the canyons had been killed by falling rocks. Indeed, a cataclysmic series of avalanches did occur near the Atsugewi lands about 300 years ago, pulverizing and burying much of what lay beneath the newly formed Chaos Jumbles in what is now Lassen Volcanic National Park. Elsewhere in the region, the most recent eruptions on the Medicine Lake Highlands, which sent lava flows to the shores of Tule Lake, spewing rhyolite pumice and scattering airborne ash 35 miles west to Shasta, occurred less than 1,100 years ago. Such dramatic displays of natural power must have struck terror among the early tribal peoples of California—much as they affect us today.

The earliest archaeological sites along the upper Pit River date back to 3000 BC. One site there, which dates to 1350 BC, has been associated with the transition between the Hokan people of the Early Horizon and the Penutian people of the Middle and Late Horizons. In addition, earlier peoples inhabited the Tule Lake Basin prior to the Modoc. The oldest-known archaeological site in Northern California lies on the west shore of Tule Lake and dates back 11,450 years. Tule Lake was then a lush valley grazed by bison. Spear points of the type used to kill mastodon have been found along its shores.

Natural Resources and Material Culture

Proximity to cultures of the Pacific Northwest influenced the unique material culture in northeast California. One traditional plant food of the Modoc was *wocus* (water lily seed), ground in mortars made of lava. To this staple were added wild parsley roots and *epos* (wild potatoes) gathered near Tule Lake. Salmon-spawning runs extended inland as far as the lower Pit River. In the autumn, pine nuts and manzanita berries were gathered. The Modoc both trapped waterfowl in Tule Lake and collected eggs from the nests. Bighorn sheep and pronghorn were hunted in the lava beds. The Modoc utilized a fighting armor made of a double thickness of elk skin. Their baskets and canoes were made of tule.

Houses were conical structures covered with bark. Along the upper Klamath River, the Shasta built plank houses similar to those of the Yurok. The summer house was a roofless windbreak of brush. The mortars found in the region were not used by the Shasta people, because they pounded acorns in strong, supple baskets against rock slabs. Dugout canoes of pine or cedar were used in navigating the Klamath and Pit rivers. Dentalia shells and woodpecker scalps served as currency. The Shasta fashioned containers out of deerskin.

Obsidian was the most desired commodity in the region, and was traded in all directions. The Atsugewi and Achomawi offered furs to the Wintu and other neighboring lowland peoples in exchange for shell beads. The Shasta traded obsidian, deerskin, and sugar pine nuts to the Karok in exchange for dentalia, salt, seaweed, baskets, acorns, and canoes. The Shasta subsequently traded the obtained dentalia to the Wintu for acorns. The Modoc traded mainly with their neighbor to the north, the Klamath.

People traveled great distances to obtain the higher grades of obsidian found throughout this region. Mahogany obsidian from the Warner Mountains, prized both for its brown color and its worth as a tool material, has been found in chipping sites throughout the Southwest. Glass Mountain in Modoc territory was an important obsidian mine, supplying most northern California tribes with the materials to make arrow points.

Within the caves of Modoc territory are colorful pictographs, which are rare in northern California. Some are thought to date to AD 500. Petroglyphs are also found at Petroglyph Point near Tule Lake. A Shastan rain rock bearing cupules, which was salvaged from a Caltrans project in Siskiyou County, is now on display at the Fort Jones Museum. This piece of soapstone dating to AD 1000 represents another style of petroglyph. Its pits and grooves were carved for the scraped dust by shamans on a rain quest or women seeking fertility; they would drink it to obtain power.

Museums and Interpretive Sites

In front of the **Fort Jones Museum** in Scott Valley lies the aforementioned Shastan rain rock. Inside the museum are baskets, mortars, and pestles gathered from throughout Siskiyou County, (530) 468-5568.

Achomawi baskets twined of hazelnut are displayed in the Recent Acquisitions section at the **California Academy of Sciences** in San Francisco. The museum is open daily from 10 A.M. until 5 P.M., (415) 750-7145.

The **Siskiyou County Museum** in Yreka contains artifacts and exhibits of the local Shasta culture as well as others. The museum is open Tuesday through Saturday from 9 A.M. until 5 P.M., (530) 842-3836.

The **Lava Beds National Monument Visitor Center** features a model of a Modoc summer encampment. In addition, one exhibit portrays the finding of obsidian chips in a squirrel den that led to the documentation resulting in the formation of the archaeological district. The visitor center is open daily from 8 A.M. until 5 P.M., (530) 667-2282.

hike 92   Burney Falls Trail

Roundtrip Distance	2 miles
Location	Lakeside archaeological site of the Achomawi
Administration	McArthur-Burney Falls Memorial State Park (530) 335-2777
Map	McArthur-Burney Falls Memorial State Park

The McArthur-Burney Falls Memorial State Park protects some former lands of the Ilmawi band of the Achomawi people, which in prehistoric times extended along the Pit River between Hat and Burney creeks. The Ilmawi lived in semi-permanent villages along the river, now flooded by waters of Lake Britton. The Achomawi traditionally believe that prominent natural features possess great power. As such, Burney Falls is held sacred. The Atsugewi and other neighboring tribes shared this site, visiting the falls to fast and experience visions.

Today, the Lake Britton Archaeological Project is listed on the National Register of Historic Places. Managed by Pacific Gas and Electric in cooperation with the Ilmawi people living nearby, the project contains 27 excavated archaeological sites at the lake. Remains of river mussel shells here have contributed a great deal of archaeological information. Growth rings on unearthed shells reveal the age of the shellfish at the time of harvest. Archaeologists attribute harvest-age fluctuation over time to changes in demand for this food source. Remains indicate there was a plentiful supply of mussels in the Pit River 4,500 years ago, the discarded shells showing harvest at a mature age. But by 3,200 years ago, smaller and younger mussels were being harvested, indicating an increase in demand. By 2,800 years ago, the mussel age at harvest increased again, revealing a lessening demand coinciding with a region-wide change in methods of subsistence. From the cultural shift forward, demand likely increased as harvest age began to drop again, continuing to do so until 200 years ago, when harvest stopped.

Burney Falls are held sacred by the Achomawi and the Atsuwegi

Trailhead

Exit Hwy. 299 at Hwy. 89, 5 miles east of Burney. Go 5.8 miles north on Hwy. 89 to the McArthur-Burney Falls Memorial State Park entrance (fee required) on the west side of the highway. Park by the visitor center.

On The Trail

At 3,000 feet, this forested park near the edge of the Modoc Plateau provides a cool escape from the hot summer temperatures of the Sacramento Valley. The Burney Falls Trail visits the falls, and then follows Burney Creek to the archaeologically rich shores of Lake Britton. The well-marked trail begins at the west side of the parking area. The paved walkway descends a steep hill along switchbacks, with interpretive signs indicating the native plants. The pavement ends at the pool below the falls at 0.25 mile, where mist from the awesome splash cools visitors.

Crossing the foot of a talus slope of basalt boulders, the trail continues north down Burney Creek to a footbridge at 0.5 mile and the junction with the Burney Creek Trail. Where the Burney Falls Trail crosses the bridge, go straight, continuing north along the Burney Creek Trail. White patches you find along the route are diatomaceous earth deposits, which rarely coincide with volcanic rock formations. Originating from organisms that fell to the bottom of the ancient sea preceding the uplift and volcanism here, these chalky deposits provide a stark contrast to the black basalt. You reach the beach at Lake Britton's south shore at 1 mile. The beaches of Lake Britton are backed by conifer forest that covers the Pit River canyon. Radiocarbon-dating of artifacts excavated nearby establishes that there was a village here 5,000 years ago. Swimming is often a good recreational option at this popular, summer beach. When you're ready, retrace your steps to the parking lot.

hike 93

Medicine Lake Loop

Roundtrip Distance	4.5 miles
Location	Summer lakeside Modoc village site
Administration	Doublehead Ranger District, Modoc National Forest (530) 667-2246
Map	Modoc National Forest, Medicine Lake Highlands

At the center of the Modoc Plateau's volcanic highlands lies Medicine Lake. The Modoc maintained the seasonal village of Lani'shwi here in summer. Volcanic activity has been so recent in some areas of the Medicine Lake Highlands that vegetation has not reestablished. Elsewhere, sugar and lodgepole pine, red and white fir, and a low cover of manzanita and bitterbrush break up the lava fields.

When the huge Medicine Lake volcano erupted, its peak collapsed, leaving a six-mile-wide, 500-foot-deep caldera. Its bottom has since filled with the waters of Medicine Lake. Without tributary streams, the lake appears to replenish itself from underwater springs. The Shasta people traveled here to perform initiation ceremonies. Many Native Californian cultures believed the lake had curing properties; the healing that took place here is still honored in the lake's English name.

Trailhead

Exit I-5 at Hwy. 89 about 5 miles north of Dunsmuir, and go 29 miles east to Harris Springs Rd. (FS Rd. 15) near Bartle. Turn left and drive 4 miles to Powder Hill Rd. (FS Rd. 49). Make a right and go 31 miles northeast to Medicine Lake Rd. Follow Medicine Lake Rd. left to the campground at the lakeshore (no fee). (Call the Doublehead Ranger District of Modoc National Forest for conditions. The area is snow free by summer.)

On The Trail

Paths encircle the lake that partially fills the caldera of Medicine Lake volcano. From the campground, follow the tree-lined shore. While there is no formal trail, you can easily join trails between the three camp-grounds and shoreline paths to either encircle the lake or make a partial loop. En route are beaches backed by conifer forest. With a depth of 150 feet, the clear lake waters are used for swimming, boating, and fishing. On the lake's west side is a (5-mile-round-trip) road leading to the summit of 7,309-foot Little Mount Hoffman. This is one of the best places from which to view Mount Shasta to the west, as well as the volcanic landscape surrounding Medicine Lake.

In the Shastan worldview, the towering volcano we call Mt. Shasta was known as the home of Skell, a spirit chief who created it by blowing ice and snow through a slit he had cut in the sky with his sharp, stone knife. By pushing more and more snow down through the cloud opening, he built the mountain tall enough to reach him. He then slightly descended to inhabit Shasta's 14,162-foot summit. Smoke and fire periodically emitted from the mountain are how Skell makes his presence known.

hike 94   Glass Mountain

Roundtrip Distance	2 miles (more or less along informal paths)
Location	Prehistoric obsidian quarry
Administration	Doublehead Ranger District, Modoc National Forest (530) 667-2246
Map	Modoc National Forest, Medicine Lake Highlands

The Medicine Lake Highlands are a land of volcanic glass flows, pumice deposits, and lava tubes—impressive leftovers from eruptions of the Medicine Lake volcano. Yet, unlike the dramatic profiles of the stratovolcanoes that formed the peaks of Shasta and Lassen, the Medicine Lake volcano is a shield volcano with gently sloping sides. Its magma chamber emptied through side vents leaving a huge dome on the landscape. On the east, the highlands are made up of 950-year-old lava flows. Highland glass flows include Grasshopper Flat, Little Glass Mountain, Glass Mountain, and Sugar Hill. Above the Modoc Plateau, the highlands described a natural boundary between Modoc and Achomawi lands. The Ilmawi band of Achomawi, who lived along the Pit River, traveled far to obtain the better-chipping obsidian found at Grasshopper Flat. Because both the Modoc and the Achomawi claimed the obsidian quarry at Sugar Hill, there were occasional conflicts. The ancient quarries remain evident today. Obsidian mined here was traded throughout Northern California.

Trailhead

Exit I-5 at Hwy. 89 about 5 miles north of Dunsmuir, and go 29 miles east to Harris Springs Rd. (FS Rd. 15) near Bartle. Turn left and drive 4 miles to Powder Hill Rd. (FS Rd. 49). Make a right and go 29 miles northeast to Forest Service Rd. 97. Turn right and go 6 miles north to Forest Service Rd. 43N99. Turn left (north) and go to the southern edge of the Glass Mountain Geologic Area. Park along the road (no fee). (Call the Doublehead Ranger District for conditions.)

On The Trail

A Glass Mountain walk takes in the prehistoric obsidian mines along a glass flow, which because of its rare geologic formation, has been designated a Special Interest Area in Modoc National Forest. Because dacite and rhyolite obsidian were emitted here simultaneously from the same vent—swirling but not mixing—they created a stronger, higher grade of glass. Quarried by Modoc, Atsugewi, Achomawi, and Wintu, the obsidian was traded to villages over 100 miles away. The Wintu used fire to break off the weathered surface layer of obsidian to expose the high-grade subsurface material. Since the quarrying activity has not been entirely obscured by weathering and vegetation growth, certain places on Glass Mountain remain as though they were only recently altered by Native miners. Pick your route along informal paths of gray dacite. Avoid walking on the slippery and sharp rhyolite glass. Wander as much of the 4,000-acre flow as you like before returning to your car.

hike 95

Petroglyph Point

Roundtrip Distance	0.2 mile
Location	Petroglyph site in Modoc territory
Administration	Lava Beds National Monument (530) 667-2282
Map	Lava Beds National Monument, interpretive brochure

In prehistoric times, Petroglyph Point was an island in ancient Lake Modoc, which once covered the Klamath-Tule lakes basin. According to the Modoc creation myth, the world was fashioned by Kamookumpts. It was here at Petroglyph Point that Kamookumpts made the first hill from mud he had dug on the lake bottom. Then, he created the surrounding mountains also from this mud. He made the world's streams, plants, and animals before sleeping in a hole beneath the lake. Kamookumpts left the original hill to mark his resting place. Its mud soon dried and became stone and is known today as Petroglyph Point.

The earliest carvings here are perhaps 2,500–4,500 years old, and correspond to a time when the lake level almost reached the petroglyphs on the cliff face. Tule-balsa canoes were used to navigate the lake to Kamookumpts' hill. The petroglyphs were carved from canoes on the water to record important events.

Trailhead

Exit I-5 at Hwy. 299 in Redding and go 133 miles northeast to Hwy. 139 at Canby. Turn left (north) and go 27 miles to the signed turnoff for Lava Beds National Monument. Make a left and drive northwest to the park entrance and visitor center (fee required). From the visitor center, follow the park road 18 miles north. Turn right on the dirt road signed PETROGLYPH SECTION and go 0.25 mile to the Petroglyph Point parking area on the right.

On The Trail

The interpretive walk at Petroglyph Point includes over 5,000 carvings, making this one of the most extensive petroglyph sites in North

Petroglyphs

America. Petroglyphs often exist at impressive natural landmarks such as these cliffs, as they signify power and denote passages to the spirit world. The number of petroglyphs indicates that this was considered a very powerful site for many thousands of years.

From the parking area, walk left to the end of the barbed-wire fence protecting the petroglyphs. Follow the fence, pausing at the numbered signposts that correspond to numbered sections of the brochure (available at the trailhead). Geometric shapes and animal figures—similar in style to those of the Great Basin—were created by incision, pecking, abrasion, and drilling, and then connecting the tiny pits. Unfortunately, the fragile petroglyphs are slowly deteriorating in the abrasive wind. The trail continues south to the end of the carvings at 0.1 mile. When you're ready, retrace your steps to the parking area.

hike 96   Big Painted Cave and Symbol Bridge

Roundtrip Distance	1.6 miles
Location	Pictograph site in Modoc territory
Administration	Lava Beds National Monument (530) 667-2282
Map	Lava Beds National Monument

A comprehensive archaeological study in Lava Beds National Monument revealed so much prehistory that in 1991, Modoc Lava Beds Archaeological District was placed on the National Register of Historic Places. In their random diggings, even squirrels had helped uncover some of the obsidian-flaking sites. Archaeologists have since unearthed village sites on Nightfire Island and on the shores of Tule Lake. The trail to the pictographs traverses the distinctive landscape of these Modoc lands. Sage, juniper, and wildflowers grow among the lava beds. Modoc women once collected more than a dozen different types of roots, as many different types of berries, and several dozen types of seeds here. Beneath the rock the area is festooned with lava tubes and caves. Occasional open pits of jumbled rock and bridges mark collapsed remnants of caves. Whether the heat of summer or the snows of winter make the surface uncomfortable, the temperature in the caves remains a constant 65 degrees Fahrenheit. The Modoc used this network of caves as one might use a cathedral. They sought refuge in them during the Modoc War. Several of the caves contain pictographs which mark sacred places and record important events. A smattering of light pumice from an eruption in the Medicine Lake Highlands—deposited about 1,000 years ago—dusts the ground of Lava Beds. During this time the Modoc were living here, and they may have recorded the event in these pictographs.

Trailhead

Exit I-5 at Hwy. 299 in Redding and go 133 miles northeast to Hwy. 139 at Canby. Turn left (north) and go 27 miles to the signed turnoff for

Pictographs

Lava Beds National Monument. Make a left and drive northwest to the park entrance and visitor center (fee required). From the visitor center, head 1.5 miles north on the park road to the Skull Cave turnoff. Turn right and go 1 mile east to the Big Painted Cave/Symbol Bridge trailhead on the left.

On The Trail

Though neither Big Painted Cave nor Symbol Bridge requires flashlights—they are day-lit for as far as passage is possible—flashlights may aid visibility in the shadows. The nearly level trail tours cave wall paintings of human figures, stars (or cog wheels), the moon, and animals as seen through the eyes of a shaman while in an altered vision state. From the trailhead, the signed path leads northwest across a plateau, with a view south of the Medicine Lake Highlands. As you pass through sagebrush and lava fields along the way, several smaller, partially collapsed tubes and caves fail to prepare you for the bigger caverns that lie ahead.

In 0.5 mile take a spur trail marked BIG PAINTED CAVE. It leads southwest, descending several hundred yards into the lava cavern. Just as you pass into the shadows of the cave, you can see pictographs drawn in black on the smooth boulders along the trail. Painted by the Modoc people over thousands of years, the Big Painted Cave pictographs include geometric shapes and parallel zigzag lines. The spur trail continues only several yards farther into the cave. Returning to the main trail, continue northwest to an interpretive sign describing Symbol Bridge at 0.8 mile. A footpath descends 100 feet into the cave to approach the bridge. The Symbol Bridge pictographs are more numerous, more varied, and better preserved than those at the Big Painted Cave. Though the Lava Beds pictographs have no direct similarities to those of any other region, the style of figures outlined in one color, then another, is also found in the Klamath Basin in southern Oregon. Approach the bridge as you would any sacred place. Viewing figures painted 380 to 1,480 years ago in this setting can be a profound experience. When you're ready, retrace your steps to the parking area.

Guided Walks

Ahjumawi Lava Springs State Park. *Ahjumawi* means "where waters come together." Aptly named, this park is surrounded by water, roadless Thousand Lakes Wilderness, and private land, making it accessible only by boat. From this land, vividly reflecting its volcanic origin, you can see lava tubes and a spatter cone, as well as Burney Mountain, Lassen Peak, and Mount Shasta. The remoteness and beauty of the place alone are worth the journey. Mortar holes remain in the lava near the many village sites that line the shore. Blue Water Kayaking at (415) 669-2600 in Inverness, California, offers weekend-length guided tours of this beautiful but difficult-to-reach state park in spring and fall. Or Lava Creek Lodge at (530) 336-6288 will either rent you a boat to make the 1-mile paddle yourself, or shuttle you out and back for a walk on your own.

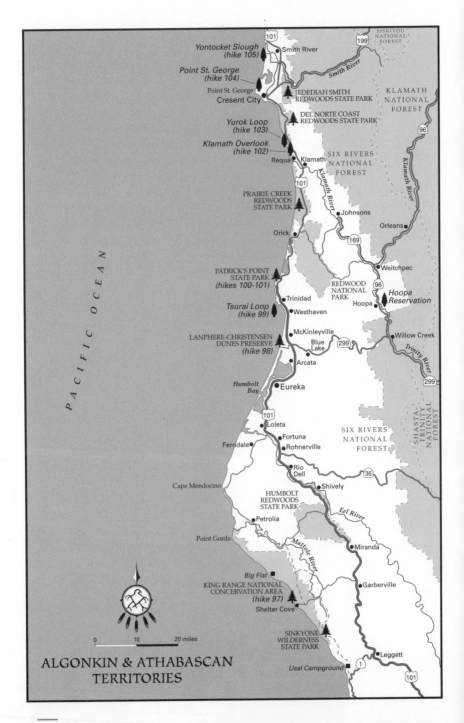

Yontocket Slough
(hike 105)
Smith River

Point St. George
(hike 104)
Point St. George
Cresent City

Yurok Loop
(hike 103)

Klamath Overlook
(hike 102)
Requa • Klamath

Smith River

SISKIYOU
NATIONAL
FOREST

JEDEDIAH SMITH
REDWOODS STATE PARK

KLAMATH
NATIONAL
FOREST

DEL NORTE COAST
REDWOODS STATE PARK

SIX RIVERS
NATIONAL
FOREST

PRAIRIE CREEK
REDWOODS
STATE PARK

Johnsons

Orleans

Orick

Weitchpec

PATRICK'S POINT
STATE PARK
(hikes 100-101)

REDWOOD
NATIONAL
PARK

Hoopa
Reservation

Trinidad
Tsurai Loop
(hike 99)
Westhaven

Hoopa

McKinleyville

LANPHERE-CHRISTENSEN
DUNES PRESERVE
(hike 98)

Blue
Lake
Arcata

Willow Creek

P A C I F I C   O C E A N

Humbolt
Bay
Eureka

Loleta

Fortuna
Ferndale
Rohnerville

SIX RIVERS
NATIONAL
FOREST

Rio
Dell
Cape Mendocino
Shively

SHASTA-
TRINITY
NATIONAL
FOREST

HUMBOLT
REDWOODS
STATE PARK

Eel River

Petrolia

Point Gorda

Mattole River

Miranda

Big Flat

KING RANGE NATIONAL
CONCERVATION AREA
(hike 97)
Shelter Cove

Garberville

0   10   20 miles

ALGONKIN & ATHABASCAN
TERRITORIES

SINKYONE
WILDERNESS
STATE PARK

Usal Campground

Leggett

Algonkin & Athabascan

North Coast

Landscape and People

The North Coast contained one of the largest populations in the state before European contact, estimated at over 20,000. In their way of life, the tribes of this region blend the material cultures of California with those of the Pacific Northwest. The Yurok culture is respected as one of the more materially elaborate in the region. Pacific Northwest culture is epitomized here by the Yurok, and is seen in lesser degrees of elaboration among neighboring tribes. Yurok customs are shared almost entirely with Hupa and Karok, and to a lesser degree by Tolowa, Wiyot, and Chilula. The Shasta, Chimariko, Nongatl, and Whilkut have fewer similarities with the Yurok, and the Sinkyone and Lassik peoples share even less. The Pacific Northwest cultural repertoire is entirely absent among the Kato, a people who migrated from Central California, sharing only a linguistic family with the Yurok.

Algonkin

The Algonkin language family in California includes Yurok and Wiyot. As they have for millennia, the Yurok people live along the lower Klamath River. Their homeland extends upstream to the Karok lands, and along the Pacific Coast from the Klamath River mouth south to Trinidad Head. The central gathering place of the Yurok culture lies at the confluence of the Trinity and the Klamath rivers. This is the site of the Yurok village, Weitchpec. In the Yurok language, the word for the Klamath mouth translates as the "end of the world." *Yurok* is actually a Karok word meaning "downstream." The prehistoric Yurok population is estimated to have once reached 3,100.

Centered along Humboldt Bay, the Wiyot homeland extends inland along the lower Eel River. *Wiyot* is an Algonkin word referring to the southern portion of their lands. The prehistoric Wiyot population is thought to have reached 3,300.

Athabascan

Tribes speaking languages in the Athabascan family inhabited the northernmost corner of California, including northern Del Norte County, and extending into Oregon's Rogue River Valley. The California Athabascans include the Tolowa along the northern coast, the Hupa (including Whilkut and Chilula) along the lower Trinity River, the Mattole at Cape Mendocino and along the Bear and Mattole rivers, and the Wailaki (including Nongatl, Lassik, Sinkyone, and Kato) along the drainage of the Eel River.

Within the Hupa culture, the Chilula homeland lies along lower Redwood Creek south of the Klamath. The Whilkut homeland lies along the Mad River and upper Redwood Creek. The Hupa people live along the lower Trinity River, with a cultural hub in the Hoopa Valley, which they call *Natinook*. (The people are "Hupa," and the land is "Hoopa.")

Of the California Athabascans, the only grouping culturally much different from the Yurok is the Wailaki, especially the Sinkyone and the Kato. The Sinkyone lands occupied a cultural crossroads between the people of Central California and those of Northwestern California. More closely reflecting cultural aspects of Central California tribes, the Sinkyone differed from other regional peoples by including abalone in their diet and by not using boats. Sinkyone lands extended the length of the Lost Coast from the Mattole River south to Yuki territory beginning around Rockport. From the coast, Sinkyone villages lined the South Fork of the Eel River inland to its headwaters near Branscomb, where the Kato people lived. The name "Sinkyone" is derived from *sinkyoko*, an Athabascan word designating the South Fork of the Eel River. Athabascan people came to the North Coast around 3000 BC. One well-known Athabascan group outside California is the Navajo. The Athabascan population in northwest California prior to European contact is thought to have reached 14,000.

The landscape is the rainforest of the North Coast. Villages were located along stream banks, river mouths, and lagoons—such as Stone and Big lagoons in Humboldt Lagoons State Park, and Espa Lagoon in Prairie Creek Redwoods State Park. This is a landscape through which travel was facilitated by the dugout canoe. Canoes were made by the Yurok, the Tolowa, and the Wiyot. The Yurok also made boats to be sold to the Hupa and the Karok. While the northwestern people were not ruled traditionally by chiefs, they lived in a society structured by respect for wealthy individuals and families. The social system was highly stratified and hereditary. With a concept of private property, an individual owning a particular oak grove, a mussel-rich sea stack, or a fishing hole gained influence and respect.

The Yurok traded with their neighbors, but rarely ventured into unknown lands. A man of wealth might travel only where relatives or friends welcomed him. Nor did the Yurok welcome strangers, which generally holds true for visitors today. Unlike Central Californian cultures, in the northwest animals do not figure in traditional tales. The Yurok creator was a man, but shamans were traditionally female. The Yurok hold a series of gatherings annually to honor the land and ward off disasters in the coming year, called the World Renewal Ceremony. Bringing families from various villages together, these gatherings helped unify the Yurok. Certain parts of the World Renewal Ceremony, such as the White Deerskin Dance and the Brush Dance, may be attended today at Sunmeg and on the Hoopa Reservation.

Villages of earlier cultures may have existed along the North Coast at a time of lower sea levels, with their artifacts now underwater. Archaeological records reveal an early site at Point St. George, where chipped stone tools date back to 300 BC. These are associated with an Athabascan group that predates the Tolowa. Additional sites dating to AD 900 have been excavated along the Klamath River. Remains here are associated with sea lion hunting, surf fishing, shellfish gathering, and the acorn harvest. Items of wealth include stone animal effigies up two feet in length carved in dark, polished slate. Many 5-inch-tall, fired-clay human figurines were excavated at a site near Humboldt Bay. The figurines are thought to date to some time after AD 1500.

Middens along the North Coast contain stone fishhooks, grooved-stone fishnet sinkers, barbed stone harpoons, elaborate handles for shell blades used in milling redwood planks, and steatite bowls for catching the juices of cooking salmon. The chronological change of artifacts found in this region documents the appearance of elaborate material culture and probable social ranking comparable to that of the Chumash.

Natural Resources and Material Culture

This food-rich region sustained one of California's largest and most advanced material cultures, and went beyond providing for subsistence to allow the accumulation of wealth. Traditional food staples included salmon and acorns. The latter were ground on a stone slab with a stone pestle. Hazelnuts and pine nuts, lily bulbs, greens, and a pinole made of seeds greatly extended the larder. Relied upon more here than in any other region in Native California, salmon were taken from the rivers year-round. Fish not eaten right away were dried. Salmon jerky is still made here and is available at roadside cafes near Requa. Lampreys and sturgeon were also taken from the rivers with fishing nets made of rolled iris fibers. Sea lion hunters disguised themselves in bear- or deer-skins and hid among the rocks. Other traditional seafoods included surf fish, smelt, and large ocean mussels, whose remnant shells paved dwelling floors. Though an important food source, the filter-feeding mussel was not harvested during the summer, for the same reason it is now quarantined during the toxic "red tide." Among the sea stacks, eggs were collected from the nests of shorebirds. The Yurok preferred whale meat above all else, and greatly celebrated all beachings. Deer meat was also greatly enjoyed. Salt was obtained from seaweed that had been dried in small black cakes. To the extent that they cultivated native tobacco, the Yurok practiced a limited agriculture.

Large, rectangular houses were made traditionally of redwood or cedar planks. They were partially subterranean with gabled roofs and round doorways. Large, flat river stones paved the entranceways. As emulated by the architect of the modern tribal office building on the Hupa Reservation, this style has a very pleasing and dramatic effect. A house typically bore a name, which was usually a reference to its geographic location. You may visit northwest-style plank houses on the Hoopa Reservation and at Sunmeg in Patrick's Point State Park.

The Yurok were well known for the craftsmanship of their *Yack*, a dugout canoe made of redwood. Specific sections of the canoe correspond to parts of the human body. Carved with elkhorn tools, each canoe has heart, nose, lungs, and kidneys. To seal the wood and drive away bad spirits, the finished art was passed through fire. These canoes were so stable in the water that sea lions could be hauled aboard. Besides using them for hunting and travel, the Yurok—as a matter of law—provided a free ferry service across the Klamath to anyone who needed it. You can see their canoes displayed at Sunmeg and at the Hiouchi Visitor Center in Redwood National Park.

In addition to the canoe, more than 100 types of wood items—from acorn soup spoons to dance adornments—were crafted by the cultures of northwest California. Ornate spoons and stirrers were also made of elk antlers. Other treasures included scarlet woodpecker scalps, deerskins in rare hues, large obsidian blades, and knives of white chert. Wooden stools and pillows made by the Yurok were two of the limited instances of furniture-craft in prehistoric California. Women's clothing might be adorned with olivella shells, abalone shells (from south of Cape Mendocino), and obsidian prisms. Dentalia shells, obtained through trade from the tribes of Vancouver Island, were used as money.

Regional baskets were constructed by twining, with overlaid designs worked in. This basketry style ranged from the Wailaki in the south to the Achomawi in the east, as well as the Oregon Athabascan. Materials included hazel shoots and split roots of redwood or willow. Designs were created with white blades of bear grass, glossy-black maidenhair fern stems, fibers of giant fern dyed red with alder bark, or bear grass steeped yellow with lichen.

Museums and Interpretive Sites

The **Hoopa Valley Tribal Council Museum** in Hoopa displays traditional artifacts and basketry of the Hupa people, as well as the work of modern Hupa artists, some of which are for sale. Located on the Hoopa Reservation, the museum is staffed by tribal members who also host village tours. It is open weekdays from 8 A.M. until 5 P.M., (530) 625-4110. (See also the "Guided Walk" for this chaper.)

The **Trees of Mystery Indian Museum** in Klamath contains five rooms of artifacts, one of which is dedicated to the Yurok and the Karok. The main gallery has art for sale and is open daily from 8 A.M. until 6 P.M., (707) 482-2251.

The Native American room at the **Clark Memorial Museum** in Eureka displays baskets and other ceremonial artifacts. Their collection is so large that they have to rotate exhibits. The museum is open from Tuesday through Saturday from 12 P.M. until 4 P.M., (707) 443-1947.

hike 97

Shelter Cove to Big Flat
(via Coast Trail)

Roundtrip Distance	16 miles
Location	Coastal Sinkyone summer encampments
Administration	BLM, Arcata Resource Area (707) 825-2300
Map	Trails of the Lost Coast (King Range National Conservation Area)

In summer the Sinkyone camped along the Lost Coast. Their seasonal village of Tangatin was located at Shelter Cove. Camping there in conical houses made of redwood bark, they were able to replenish depleted supplies of abalone, mussels, salmon, and sea lion meat. They also gathered clamshells for trade with the Pomo people to the south. Middens along the shore here date back 4,000 years.

The walk between Shelter Cove and Big Flat is a long one, and in loose sand, at that. Between the fog, the ocean, and all of the creeks and seeps along the way, your clothes will never be dry here. But this is one of the most beautiful walks in California. To the Sinkyone, the Lost Coast is a place of healing. Indeed, perhaps this is the most tangible aspect of Native California to be found here. Because of the steepness of the King Range, the area's remoteness, and heavy rains (and fogs), the Lost Coast offers an invigorating walk along an incredibly pristine and dramatic coastline. The shoreline is backed by rugged mountains, which have well preserved the area's natural ecosystem. Between exposed cliffs, the forest of Douglas-fir, madrone, tanbark oak, and sugar pine intermittently plunges down to the black sand beach. You might see bald eagles and peregrine falcons here if you are lucky. Rare native grasses—such as leafy reed grass—still grow in the meadow near Big Flat. If there is a fog-free moment during your time there, the views are breathtaking. Big Flat Creek cuts a wedge through forest that frames the more than 4,000-foot summit of Kings

Peak. Big Flat was a Sinkyone campsite used for thousands of years. If you don't have to hike out before dark (or high tide), there are primitive campsites along the beach.

Trailhead

Exit Hwy. 101 at the GARBERVILLE/REDWAY exit in Garberville. Following signs to Shelter Cove/King Range National Conservation Area, drive 18 miles west. In the town of Shelter Cove, turn right onto Beach Rd., and follow signs to Black Sands Beach. (Plan your walk so that you have a low tide permitting an 8-mile beach hike and back.)

On The Trail

From Shelter Cove the Coast Trail follows the shoreline for 8 miles to Big Flat, making this trip ideal for a weekend camp-over. The rugged shoreline is backed by steep, unstable cliffs, hardly tamed by the creeks flowing into the ocean. From the trailhead at Black Sands Beach, follow the shoreline to the right, heading north along the wet sand. (Though off-road vehicles are permitted along the sand at Shelter Cove, they are banned north of Gitchell Creek.) From Gitchell Creek at mile 3.5 to Buck Creek at mile 5.5, the beach is broad. North of Buck Creek, seaward cliffs permit only a narrow beach. Springs in the cliff faces can be identified where ferns are dripping. Since the King Range rises abruptly from the shore, there are several rocky points that require a low tide to pass. To gauge your progress, Big Flat is visible before you reach it. Well named, Big Flat is a wide alluvial deposit at the mouth of Big Flat Creek at 8 miles. When choosing a picnic area or a campsite, be aware that rattlesnakes can live among the scattered driftwood not far from the beach here. When you're ready, retrace your footprints to Shelter Cove.

The black sand beach at Big Flat

hike 98 Lanphere-Christensen Dunes

Roundtrip Distance	1.25 miles
Location	Coastal Wiyot village site
Administration	Lanphere Dunes Unit, Humboldt Bay National Wildlife Reserve (707) 822-6378
Map	Lanphere Dunes

The Yurok knew of a Wiyot village they called Tegwol, located at the mouth of the Mad River on its south bank. A large sandspit extending from here south to the entrance to Humboldt Bay formed over many years as the Mad River deposited sand where it met the ocean. In prehistoric times, the Mad River flowed into Humboldt Bay. The Mad River Slough is a remnant of this drainage. Sand blown up the dunes is secured by the roots and the rhizomes of native dune grass, beach pea, coast buckwheat, and sand verbena. The Wiyot people camped in the dune system here. They collected clams in the mudflats, fished in the Mad River and along the beach, and hunted game in the forest. Over the years, middens in the sand dunes have been uncovered by the wind. Attributed to the Wiyot culture, archaeologists have recorded stone sinkers used on fishing nets, spear points, arrow points, knives, and drills. All of these had been used here more than one thousand years ago.

Trailhead

Exit Hwy. 101 at Spear Ave. just north of Arcata. Heading west, Spear soon becomes Jane's Rd. and swings north, paralleling Hwy. 101 for several hundred yards. Turn left (west) on Upper Bay Rd. and follow it 0.5 mile until it becomes Lanphere Road; continue 1.25 miles west to its end at the preserve's gate. Park beside the road. (Call before you come to get a permit, or call to check on guided walks.)

On The Trail

The Beach Trail takes in the spruce and pine forest, the coastal wetlands, and the fragile dunes of shifting sand. From the preserve entrance, the trail passes through a kind of tunnel the canopy makes here and continues through forest. Growing in the shelter of the trees are several species of orchids, such as ladies' tresses, calypsos, Rein orchids, and rattlesnake plantains. You soon reach the transition zone between forest and dunes, which is signaled by the presence of willow and huckleberry. Continue—treading carefully to minimize your impact on the dune plants—down to the water's edge at 0.5 mile. The trail along the shore is brief. Since even walking on the dunes can damage plants, inhibiting their ability to stabilize the sand and stop coastal erosion, access has been limited here to a permit basis. Head left (south) along the shore for several hundred yards until the South Hollow Trail, on your left, loops back across the bleached white sand of the dunes and into the forest. The route intersects the Beach Trail at 0.75 mile. From here, you retrace your steps (right) along the Beach Trail to the parking area.

The Wiyot village of Tegwol was at the Mad River mouth

hike 99 Tsurai Loop

Roundtrip Distance	1.5 miles
Location	Coastal village site in Yurok territory
Administration	City of Trinidad (707) 677-0223
Maps	Not necessary

Tsurai was the southernmost and largest of Yurok coastal villages. From its beginning 5,000 years ago, Tsurai continued to function as a village until 1916. Though most Yurok villages were loosely configured with several smaller nearby villages, *Tsurai* (mountain) stood alone above the cove sheltered by Trinidad Head. The village site is located in a grove of alders between the bluff and Indian Beach. A plaque at the south end of Ocean Street marks the spot. *Ktlonechk* is the Yurok name for Trinidad Head. A place of meditation, a protector from storms, and a place where people could collect foods from the sea were some of the attributes of Ktlonechk for the Yurok.

The City of Trinidad consulted with Tsurai descendants in placing benches along the Tsurai Loop on Trinidad Head. Trinidad Head and offshore waters were used by the Yurok as hunting and gathering grounds. You'll have great views of the offshore waters and surrounding coastline from the summit. To the north, Trinidad State Beach provides a contrast to a group of sea stacks scattered offshore known collectively as the Offshore Rocks. Isolated from land predators, the Offshore Rocks include several important shorebird rookeries. You may notice sea lions hauling out among the nesting shorebirds here. The Yurok used dugout canoes to fish, hunt sea lions, snare shorebirds, collect eggs from the rocks, and harvest the rich kelp beds.

Trailhead

Take the Trinidad exit from Hwy. 101 leading into Main St. Follow Main St. west to Trinity St. Turn left on Trinity and go several blocks to its end at Edwards St. Turn right on Edwards and follow it to the end at the parking area (no fee).

On The Trail

The Tsurai Loop Trail encircles Trinidad Head, climbing through chaparral and Sitka spruce to the 362-foot summit overlooking the coast. From the south end of the parking area, climb the steps marked by the TRINIDAD HEAD TRAILS sign to the paved Coast Guard road. Your route climbs steeply along the road for several hundred yards before the road turns left at a gate. The actual trail begins here, next to the benches on the right. Go straight to pick up the trail traversing the west side of Trinidad Head. Pass through the dense chaparral to a clearing. Benches form an outdoor amphitheater here for viewing the sea lion rookery offshore. Sea lions feed off of the ample supply of salmon swimming these waters. To the northwest is Flatiron Rock, where sea lions haul-out among a colony of murres. Farther north on thickly-forested Pewetole Island is a black oystercatcher colony. The trail bears east from the sea lion viewing station, and passes above the lighthouse before climbing to the summit. Enjoy 360-degree views of this impressive meeting of land and sea before descending to the east. You soon have fine views of Trinidad Bay. The Tsurai site is now visible, just south of the Memorial Lighthouse in the cove. Your trail leads to a gravel road, which joins the paved road back to the parking area.

hike 100   Rim Trail

Roundtrip Distance	4 miles
Location	Coastal Yurok summer encampments
Administration	Patrick's Point State Park (707) 677-3570
Map	Patrick's Point State Park

An important area in their tradition, the Yurok know Patrick's Point as *Sunmeg*. Sunmeg is the domain of the last of the immortals, living in the guise of porpoises. Once human beings had populated the world, the porpoise/immortals came to live here.

A quarter of a mile off Palmer Point stands Cone Rock, where over 1,000 sea lion skulls were uncovered by archaeologists, each with a 2-inch hole drilled through the top. As no other bones were found on Cone Rock, the archaeologists assumed that skulls were brought here as an offering to Sunmeg for successful sea lion hunting. Findings among early Arctic cultures, where similar bore holes in polar bear and walrus skulls remain from a ritual to sustain their hunt, seem to substantiate this theory.

Trailhead

To reach the trailhead, 5 miles north of Trinidad exit Hwy. 101 at the Patrick's Point State Park Rd. Turn left at the stop sign and drive for 1 mile to the park entrance (fee required). Continue 0.25 mile to the Palmer Point trailhead.

On The Trail

The Rim Trail follows a Yurok route among the bluffs of Patrick's Point State Park. The Rim Trail is wheelchair-accessible from the Wedding Rock parking area south to Patrick's Point. The trail leads from Palmer Point to Agate Beach, with six spur trails accessing tidepools, gravel beaches, and scenic overlooks. From the parking area, walk west to the interpretive panel explaining the sea lion skulls at Cone Rock. A spur trail descends to the shore here. Following the edge of the parking area north for several hundred feet, the Rim Trail veers off into the thickly vegetated ravine below. After spanning two drainages, the trail skirts Abalone Campground at 0.5 mile. The seasonal Yurok village at Abalone Point sheltered and sustained people who had traveled here to hunt sea lion and other game, and to gather shellfish and berries, for hundreds of summers. Another spur trail accesses sites of early Yurok seasonal encampments along the beach. Please respect signs cautioning you of the area's archaeological fragility. Back on the Rim Trail, your route follows the bluffs through woods to access trails for Rocky Point at 0.75 mile, Patrick's Point at 1 mile, and Wedding Rock and Mussel Rock at 1.5 miles. From here, there are views through the woods north to Agate Beach, and beyond that, Big Lagoon. Discovered along Big Lagoon's shores was the village site of Oketo with its four, small outlying communities. At 2 miles, the trail joins a road through the campground to reach the parking area at Agate Beach, where stairs descend the bluff to the beach. When you're ready, retrace your path to the trail-head.

hike 101   Sunmeg Village

Roundtrip Distance	0.25 mile
Location	Reconstructed Yurok village
Administration	Patrick's Point State Park (707) 677-3570
Map	Patrick's Point State Park

Though authentically constructed according to traditional methods, Sunmeg was not a Yurok village in prehistoric times. Its plank houses were faithfully built by members of the Yurok Tribe and park staff to educate visitors and to be used in Native American ceremonies. One such ritual is the annual Brush Dance, which is held to cure existing illness and ensure children's health in the coming year. If you get to see the Brush Dance, keep in mind that everyone in the audience is part of the ceremony and think positive thoughts.

Sunmeg contains three family houses, a dance pit, a sweathouse, and a canoe. In their language, the Yurok make no distinction between the English words "house" and "family." Women, girls, and young boys lived in the main houses. When boys reached the age of six or seven, they went to live with their fathers and uncles in the

The architecture of the Yurok at Sunmeg

sweathouse. In a traditional Yurok community, the sweathouse is entered only by men. All buildings are entered with respect: women enter backwards; men headfirst. A native plant garden at Sunmeg's east corner contains many of the plants used traditionally by the Yurok.

Trailhead

To reach the trailhead, 5 miles north of Trinidad exit Highway 101 at the Patrick's Point State Park Rd. Turn left at the stop sign and drive 1 mile to the park entrance (fee required). Park in the lot next to the entrance station.

On The Trail

A walk through Sunmeg takes in the buildings of a reconstructed Yurok village. The trailhead is at the east end of the parking area, across from the bookstore. Passing through a wooded area, you reach a clearing at the center of Sunmeg in 0.25 mile. The trail ends here, and informal paths connect to village buildings. The newest of buildings, the sweathouse is rebuilt every six years as part of a ritual. Its roof is lower than other buildings. At its cornice is a retired canoe. The entry door is rectangular, while the exit door is round. Recessed areas in the sweathouse were used for cooking and sleeping, while upper areas were used for storage. Under a smoke hole in the roof, a fire centered the room. The sweathouse you see at Sunmeg was built for public use. (Another is used only in rituals, and is not open to the public.) The main houses here may be also entered by the public. Sunmeg provides a rare opportunity to acquaint yourself with this unique and beautiful architecture. When you're ready, retrace your steps to the parking area.

A Yurok dugout canoe at Sunmeg

hike 102   Klamath Overlook

Roundtrip Distance	1 mile
Location	Coastal overlook in Yurok territory
Administration	Redwood National Park (707) 464-6101
Map	Redwood National Park

On a clear day here, you can see at the horizon the earth's curve. Closer, you behold the Klamath River estuary. This is the center of the Yurok world. All directional words in their language refer to the Klamath River's flow. Before European contact, over 2,500 Yurok lived in the environs of this river. At its mouth is the town of Requa. *Re'kwoi* is the Yurok word for "river mouth," and the name of the village that occupied this place for over 2,000 years. A reconstructed Yurok family's plank house remains on the Klamath's north bank.

To the Yurok, the unmistakable stone pillar at the river mouth represents Oregos, who ensures the healthy salmon runs year after year. At the beginning, the Maker called the spirit people together so that each might choose a part in filling the world with animals and trees. *Oregos* (the helpful one), chose to be a guardian rock here at the Klamath River mouth, calling the salmon to spawn here each year. Indeed, the Klamath River supports the largest salmon and steelhead runs in California. The Salmon Festival is held in Klamath each June, featuring ceremonial dances and traditional crafts of the local Native American community.

Trailhead

Exit Hwy. 101 at Requa Rd. in Redwood National Park, just north of the Klamath River (and 18 miles south of Crescent City). Go 2.5 miles east on Requa Rd. to the Klamath Overlook on the left (no fee).

On The Trail

The Klamath Overlook offers the optimal vantage point. A interpretive panel near the trailhead depicts the Yurok myth of Oregos. The trailhead is at the south end of the parking area, by a COASTAL TRAIL sign. Within several steps, a spur trail marked OVERLOOK leads (right) down toward the water. In season, butterflies and scarlet pimpernels may brighten the sometimes steep switchbacks ahead. Stairs lead through chaparral to the fenced overlook atop an ancient sea stack in 0.5 mile. From this promontory 200 feet above the water, you can see Requa and the Klamath River mouth, guarded by Oregos. On a clear day from January through April, this is also a good place to watch for passing whales. When you're ready, climb back up to the parking area.

The vantage point at Klamath Overlook

hike 103

Yurok Loop

Roundtrip Distance	1 mile
Location	Coastal Yurok village site
Administration	Redwood National Park (707) 464-6101
Map	Redwood National Park, Yurok Loop brochure

R edwood National Park protects part of the ancestral homeland of the Yurok, Tolowa, and Chilua peoples. Redwood trees are sacred to the northwest California peoples. The Great Creator, who made all things, mixed a bit of each tree with the blood of the people to make the redwood. As the tallest, most powerful and beautiful of the world's trees, redwoods remain as demonstrable signs of the Creator's love. Redwoods also contribute to an ecosystem whose abundant resources enabled the Yurok to attain one of the highest hunter-gatherer population densities and one of the most complex material cultures known in early California. An interpretive trail, the Yurok Loop, details the native culture of the coastal redwood forest. The trail explores a wooded area along Lagoon Creek and takes in a promontory overlooking the rocky coastline near False Klamath Rock. Offshore are fishing grounds and sea stacks, which the Yurok used for sea lion hunting and mussel gathering.

Trailhead

Exit Hwy. 101 at Redwood National Park's Lagoon Creek Parking Area, 14 miles south of Crescent City (and 4 miles north of the Requa Rd. exit for Klamath Overlook). Park by the restrooms.

On The Trail

The Yurok Loop introduces the culture of the people who lived here. Numbered signposts correspond to explanations in the interpretive trail guide (available at the trailhead). Beginning at the southwest end of the parking area, the trail passes through forest cover and immediately veers left across Lagoon Creek. The trail now explores the vicinity of *O'men* (where land opens inward). This was the northernmost of Yurok villages. Across Wilson Creek—visible to the north—is the Tolowa home-land. The loop section begins ahead where two adjacent paths make openings in the canopy. Choose the one on the right and traverse a small bluff overlooking a sandy beach. Along the way are several plant specimens and other interpretive panels on Yurok culture. The Yurok fished along the beach with throw lines and dip nets for surfperch and smelt. At the point are several benches overlooking False Klamath Rock; its Yurok name translates as "brodiaea bulb digging place." Noticing the ocean view here, the brochure describes the Yurok belief that the sun follows the moon across the sky, passing under the earth after sunset to light the world of the dead. For the Yurok, it is unwise to watch the sun go down as doing so may imply a wish to join the ancestors. The trail heads south around the hill behind the village site. Along the route is a traditional resting place where travelers would stop. A Yurok traveler would ask, "May I come this way again?" To do otherwise would show a lack of respect. When you return to the beginning of the loop, retrace your steps to the parking area.

The rocky coastline from the Yurok Loop

hike 104   Point St. George

Roundtrip Distance	2 miles
Location	Coastal Tolowa seasonal village sites
Administration	Del Norte County Parks (707) 464-7237
Map	Not necessary

The Yurok people speak of a Tolowa village they called "where the waves dash against a bluff." Such is the landscape of Point St. George. A culture that predates the Tolowa camped here while gathering shellfish and hunting sea lions offshore. The waters around Castle Rock and St. George Reef, which extends 7 miles into the ocean, are part of an ancient hunting ground. Artifacts have been uncovered here that radiocarbon-date to 300 BC. *Pekwutsu*, the Tolowa name for the large rock where seal lions were hunted, lies among the Seal Rocks protruding from St. George Reef. Middens remain among the bluffs. At the Pebble Beach Public Fishing Access 2 miles south of here, a State Historical Landmark plaque lists regional Tolowa villages sites: Ta'atun is near Battery Point in Crescent City by the lighthouse; Meslteltun is at Pebble Beach; just south of Point St. George is Tatintun, and to the north is Tawaitun.

Trailhead

Exit Hwy. 101 at Washington Blvd. in Crescent City. Go west until Washington Blvd. becomes Radio Rd. Continue northwest on Radio Rd. to its end at the Coast Guard facility parking area (no fee).

On The Trail

A beach walk here explores the coastal gathering grounds that sustained the Tolowa villages in the Point St. George area. From the trailhead, pass the gate and head north through hillocks of grasses and seasonal wildflowers for several hundred yards to the shore. Bits of shell discarded long ago in a midden whiten your trail. Follow the shore left (south) for 1 mile to the tidepools below the headland. These waters and offshore rocks make up the Castle Rock National Wildlife Refuge protecting one of the state's most important seabird rookeries. The tidepools here contain an unusually rich assortment of sea life, washed by kelp and sea palms. (For a longer walk, the sandy beach to the north skirts windy Pelican Bay all the way to the Smith River mouth.) Explore this productive shoreline with care before retracing your steps to the parking area.

hike 105   Yontocket Slough

Roundtrip Distance	3 miles
Location	Coastal Tolowa village site
Administration	Del Norte County Parks (707) 464-7237
Map	Del Norte County Parks

Several Tolowa villages were located near the Smith River mouth, and others lined the riverbanks inland. The Tolowa, occupying this rich convergence of habitats, enjoyed a constant and varied food supply. In the riparian woodland, the Tolowa found berries. Surfperch, smelt, and mussels were harvested along the coast. Sea lions were hunted from dugout canoes in the offshore waters. Deer and rabbit were hunted in the forest. Offshore, Prince Island and Hunter Rock host shorebird rookeries where waterfowl were snared and eggs collected. Salmon, steelhead, sturgeon, and lamprey were fished in the river. With its Wild and Scenic River designation, the Smith River is the only river in California without a dam. Yontocket Slough is a drying arm of the Smith River. Its name is derived from *yan'daged*, a Tolowa word meaning "uphill facing south." This was the name of a Tolowa village that occupied this site for centuries.

Trailhead

Exit Hwy. 101 at Lake Earl Dr., 9 miles north of Crescent City. Go 4.7 miles northwest on Lake Earl Dr. to Lower Lake Rd. Turn left on Lower Lake Rd. and drive 5.3 miles north until the road deadends at Pala Rd.

Go left (you can't go right) and go 0.8 mile west to the road's end at the state park boundary (no fee). Park along the side of the road.

On The Trail

The trail takes in the Yontocket village site and the Smith River mouth. From the trailhead, walk west along a levee road across the wetland. At 0.25 mile, a hitching rail marks the junction of trails to the river. The site of Yontocket is on the knoll to the south. The fenced cemetery demarcates the site. The main trail continues straight ahead (southwest) to the knoll that protected Yontocket from Smith River floodwaters. From the hitching rail, go right, heading toward the Smith River mouth. Cross the dunes to the river mouth/overlook trail junction in 0.4 mile. To the right you reach the overlook in 0.2 mile. To the left you reach the beach in 0.9 mile. When you're ready, retrace your steps to the parking area.

The site and cemetery of the Tolowa village, "uphill facing north"

Guided Walks

The **Hoopa Reservation** includes the Hoopa Valley Tribal Council Museum, with its displays of artifacts and various crafts. Traditional villages, such as Djictanadin, Medildian, Tsemeta, and Tsuldin are still in use. Hoopa village walks, touring villages in continual operation for thousands of years, are guided by Hupa Tribal members and can be arranged through the museum. Sites include plank houses, sweathouses, calendar stones, and dance pits. Fire pit remains here have been carbon-dated back 10,000 years. In all, the reservation contains 13 restored Hupa village sites. Knowledgeable guides describe dwellings, dances, and traditions, and can answer your questions, (530) 625-4110.

Glossary

band	a group of families sharing a homeland and a number of smaller villages. This form of social organization is typical in the desert region.
cupule	a walnut-sized depression worked into a rock surface. While their use is unclear, it is thought that both women seeking fertility and shamans seeking to affect the weather made cupules.
ethnography	an area of anthropology that specifically addresses the comparative and analytical aspects of differing cultures.
horizon	a term used by archaeologists to classify similar cultural elements from a set time period that are found within a specific geographical region. Early, Middle, and Late Horizons are specified for the Central California culture.
intaglio	a large figure made by scraping away the dark desert pavement, exposing the lighter soil underneath. Examples can be found in the lower Colorado River desert region.
language family	(also referred to as a **stock**) it includes several tribes, tribelets, or bands related by linguistics. Those in California include Algonkin, Athabascan, Hokan, Penutian, Uto-Aztecan, Yukian, and Yuman.
mano	a hand-held stone used in a mortar or metate to grind seed kernels.
metate	a shallow depression worked into a rock surface for the purpose of grinding seeds.
midden	the village refuse heap, containing discarded food remains, artifacts, and soil.
mortar	(also known as a **mortero**) a large, deep depression worked into a rock surface for the purpose of grinding acorns or seeds with a pestle or a mano.
myth	told by a traditional storyteller to pass on a belief about the structure, the origin, or the workings of

the natural world. Within a myth there may be mention or explanation of a geologic event that took place long ago.

petroglyph   an engraving on a rock surface.

pictograph   a painting on a rock surface.

shaman   (also known as a **medicine man** or **woman**) Regarded as a healer, a shaman passes between the spiritual and the physical world via an altered consciousness and may record visions of such journeys in rock art.

tribelet   a group of several villages within a specific named territory governed by a chief. This form of social organization is found throughout California.

Appendix I.   Cultural Feature Listing

In the following listings, these abbreviations are used:
SB–State Beach, SHP–State Historic Park, SP–State Park, SR–State Reserve, SRA–State Recreation Area, NF–National Forest, NM–National Monument, NP–National Park, NS–National Seashore.

🌿 Ethnobotanical Exhibits, Gardens, and Native American Plant-Use Trails

⊕ Grinding Rocks

◎ Rock-Art Sites

△ Reconstructed or Re-created Villages

🐺 Places Informed by a Native Story or Myth

🏹 Archaeological Sites

Trade Routes and Prehistoric Trails

Trails and Exhibits on Tribal Lands

Appendix 2. Native American Events, Festivals, & Powwows

January

Los Angeles Native American American Film Festival at the Southwest Museum, (323) 221-2164.

April

Palm Springs Indian Market and Tribal Festival at Agua Caliente Reservation, (760) 323-0151.

Strawberry Festival at Kule Loklo, Point Reyes National Seashore, (415) 663-1092.

May

Native American Culture Day at Anderson Marsh State Historical Park, (707) 944-0688.

Day Under The Oaks at Jesse Peters Native American Art Museum, (707) 527-4479.

June

Indian Fair Days at the San Diego Museum of Man, (619) 239-2001.

Gabrieleño and Chumash Gathering and Powwow at Satwiwa, (818) 597-9192.

Summer Solstice Celebration at Mount Pinos, Chumash Wilderness, (805) 245-3731.

Indian Day Big Time at Yosemite National Park Visitor Center, (209) 372-0200.

Indian Trade Festival at Marin Museum of the American Indian, (415) 897-4064.

July

Gathering Day at Wassama Roundhouse State Historic Park, (559) 322-2332.

Big Time Celebration at Kule Loklo, Point Reyes National Seashore, (415) 663-1092.

Hoopa Rodeo (July 4) at Hoopa Reservation, (530) 625-4110.

Modoc Gathering at Lava Beds National Monument, (530) 667-2282.

August

Indian Fair at the Sierra Mono Museum, (559) 877-2115.

Indian Day at Fort Ross State Historic Park, (707) 847-3437.

September

Malki Museum Fiesta and Pow Wow (Memorial Day) at Morongo Reservation, (909) 849-7289.

Memorial Day Gathering (Memiorial Day) at the Sierra Mono Museum, (559) 877-2115.

Big Time at Indian Grinding Rock State Historic Park, (209) 296-7488.

White Deerskin Dance at Hoopa Reservation, (530) 625-4110.

November

Sunrise Ceremony (Thanksgiving) at Alcatraz Island, International Indian Treaty Council, (415) 641-4482.

Ongoing

California State Indian Museum in Sacramento features regular events, (916) 324-0971.

Appendix 3.   Recommended Reading &
                 Source Materials

General

Fentress, Jeff, 1994. "Prehistoric Rock Art Sites of Alameda and Contra Costa Counties" in *The Ohlone Past and Present: Native Americans of the San Francisco Bay Region* edited by Lowell John Bean. Palo Alto, CA: Ballena Press.

Foster, Lynne, 1987. *Adventuring in the California Desert.* San Francisco, CA: Sierra Club Books.

Holing, Dwight, 1988. *California Wild Lands: A Guide to the Nature Conservancy Preserves.* San Francisco, CA: Chronicle Books.

McKinney, John, 1988. *Coast Walks.* Santa Barbara, CA: Olympus Press.

Ostertag, Rhonda, and George Ostertag, 1995. *California State Parks.* Seattle, WA: The Mountaineers.

Whitley, David S., 1996. *A Guide to Rock Art Sites: Southern California and Southern Nevada.* Missoula, MT: Mountain Press.

Natural History

Fink, Augusta, 1987. *Palos Verdes Peninsula: Time and the Terraced Land.* Santa Cruz, CA: Western Tanager Press.

Fradkin, Philip, 1995. *The Seven States of California: A Human and Natural History.* New York, NY: Henry Holt and Co.

Native Californian

Bean, Lowell, and Harry Lawton, 1995. *The Cahuilla Indians of Southern California.* Banning, CA: Malki Museum Press.

Brown, Vinson, 1985. *Native Americans of the Pacific Coast.* Happy Camp, CA: Naturegraph Publishers.

Brown, Vinson, and Douglas Andrews, 1968. *The Pomo Indians of California and Their Neighbors*. Healdsburg, CA: Naturegraph Publishers.

Eargle, Dolan H., Jr., 1986. *The Earth Is Our Mother*. San Francisco, CA: Trees Company Press.

Faber, Gail, and Michele Lasagna, 1981. *Whispers from the First California: A Story of California's First People*. Alamo, CA: Magpie Publications.

Gattuso, John, 1993. *Native America*. Insight Guides. Boston, MA: Houghton Mifflin Co.

Godfrey, Elizabeth, 1977. *Yosemite Indians*. Yosemite National Park, CA: Yosemite Association.

Heizer, Robert F., and Albert B. Elsasser, 1983. *The Natural World of the California Indians*. Berkeley, CA: University of California Press.

Heizer, R.F., and M.A. Whipple, 1973. *The California Indians, A Sourcebook*. Berkeley, CA: University of California Press.

Kroeber, A.L., 1976. *Handbook of the Indians of California*. New York, NY: Dover Publications, Inc.

O'Dell, Scott, 1960. *Island of the Blue Dolphin*. New York, NY: Dell Publishing.

Margolin. Malcolm, 1978. *The Ohlone Way*. Berkeley, CA: Heyday Books.

Murphy, Edith Van Allen, 1987. *Indian Uses of Native Plants*. Ukiah, CA: Mendocino County Historical Society.

Santa Barbara Museum of Natural History, 1991. *The Chumash People*. San Luis Obispo, CA: EZ Nature Books.

Tregg, R.E. "The Indian Story of Point Reyes" in *U.S. National Park Service Land-Use Survey, Proposed Point Reyes National Seashore*. Washington, DC: U.S. Department of the Interior.

Index